Ambassador Morgenthau's Story

A Personal Account of the Armenian Genocide

By Henry Morgenthau

*American Ambassador at Constantinople
from 1913 to 1916*

Published in 2018

Logo art adapted from work by Bernard Gagnon

ISBN-13: 978-1-387-97130-5

First published in 1918

Henry Morgenthau Sr.

Contents

Preface

By this time the American people have probably become convinced that the Germans deliberately planned the conquest of the world. Yet they hesitate to convict on circumstantial evidence and for this reason all eye witnesses to this, the greatest crime in modern history, should volunteer their testimony.

I have therefore laid aside any scruples I had as to the propriety of disclosing to my fellow countrymen the facts which I learned while representing them in Turkey. I acquired this knowledge as the servant of the American people, and it is their property as much as it is mine.

I greatly regret that I have been obliged to omit an account of the splendid activities of the American Missionary and Educational Institutions in Turkey, but to do justice to this subject would require a book by itself. I have had to omit the story of the Jews in Turkey for the same reasons.

My thanks are due to my friend, Mr. Burton J. Hendrick, for the invaluable assistance he has rendered in the preparation of the book.

Henry Morgenthau

October, 1918

Chapter I - A German Superman at Constantinople

When I began writing these reminiscences of my ambassadorship, Germany's schemes in the Turkish Empire and the Near East seemed to have achieved a temporary success. The Central Powers had apparently disintegrated Russia, transformed the Baltic and the Black seas into German lakes, and had obtained a new route to the East by way of the Caucasus. For the time being Germany dominated Serbia, Bulgaria, Rumania, and Turkey, and regarded her aspirations for a new Teutonic Empire, extending from the North Sea to the Persian Gulf, as practically realized. The world now knows, though it did not clearly understand this fact in 1914, that Germany precipitated the war to destroy Serbia, seize control of the Balkan nations, transform Turkey into a vassal state, and thus obtain a huge oriental empire that would form the basis for unlimited world dominion. Did these German aggressions in the East mean that this extensive programme had succeeded?

As I picture to myself a map which would show Germany's military and diplomatic triumphs, my experiences in Constantinople take on a new meaning.

I now see the events of those twenty-six months as part of a connected, definite story. The several individuals that moved upon the scene now appear as players in a carefully staged, superbly managed drama. I see clearly enough now that Germany had made all her plans for world dominion and that the country to which I had been sent as American Ambassador was one of the foundation stones of the Kaiser's whole political and military structure. Had Germany not acquired control of Constantinople in the early days of the war, it is not unlikely that hostilities would have ended a few months after the Battle of the Marne. It was certainly an amazing fate that landed me in this great headquarters of intrigue at the very moment when the plans of the Kaiser for controlling Turkey, which he had carefully pursued for a quarter of a century, were about to achieve their final success.

For this work of subjugating Turkey, and transforming its army and its territory into instruments of Germany, the Emperor had sent to Constantinople an ambassador who was ideally fitted for the task. The mere fact that the Kaiser had personally chosen Baron Von Wangenheim for this post shows that he had accurately gauged the human qualities needed in this great diplomatic enterprise.

The Kaiser had early detected in Wangenheim an instrument ideally qualified for oriental intrigue; he had more than once summoned him to Corfu for his vacations, and here, we may be sure, the two congenial spirits had passed many days discussing German ambitions in the Near East. At the time when I first met him, Wangenheim was fifty-four years old; he had spent a quarter of a century in the diplomatic corps, he had seen service in such different places as Petrograd, Copenhagen, Madrid, Athens, and Mexico, and he had been charg? at Constantinople, several years afterward coming there as ambassador. He understood completely all countries, including the United States; his first wife had been an American, and Wangenheim, when Minister to Mexico, had intimately studied our country and had then acquired an admiration for our energy and progress. He had a complete technical equipment for a diplomat; .he spoke German, English, and French with equal facility, he knew the East thoroughly, and he had the widest acquaintance with public men. Physically he was one of the most imposing persons I have ever known. When I was a boy in Germany, the Fatherland was usually symbolized as a beautiful and powerful woman---a kind of dazzling Valkyrie; when I think of modern Germany, however, the massive, burly figure of Wangenheim naturally presents itself to my mind. He was six feet two inches tall; his huge, solid frame, his Gibraltarlike shoulders, erect and impregnable, his bold, defiant head, his piercing eyes, his whole physical structure constantly pulsating with life and activity---there stands, I would say, not the Germany which I had known, but the Germany whose limitless ambitions had transformed the world into a place of horror. And Wangenheim's every act and every word typified this new and dreadful portent among the nations. Pan-Germany filled all his waking hours and directed his every action. The deification of his emperor was the only religious instinct which impelled him. That aristocratic and autocratic organization of German society which represents the Prussian system was, in Wangenheim's eyes, something to be venerated and worshipped; with this as the groundwork, Germany was inevitably destined, he believed, to rule the world. The great land-owning Junker represented the perfection of mankind. "I would despise myself," his closest associate once told me, and this represented Wangenheim's attitude as well, "if I had been born in a city." Wangenheim divided mankind into two classes, the governing and the governed; and he ridiculed the idea that the upper could ever be recruited from the lower. I recall with what unction and enthusiasm he used to describe the Emperor's caste organization of German estates; how he had made them non-transferable, and had even arranged it so that the possessors, or the prospective possessors, could not marry without the imperial consent. "In this way," Wangenheim would say, "we keep our governing classes pure, unmixed of blood." Like all of his social order, Wangenheim worshipped the Prussian military system; his splendid bearing showed that he had himself served in the army, and, in true German fashion, he regarded practically every situation in life from a military standpoint. I had one curious illustration of this when I asked Wangenheim one day why the Kaiser did not visit the United States. "He would like to immensely," he replied, "but it would be too dangerous. War might break out when he was at sea, and the enemy would capture him." I suggested that that could hardly happen as the American Government would escort its guest home with warships, and that no nation would care to run the risk of involving the United States as Germany's ally; but Wangenheim still thought that the military danger would make any such visit impossible.

Upon him, more than almost any diplomatic representative of Germany, depended the success of the Kaiser's conspiracy for world domination. This German diplomat came to Constantinople with a single purpose. For twenty years the German Government had been cultivating the Turkish Empire. All this time the Kaiser had been preparing for a world war, and in this war it was destined that Turkey should play an almost decisive part. Unless Germany should obtain the Ottoman Empire as its ally, there was little chance that she could succeed in a general European conflict. When France had made her alliance with Russia, the man power of 170,000,000 people was placed on her side, in the event of a war with Germany. For more than twenty years

Germany had striven diplomatically to detach Russia from this French alliance, but had failed. There was only one way in which Germany could make valueless the Franco-Russian Alliance; this was by obtaining Turkey as an ally. With Turkey on her side, Germany could close the Dardanelles, the only practical line of communication between Russia and her western allies; this simple act would deprive the Czar's army of war munitions, destroy Russia economically by stopping her grain exports, her greatest source of wealth, and thus detach Russia from her partners in the World War. Thus Wangenheim's mission was to make it absolutely certain that Turkey should join Germany in the great contest that was impending.

Wangenheim. believed that, should he succeed in accomplishing this task, he would reap the reward which for years had represented his final goal---the chancellorship of the Empire. His skill at establishing friendly personal relations with the Turks gave him a great advantage over his rivals. Wangenheim had precisely that combination of force, persuasiveness, geniality, and brutality which was needed in dealing with the Turkish character. I have emphasized his Prussian qualities; yet Wangenheim was a Prussian not by birth but by development; he was a native of Th?ringen, and, together with all the push, ambition, and overbearing traits of the Prussian, he had some of the softer characteristics which we associate with Southern Germany. He had one conspicuous quality which is not Prussian at all ---that is, tact; and, as a rule, he succeeded in keeping his less-agreeable tendencies under the surface and showing only his more ingratiating side. He dominated not so much by brute strength as by a mixture of force and amiability; externally he was not a bully; his manner was more insinuating than coercive; he won by persuasiveness, not by the mailed fist, but we who knew him well understood that back of all his gentleness there lurked a terrific, remorseless, and definite ambition. Yet the impression left was not one of brutality, but of excessive animal spirits and good nature. Indeed, Wangenheim had in combination the jovial enthusiasm of a college student, the rapacity of a Prussian official, and the happy-go-lucky qualities of a man of the world. I still recall the picture of this huge figure of a man, sitting at the piano, improvising on some beautiful classic theme---and then suddenly starting to pound out uproarious German drinking songs or popular melodies. I still see him jumping on his horse at the polo grounds, spurring the splendid animal to its speediest efforts---the horse never making sufficient speed, however, to satisfy the ambitious sportsman. Indeed, in all his activities, grave or gay, Wangenheim displayed this same restless spirit of the chase whether he was flirting with the Greek ladies at Pera, or spending hours over the card table at the Cercle d'Orient, or bending the Turkish officials to his will in the interest of Germany, all life was to him a game, which was to be played more or less recklessly, and in which the chances favoured the man who was bold and audacious and willing to pin success or failure on a single throw. And this greatest game of all---that upon which was staked, as Bernhardi has expressed it, "World empire or downfall"---Wangenheim did not play languidly, as though it had been merely a duty to which he had been assigned; to use the German phrase, he was "fire and flame" for it; he had the consciousness that he was a strong man selected to perform a mighty task. As I write of Wangenheim, I still feel myself affected by the force of his personality, yet I know all the time that, like the government which he served so loyally, he was fundamentally ruthless, shameless, and cruel. But he was content to accept all the consequences of his policy, however hideous these might be. He saw only a single goal, and, with the realism and logic that are so characteristically German, Wangenheim would brush aside all feelings of humanity and decency that might interfere with success. He accepted in full Bismarck's famous dictum that a German must be ready to sacrifice for Kaiser and Fatherland not only his life but his honour as well.

Just as Wangenheim personified Germany, so did his colleague, Pallavicini, personify Austria. Wangenheim's essential quality was a brutal egotism, while Pallavicini was a quiet, kind-hearted, delightfully mannered gentleman. Wangenheim. was always looking to the future, Pallavicini to the past. Wangenheim represented the mixture of commercialism and medieval lust for conquest which constitute Prussian weltpolitik; Pallavicini was a diplomat left over from the days of Metternich. "Germany wants this!" Wangenheim. would insist, when an important point had to be decided; "I shall consult my foreign office," the cautious Pallavicini would say, on a similar occasion. The Austrian, with little upturned gray moustaches, with a rather stiff, even slightly strutting, walk, looked like the old-fashioned Marquis that was once a stock figure on the stage. I might compare Wangenheim with the representative of a great business firm which was lavish in its expenditures and unscrupulous in its methods., while his Austrian colleague represented a house that prided itself on its past achievements and was entirely content with its position. The same delight that Wangenheim took in Pan-German plans, Pallavicini found in all the niceties and obscurities of diplomatic technique. The Austrian had represented his country in Turkey many years, and was the dean of the corps, a dignity of which he was extremely proud. He found his delight in upholding all the honours of his position; he was expert in arranging the order of precedence at ceremonial dinners, and there was not a single detail of etiquette that he did not have at his fingers' ends. When it came to affairs of state, however, he was merely a tool of Wangenheim. From the first, indeed, he seemed to accept his position as that of a diplomat who was more or less subject to the will of his more powerful ally. In this way Pallavicini played to his German colleague precisely the same part that his emperor was playing to that of the Kaiser. In the early months of the war the bearing of these two men completely mirrored the respective successes and failures of their countries. As the Germans boasted of victory after victory Wangenheim's already huge and erect figure seemed to become larger and more upstanding, while Pallavicini, as the Austrians lost battle a after battle to the Russians, seemed to become smaller and more shrinking.

The situation in Turkey, in these critical months, seemed almost to have been purposely created to give the fullest opportunities to a man of Wangenheim's genius. For ten years the Turkish Empire had been undergoing a process of dissolution, and had now reached a state of decrepitude that had left it an easy prey to German diplomacy. In order to understand the situation, we must keep in mind that there was really no orderly, established government in Turkey at that time. For the Young Turks were not a government; they were really an irresponsible party, a kind of secret society, which, by intrigue, intimidation, and assassination, had obtained most of the offices of state. When I describe the Young Turks in these words, perhaps I may be dispelling certain illusions. Before I came to Turkey I had entertained very different ideas of this organization. As far back as 1908 I remember reading news of Turkey that appealed strongly to my democratic sympathies. These reports informed me that a body of young revolutionists had swept from the mountains of Macedonia, had marched upon Constantinople, had deposed the bloody Sultan, Abdul Hamid, and had established a constitutional system. Turkey, these glowing newspaper stories told us, had become a democracy, with a parliament, a responsible ministry, universal suffrage, equality of all citizens before the law, freedom of speech and of the press, and all the other essentials of a free, liberty-loving commonwealth. That a party of Turks had for years been struggling for such reforms I well knew, and that their ambitions had become realities seemed to indicate that, after all, there was such a thing as human progress. The long welter of massacre and disorder in the Turkish Empire had apparently ended; "the great assassin", Abdul Hamid, had been removed to solitary confinement at Saloniki , and his brother, the gentle Mohammed V, had ascended the throne with a progressive democratic programme. Such had been the promise; but, by the time I reached Constantinople, in 1913, many changes had taken place. Austria had annexed two Turkish provinces, Bosnia and Herzegovina; Italy had wrenched away Tripoli; Turkey had fought a disastrous war with the Balkan states, and had lost all her territories in Europe except Constantinople and a small hinterland. The aims for the regeneration of Turkey that had inspired the revolution had evidently miscarried, and I soon discovered that four years of so-called democratic rule had ended with the nation more degraded, more impoverished, and more dismembered than ever before. Indeed, long before I had arrived, this attempt to establish a Turkish democracy had failed. The failure was probably the most complete and the most disheartening in the whole history of democratic institutions. I need hardly explain in detail the causes of this collapse. Let us not criticize too harshly the Young Turks, for there is no question that, at the beginning, they were sincere. In a speech in Liberty Square, Saloniki, in July, 1908, Enver Pasha, who was popularly regarded as the chivalrous young leader of this insurrection against a century-old tyranny, had eloquently declared that, "To-day arbitrary government has disappeared. We are all brothers. There are no longer in Turkey Bulgarians, Greeks, Servians, Rumanians, Mussulmans, Jews. Under the same blue sky we are all proud to be Ottomans." That statement represented the Young Turk ideal for the new Turkish state, but it was an ideal which it was evidently beyond their ability to translate into a reality. The races which had been maltreated and massacred for centuries by the Turks could not transform themselves overnight into brothers, and the hatreds, jealousies, and religious prejudices of the past still divided Turkey into a medley of warring clans. Above all, the destructive wars and the loss of great sections of the Turkish Empire had destroyed the prestige of the new democracy. There were plenty of other reasons for the failure, but it is hardly necessary to discuss them at this time.

Thus the Young Turks had disappeared as a positive regenerating force, but they still existed as a political machine. Their leaders, Talaat, Enver, and Djemal, had long since abandoned any expectation of reforming their state, but they had developed an insatiable lust for personal power. Instead of a nation of nearly 20,000,000, developing happily along democratic lines, enjoying suffrage, building up their industry and agriculture, laying the foundations for universal education, sanitation, and general progress, I saw that Turkey consisted of merely so many inarticulate, ignorant, and poverty-ridden slaves, with a small, wicked oligarchy at the top, which was prepared to use them in the way that would best promote its private interests. And these men were practically the same who, a few years before, had made Turkey a constitutional state. A more bewildering fall from the highest idealism to the crassest materialism could not be imagined. Talaat, Enver, and Djemal were the ostensible leaders, yet back of them was the Committee, consisting of about forty men. This committee met secretly, manipulated elections, and filled the offices with its own henchmen. It occupied a building in Constantinople, and had a supreme chief who gave all his time to its affairs and issued orders to his subordinates. This functionary ruled the party and the country something like an American city boss in our most unregenerate days; and the whole organization thus furnished a typical illustration of what we sometimes describe as "invisible government." This kind of irresponsible control has at times flourished in American cities, mainly because the citizens have devoted all their time to their private affairs and thus neglected the public good. But in Turkey the masses were altogether too ignorant to understand the meaning of democracy, and the bankruptcy and general vicissitudes of the country had left the nation with practically no government and an easy prey to a determined band of adventurers. The Committee of Union and Progress, with Talaat Bey as the most powerful leader, constituted such a band. Besides the forty men in Constantinople, sub-committees were organized in all important cities of the empire. The men whom the Committee placed in power "took orders" and made the appointments submitted to them. No man could, hold an office, high or low, who was not indorsed by this committee.

I must admit, however, that I do our corrupt American gangs a great injustice in comparing them with the Turkish Committee of Union and Progress. Talaat, Enver, and Djemal had added to their system a detail that has not figured extensively in American politics---that of assassination and judicial murder. They had wrested power from the other factions by a deed of violence. This coup d'?tat had taken place on January 26, 1913, not quite a year before my arrival. At that time a political group, headed by the venerable Kiamil Pasha, as Grand Vizier, and Nazim Pasha, as Minister of War, controlled the Government; they represented a faction known as the "Liberal Party," which was chiefly distinguished for its enmity to the Young Turks. These men had fought the disastrous Balkan War, and, in January, they had felt themselves compelled to accept the advice of the European powers and surrender Adrianople to Bulgaria. The Young Turks had been outside the breastworks for about six months looking for an opportunity to return to power. The proposed surrender of Adrianople apparently furnished them this opportunity. Adrianople was an important Turkish city, and naturally the Turkish people regarded the contemplated surrender as marking still another milestone toward their national doom. Talaat and Enver hastily collected about two hundred followers and marched to the Sublime Porte, where the ministry was then sitting. Nazim, hearing the uproar, stepped out into the hall. He courageously faced the crowd, a cigarette in his mouth and his hands thrust into his pockets.

"Come, boys," he said, good humouredly, "what's a this noise about? Don't you know that it is interfering with our deliberations?"

The words had hardly left his mouth when he fell dead. A bullet had pierced a vital spot.

The mob, led by Talaat and Enver, then forced their way into the council chamber. They forced Kiamil, the Grand Vizier, to resign his post by threatening him with the fate that had overtaken Nazim.

As assassination had been the means by which these chieftains had obtained the supreme power, so assassination continued to be the instrument upon which they depended for maintaining their control. Djemal, in addition to his other duties, became Military Governor of Constantinople, and in this capacity he had control of the police; in this office he developed all the talents of a Fouch?, and did his work so successfully that any man who wished to conspire against the Young Turks usually retired for that purpose to Paris or Athens. The few months that preceded my arrival had been a reign of terror. The Young Turks had destroyed Abdul Hamid's r?gime only to adopt that Sultan's favourite methods of quieting opposition. Instead of having one Abdul Hamid, Turkey now discovered that she had several. Men were arrested and deported by the score, and hangings of political offenders---opponents, that is, of the ruling gang---were common occurrences.

The weakness of the Sultan particularly facilitated the ascendancy of this committee. We must remember that Mohammed V was not only Sultan but Caliph---not only the temporal ruler, but also head of the Mohammedan Church. As religious leader he was an object of veneration to millions of devout Moslems, a fact which would have given a strong man in his position great influence in freeing Turkey from its oppressors. I presume that even those who had the most kindly feelings toward the Sultan would not have described him as an energetic, masterful man. It is a miracle that the circumstances which fate had forced upon Mohammed had not long since completely destroyed him. He was a brother of Abdul Hamid---Gladstone's "great assassin"----a man who ruled by espionage and bloodshed, and who had no more consideration for his own relatives than for the massacred Armenians. One of Abdul Hamid's first acts, when he ascended the throne, was to shut up his heir apparent in a palace, surrounding him with spies, restricting him for society to his harem and a few palace functionaries, and constantly holding over his head the fear of assassination. Naturally Mohammed's education had been limited; he spoke only Turkish, and his only means of learning about the outside world was an occasional Turkish newspaper. So long as he remained quiescent, the heir apparent was comfortable and fairly secure, but he knew that the first sign of revolt, or even a too curious interest in what was going on, would be the signal for his death. Hard as this ordeal was, it had not destroyed what was fundamentally a benevolent, gentle nature. The Sultan had no characteristics that suggested the "terrible Turk." He was simply a quiet, easy-going, gentlemanly old man. Everybody liked him and I do not think that he harboured ill-feeling against a human soul. He could not rule his empire, for he had had no preparation for such a difficult task; he took a certain satisfaction in his title and in the consciousness that he was a lineal descendant of the great Osman; clearly, however, he could not oppose the schemes of the men who were then struggling for the control of Turkey. In the replacement of Abdul Hamid, as his master, by Talaat, Enver, and Djemal, the Sultan had not greatly improved his personal position. The Committee of Union and Progress ruled him precisely as they ruled all the rest of Turkey---by intimidation. Indeed they had already given him a sample of their power, for the Sultan had attempted on one occasion to assert his independence, and the conclusion of this episode left no doubt as to who was master. A group of thirteen "conspirators" and other criminals, some real ones, others merely political offenders, had been sentenced to be hanged. Among them was an imperial son-in-law. Before the execution could take place the Sultan had to sign the death warrants. He begged that he be permitted to pardon the imperial son-in-law, though he raised no objection to vis?ing the hangings of the other twelve. The nominal ruler of 20,000,000 people figuratively went down upon his knees before Talaat, but all his pleadings did not affect this determined

13

man. Here, Talaat reasoned, was a chance to decide, once for all, who was master, the Sultan or themselves. A few days afterward the melancholy figure of the imperial son-in-law, dangling at the end of a rope in full view of the Turkish populace, visibly reminded the empire that Talaat and the Committee were the masters of Turkey. After this tragical test of strength, the Sultan never attempted again to interfere in affairs of state. He knew what had happened to Abdul Hamid, and he feared an even more terrible fate for himself.

By the time I reached Constantinople the Young Turks thus completely controlled the Sultan. He was popularly referred to as an "irade-machine," a phrase which means about the same thing as when we refer to a man as a "rubber stamp." His state duties consisted merely in performing certain ceremonies, such as receiving ambassadors, and in affixing his signature to such papers as Talaat and his associates placed before him. This was a profound change in the Turkish system, since in that country for centuries the Sultan had been an unquestioned despot, whose will had been the only law, and who had centred in his own person all the power of sovereignty. Not only the Sultan, but the Parliament, had become the subservient creature of the Committee, which chose practically all the members, who voted only as the predominant bosses dictated. The Committee had already filled several of the most powerful cabinet offices with its followers, and was reaching out for the several important places that, for several reasons, still remained in other hands.

Chapter II - The "Boss System" in the Ottoman Empire and How it Proved Useful to Germany

Talaat, the leading man in this band of usurpers, really had remarkable personal qualities. Naturally Talaat's life and character proved interesting to me, for I had for years been familiar with the Boss system in my own country, and in Talaat I saw many resemblances to the crude yet able citizens who have so frequently in the past gained power in local and state politics. Talaat's origin was so obscure that there were plenty of stories in circulation concerning it. One account said that he was a Bulgarian gipsy, while another described him as a Pomak---a Pomak being a man of Bulgarian blood whose ancestors, centuries ago, had embraced the Mohammedan faith. According to this latter explanation, which I think was the true one, this real ruler of the Turkish Empire was not a Turk at all. I can personally testify that he cared nothing for Mohammedanism for, like most of the leaders of his party, he scoffed at all religions. "I hate all priests, rabbis, and hodjas," he once told me---hodja being the nearest equivalent the Mohammedans have for a minister of religion. In American city politics many men from the humblest walks of life have not uncommonly developed great abilities as politicians, and similarly Talaat had started life as a letter carrier. From this occupation he had risen to be a telegraph operator at Adrianople; and of these humble beginnings he was extremely proud. I visited him once or twice at his house; although Talaat was then the most powerful man in the Turkish Empire, his home was still the modest home of a man of the people. It was cheaply furnished; the whole establishment reminded me of a moderately priced apartment in New York. His most cherished possession was the telegraph instrument with which he had once earned his living. Talaat one night told me that he had that day received his salary as Minister of the Interior; after paying his debts, he said, he had just one hundred dollars left in the world. He liked to spend part of his spare time with the rough-shod crew that made up the Committee of Union and Progress; in the interims when he was out of the cabinet he used to occupy the desk daily at party headquarters, personally managing the party machine. Despite these humble beginnings, Talaat had developed some of the qualities of a man of the world. Though his early training had not included instruction in the use of a knife and fork---such implements are wholly unknown among the poorer classes in Turkey---Talaat could attend diplomatic dinners and represent his country with a considerable amount of dignity and personal ease. I have always regarded it as indicating his innate cleverness that, though he had had little schooling, he had picked up enough French to converse tolerably in that language. Physically, he was a striking figure. His powerful frame, his huge sweeping back, and his rocky biceps emphasized that natural mental strength and forcefulness which had made possible his career. In discussing matters Talaat liked to sit at his desk, with his shoulders drawn up, his head thrown back, and his wrists, twice the size of an ordinary man's, planted firmly on the table. It always seemed to me that it would take a crowbar to pry these wrists from the board, once Talaat's strength and defiant spirit had laid them there. Whenever I think of Talaat now I do not primarily recall his rollicking laugh, his uproarious enjoyment of a good story, the mighty stride with which he crossed the room, his fierceness, his determination, his remorselessness---the whole life and nature of the man take form in those gigantic wrists.

Talaat, like most strong men, had his forbidding, even his ferocious, moods. One day I found him sitting at the usual place, his massive shoulders drawn up, his eyes glowering, his wrists planted on the desk. I always anticipated trouble whenever I found him in this attitude. As I made request after request, Talaat, between his puffs at his cigarette, would answer "No!" "No!" " No!"

I slipped around to his side of the desk.

"I think those wrists are making all the trouble, Your Excellency," I said. "Won't you please take them off the table?"

Talaat's ogre-like face began to crinkle, he threw up his arms, leaned back, and gave a roar of terrific laughter. He enjoyed this method of treating him so much that he granted every request that I made.

At another time I came into his room when two Arab princes were present. Talaat was solemn and dignified, and refused every demand I made. "No, I shall not do that"; or, "No, I haven't the slightest idea of doing that," he would answer. I saw that he was trying to impress his princely guests; to show them that he had become so great a man that he did not hesitate to "turn down" an ambassador. So I came up nearer and spoke quietly.

"I see you are trying to make an impression on these princes," I said. "Now if it's necessary for you to pose, do it with the Austrian Ambassador---he's out there waiting to come in. My affairs are too important to be trifled with."

Talaat laughed. "Come back in an hour," he said. I returned; the Arab princes had left, and we had no difficulty in arranging matters to my satisfaction.

"Someone has got to govern Turkey; why not we?" Talaat once said to me. The situation had just about come to that. "I have been greatly disappointed," he would tell me, "at the failure of the Turks to appreciate democratic institutions. I hoped for it once, and I worked hard for it---but they were not prepared for it." He saw a government which the first enterprising man who came along might seize, and he determined to be that man. Of all the Turkish politicians whom I met I regarded Talaat as the only one who really had extraordinary native ability. He had great force and dominance, the ability to think quickly and accurately, and an almost superhuman insight into men's motives. His great geniality and his lively sense of humour also made him a splendid manager of men. He showed his shrewdness in the measures which he took, after the murder of Nazim, to gain the upper hand in this distracted empire. He did not seize the government all at once; he went at it gradually, feeling his way. He realized the weaknesses of his position; he had several forces to deal with---the envy of his associates on the revolutionary committee which had backed him, the army, the foreign governments, and the several factions that made up what then passed for public opinion in Turkey. Any of these elements might destroy him, politically and physically. He understood the dangerous path that he was treading, and he always anticipated a violent death. "I do not expect to die in my bed," he told me. By becoming Minister of the Interior, Talaat gained control of the police and the administration of the provinces, or vilayets; this gave him a great amount of patronage, which he used to strengthen the power of the Committee. He attempted to gain the support of all influential factions by gradually placing their representatives in the other cabinet posts. Though he afterward became the man who was chiefly responsible for the massacre of hundreds of thousands of Armenians, at this time Talaat maintained the pretense that the Committee stood for the unionization of all the races in the empire, and for this reason his first cabinet contained an Arab-Christian, a Deunme (a Jew by race, but a Mohammedan by religion), a Circassian, an Armenian, and an Egyptian.

He made the latter Grand Vizier, the highest post in the Government, a position which roughly corresponds to that of Chancellor in the German Empire. The man whom he selected for this office, which in ordinary times was the most dignified and important in the empire, belonged to quite a different order of society from Talaat. Not uncommonly bosses in America select high-class figureheads for mayors or even governors, men who will give respectability to their faction, yet whom, at the same time, they think they can control. It was some such motive as this which led Talaat and his associates to elevate Sa?d Halim to the Grand Vizierate. Sa?d Halim was an Egyptian prince, the cousin of the Khedive of Egypt, a man of great wealth and great culture. He spoke English and French as fluently as his own tongue and was an ornament to any society in the world. But he was a man of unlimited vanity and ambition. His great desire was to become Khedive of Egypt, and this had led him to trust his political fortunes to the gang that was then ascendant in Turkey. He was the heaviest "campaign contributor," and, indeed, he had largely financed the Young Turks from their earliest days. In exchange they had given him the highest office in the empire, with the tacit understanding that he should not attempt to exercise the real powers of his office, but content himself with enjoying its dignities.

Germany's war preparations had for years included the study of internal conditions in other countries; an indispensable part of the imperial programme had been to take advantage of such disorganizations as existed to push her schemes of pene-

16

tration and conquest. What her emissaries have attempted in France, Italy, and even the United States is apparent, and their success in Russia has greatly changed the course of the war. Clearly such a situation as that which prevailed in Turkey in 1913 and 1914 provided an ideal opportunity for manipulations of this kind. And Germany had one great advantage in Turkey which was not so conspicuously an element in other countries. Talaat and his associates needed Germany almost as badly as Germany needed Talaat. They were altogether new to the business of managing an empire. Their finances were depleted, their army and navy almost in tatters, enemies were constantly attempting to undermine them at home, and the great powers regarded them as seedy adventurers whose career was destined to be brief. Without strong support from an outside source, it was a question how long the new regime could survive. Talaat and his Committee needed some foreign power to organize the army and navy, to finance the nation, to help them reconstruct their industrial system, and to protect them against the encroachments of the encircling nations. Ignorant as they were of foreign statecraft, they needed a skilful adviser to pilot them through all the channels of international intrigue. Where was such a protector to be obtained? Evidently only one of the great European powers could perform this office. Which one should it be? Ten years before Turkey would naturally have appealed to England. But now the Turks regarded England as merely the nation that had despoiled them of Egypt and that had failed to protect Turkey from dismemberment after the Balkan wars. Together with Russia, Great Britain now controlled Persia and thus constituted a constant threat---at least so the Turks believed---against their Asiatic dominions. England was gradually withdrawing her investments from Turkey, English statesmen believed that the task of driving the Turk from Europe was about complete, and the whole Near-Eastern policy of Great Britain hinged on maintaining the organization of the Balkans as it had been determined by the Treaty of Bucharest ---a treaty which Turkey refused to regard as binding and which she was determined to upset. Above all, the Turks feared Russia in 1914, just as they had feared her ever since the days of Peter the Great. Russia was the historic enemy, the nation which had given freedom to Bulgaria and Rumania, which had been most active in dismembering the Ottoman Empire, and which regarded herself as the power that was ultimately to possess Constantinople. This fear of Russia, I cannot too much insist, was the one factor which, above everything else, was forcing Turkey into the arms of Germany. For more than half a century Turkey had regarded England as her surest safeguard against Russian aggression, and now England had become Russia's virtual ally. There was even then a general belief, which the Turkish chieftains shared, that England was entirely willing that Russia should inherit Constantinople and the Dardanelles.

Though Russia, in 1914, was making no such pretensions, at least openly, the fact that she was crowding Turkey in other directions made it impossible that Talaat and Enver should look for support in that direction. Italy had just seized the last Turkish province in Africa, Tripoli, at that moment, was holding Rhodes and other Turkish islands, and was known to cherish aggressive plans in Asia Minor. France was the ally of Russia and Great Britain, and was also constantly extending her influence in Syria, in which province, indeed, she had made great plans for "penetration" with railroads, colonies, and concessions. The personal equation played an important part in the ensuing drama. The ambassadors of the Triple Entente hardly concealed their contempt for the dominant Turkish politicians and their methods. Sir Louis Mallet, the British Ambassador, was a high-minded and cultivated English gentleman; Bompard, the French Ambassador, was a similarly charming, honourable Frenchman, and both were personally disqualified from participating in the murderous intrigues which then comprised Turkish politics. Giers, the Russian Ambassador, was a proud and scornful diplomat of the old aristocratic r?gime. He was exceedingly astute, but he treated the Young Turks contemptuously, manifested almost a proprietary interest in the country, and seemed to me already to be wielding the knout over this despised government. It was quite apparent that the three ambassadors of the Entente did not regard the Talaat and Enver r?gime as permanent, or as particularly worth their while to cultivate. That several factions had risen and fallen in the last six years they knew, and they likewise believed that this latest usurpation would vanish in a few months.

But there was one active man in Turkey then who had no nice scruples about using such agencies as were most available for accomplishing his purpose. Wangenheim clearly saw, what his colleagues had only faintly perceived, that these men were steadily fastening their hold on Turkey, and that they were looking for some strong power that would recognize their position and abet them in maintaining it. In order that we may clearly understand the situation, let us transport ourselves, for a moment, to a country that is nearer to us than Turkey. In 1913 Victoriano Huerta and his fellow conspirators gained control of Mexico by means not unlike those that had given Talaat and his Committee the supreme power in Turkey. Just as Huerta murdered Madero, so the Young Turks had murdered Nazim, and in both countries assassination had become a regular political weapon. Huerta controlled the Mexican Congress and the offices just as Talaat controlled the Turkish Parliament and the chief posts of that state. Mexico under Huerta was a poverty-stricken country, with depleted finances, exhausted industries and agriculture, just as was Turkey under Talaat. How did Huerta seek to secure his own position and rehabilitate his distracted country? There was only one way, of course---that was by enlisting the support of some strong foreign power. He sought repeatedly to gain recognition from the United States for this reason and, when we refused to deal with a murderer, Huerta looked to Germany. Let us suppose that the Kaiser had responded; he could have reorganized Mexican finances, rebuilt her railroads, reestablished her industries, modernized her army, and in this way obtained a grip on the country that would have amounted to virtual possession.

Only one thing prevented Germany from doing this ---the Monroe Doctrine. But there was no Monroe Doctrine in Turkey, and what I have described as a possibility in Mexico is in all essentials an accurate picture of what happened in the Ottoman Empire. As I look back upon the situation, the whole thing seems so clear, so simple, so inevitable. Germany, up to that time, was practically the only great power in Europe that had not appropriated large slices of Turkish territory, a fact which gave her an initial advantage. Germany's representative at Constantinople was far better qualified than that of any other country, not only by absence of scruples, but also by knowledge and skill, to handle this situation. Wangenheim, was not the only capable German then on the ground. A particularly influential outpost of Pan-Germany was Paul Weitz, who had represented the Frankfurter Zeitung in Turkey for thirty years. Weitz had the most intimate acquaintance with Turks and Turkish affairs; there was not a hidden recess to which he could not gain admittance. He was constantly at Wangenheim's elbow, prompting, advising, informing. The German naval attach?, Humann, the son of a famous German archaeologist, had been born in Smyrna, and had passed practically his whole life in Turkey; he not only spoke Turkish, but he could also think like a Turk, and the whole psychology of the people was part of his mental equipment. Moreover, Enver, one of the two main Turkish chieftains, was on friendly terms with Humann. When I think of this experienced trio, Wangenheim, Weitz, and Humann, and of the charming and honourable gentlemen who were opposed to them, Mallet, Bompard, and Giers, the events that now rapidly followed seem as inevitable as the orderly processes of nature. By the spring of 1914 Talaat and Enver, representing the Committee of Union and Progress, practically dominated the Turkish Empire. Wangenheim, always having in mind the approaching war, had one inevitable purpose: that was to control Talaat and Enver.

Early in January, 1914, Enver became Minister of War. At that time Enver was thirty-two years old; like all the leading Turkish politicians of the period he came of humble stock and his popular title, "Hero of the Revolution," shows why Talaat and the Committee had selected him as Minister of War. Enver enjoyed something of a military reputation, though, so far as I could discover, he had never achieved a great military success. The revolution of which he had been one of the leaders in 1908 had cost very few human lives; he commanded an army in Tripoli against the Italians in 1919 ---but certainly there was nothing Napoleonic about that campaign. Enver himself once told me how, in the Second Balkan War, he had ridden all night at the head of his troops to the capture of Adrianople, and how, when he arrived there, the Bulgarians had abandoned it and his victory had thus been a bloodless one. But certainly Enver did have one trait that made for success in such a distracted country as Turkey---and that was audacity. He was quick in making decisions, always ready to stake his future and his very life upon the success of a single adventure; from the beginning, indeed, his career had been one lucky crisis after another. His nature had a remorselessness, a lack of pity, a cold-blooded determination, of which his cleancut handsome face, his small but sturdy figure, and his pleasing manners gave no indication. Nor would the casual spectator have suspected the passionate personal ambition that drove him on. His friends commonly referred to him as "Napoleonlik"---the little Napoleon---and this nickname really represented Enver's abiding conviction. I remember sitting one night with Enver, in his house; on one side hung a picture of Napoleon; on the other one of Frederick the Great; and between them sat Enver himself! This fact gives some notion of his vanity; these two warriors and statesmen were his great heroes and I believe that Enver thought fate had a career in store for him not unlike theirs. The fact that, at twenty-six, he had taken a leading part in the revolution which had deposed Abdul Hamid, naturally caused him to compare himself with Bonaparte; several times he has told me that he believed himself to be "a man of destiny." Enver even affected to believe that he had been divinely set apart to reestablish the glory of Turkey and make himself the great dictator. Yet, as I have suggested, there was something almost dainty and feminine in Enver's appearance. He was the type that in America we sometimes call a matin?e idol, and the word women frequently used to describe him was "dashing." His face contained not a single line or furrow; it never disclosed his emotions or his thoughts; he was always calm, steely, imperturbable. That Enver certainly lacked Napoleon's penetration is evident from the way he had planned to obtain the supreme power, for he early allied his personal fortunes with Germany. For years his sympathies had been with the Kaiser. Germany, the German army and navy, the German language, and the German autocratic system exercised a fatal charm upon this youthful preacher of Turkish democracy. After Hamid fell, Enver went on a military mission to Berlin, and here the Kaiser immediately detected in him a possible instrument for working out his plans in the Orient, and cultivated him in numerous ways. Afterward Enver spent a considerable time in Berlin as military attach?, and this experience still further endeared him to Germany. The man who returned to Constantinople was almost more German than Turkish. He had learned to speak German fluently, he was even wearing a moustache slightly curled up at the ends; indeed, he had been completely captivated by Prussianism. As soon as Enver became Minister of War, Wangenheim flattered and cajoled the young man, played upon his ambitions, and probably promised him Germany's complete support in achieving them. In his private conversation Enver made no secret of his admiration for Germany.

Thus Enver's elevation to the Ministry of War was virtually a German victory. He immediately instituted a drastic reorganization. Enver told me himself that he had accepted the post only on condition that he should have a free hand, and this free hand he now proceeded to exercise. The army still contained a large number of officers, many of whom were partisans of the murdered Nazim. and favoured the old r?gime rather than the Young Turks, Enver promptly cashiered 268 of these, and put in their places Turks who were known as "U. and P." men, and many Germans. The Enver-Talaat group always feared a revolution that would depose them as they had thrown out their predecessors. Many times did they tell me that their own success as revolutionists had taught them how easily a few determined men could seize control of the country; they did not propose, they said, to have a little group in their army organize such a coup d'?tat against them. The boldness of Enver's move alarmed even Talaat, but Enver showed the determination of his character and refused to reconsider his action, though one of the officers removed was Chukri Pasha, who had defended Adrianople in the Balkan war. Enver issued a circular to the Turkish commanders, practically telling them that they must look only to him for preferment and that they could make no headway by playing politics with any group except that dominated by the Young Turks.

Thus Enver's first acts were the beginnings in the Prussification of the Turkish army, but Talaat was not an enthusiastic German like his associate. He had no intention of playing Germany's game; he was working chiefly for the Committee and for himself. But he could not succeed unless he had control of the army; therefore, he had made Enver, for years his intimate associate in "U. and P." politics, Minister of War. Again he needed a strong army if he was to have any at all, and therefore he turned to the one source where he could find assistance, to Germany. Wangenheim and Talaat, in the latter part of 1913, had arranged that the Kaiser should send a military mission to reorganize the Turkish forces. Talaat told me that, in calling in this mission, he was using Germany, though Germany thought that it was using him. That there were definite dangers in the move he well understood. A deputy who discussed this situation with Talaat in January, 1914, has given me a memorandum of a conversation which shows well what was going on in Talaat's mind.

"Why do you hand the management of the country over to the Germans?" asked this deputy, referring to the German military mission. "Don't you see that this is part of Germany's plan to make Turkey a German colony---that we shall become merely another Egypt? "

"We understand perfectly," replied Talaat, "that that is Germany's programme. We also know that we cannot put this country on its feet with our own resources. We shall, therefore, take advantage of such technical and material assistance as the Germans can place at our disposal. We shall use Germany to help us reconstruct and defend the country until we are able to govern ourselves with our own strength. When that day comes, we can say good-bye to the Germans within twenty-four hours."

Certainly the physical condition of the Turkish army betrayed the need of assistance from some source. The picture it presented, before the Germans arrived, I have always regarded as portraying the condition of the whole empire. When I issued invitations for my first reception, a large number of Turkish officials asked to be permitted to come in evening clothes; they said that they had no uniforms and no money with which to purchase or to hire them. They had not received their salaries for three and a half months. As the Grand Vizier, who regulates the etiquette of such functions, still insisted on full uniform, many of these officials had to remain absent. About the same time the new German mission asked the commander of the second army corps to exercise his men, but the commander replied that he could not do so as his men had no shoes!

Desperate and wicked as Talaat subsequently showed himself to be, I still think that he at least was not then a willing tool of Germany. An episode that involved myself bears out this view. In describing the relations of the great powers to Turkey I have said nothing about the United States. In fact, we had no important business relations at that time. The Turks regarded us as a country of idealists and altruists, and the fact that we spent millions building wonderful educational institutions in their country purely from philanthropic motives aroused their astonishment and possibly their admiration. They liked Americans and regarded us as about the only disinterested friend whom they had among the nations. But our interests in Turkey were small; the Standard Oil Company did a growing business, the Singer Company sold sewing machines to the Armenians and Greeks; we bought a good deal of their tobacco, figs, and rugs, and gathered their licorice root. In addition to these activities, missionaries and educational experts formed about our only contacts with the Turkish Empire. The Turks knew that we had no desire to dismember their country or to mingle in Balkan politics. The very fact that my country was so disinterested was perhaps the reason why Talaat discussed Turkish affairs so freely with me. In the course of these conversations I frequently expressed my desire to serve them, and Talaat and some of the other members of the Cabinet got into the habit of consulting me on business matters. Soon after my arrival, I made a speech at the American Chamber of Commerce in Constantinople; Talaat, Djemal, and other important leaders were present. I talked about the backward economic state of Turkey and admonished them not to be discouraged. I described the condition of the United States after the Civil War and made the point that our devastated Southern States presented a spectacle not unlike that of Turkey at that present moment. I then related how we had gone to work, developed our resources, and built up the present thriving nation. My remarks apparently made a deep impression, especially my statement that after the Civil War the United States had become a large borrower in foreign money markets and had invited immigration from all parts of the world. This speech apparently gave Talaat a new idea. It was not impossible that the United States might furnish him the material support which he had been seeking in Europe. Already I had suggested that an American financial expert should be sent to study Turkish finance and in this connection I had mentioned Mr. Henry Bru?re, of New York---a suggestion which the Turks had received favourably. At that time Turkey's greatest need was money. France had financed Turkey for many years, and French bankers, in the spring of 1914, were negotiating for another large loan. Though Germany had made some loans, the condition of the Berlin money market at that time did not encourage the Turks to expect much assistance from that source.

In late December, 1913, Bust?ny Effendi---a Christian Arab, and Minister of Commerce and Agriculture, who spoke English fluently (he had been Turkish commissioner to the Chicago World's Fair in 1893)----called and approached me on the question of an American loan. Bust?ny asked if there were not American financiers who would take entire charge of the reorganization of' Turkish finance. His plea was really a cry of despair---and it touched me deeply. As I wrote in my diary at the time, "They seem to be scraping the box for money."' But I had been in Turkey only six weeks, and obviously I had no information on which I could recommend such a large contract to American bankers. I informed Bust?ny that my advice would not carry much weight in the United States unless it were based on a complete knowledge of economic conditions in Turkey. Talaat came to me a few days later, suggesting that I make a prolonged tour over the empire and study the situation at first hand. He asked if I could not arrange meanwhile a small temporary loan to tide them over the interim. He said there was no money in the Turkish Treasury; if I could get them only $5,000,000, that would satisfy them. I told Talaat that I would try to raise this amount for them, and that I would adopt his suggestion and inspect his Empire with the possible idea of interesting American investors. After obtaining the consent of the State Department, I wrote to my nephew and business associate, Mr. Robert E. Simon, asking him to sound certain New York institutions and bankers, on making a small short-time collateral loan to Turkey. Mr. Simon's investigations soon disclosed that a Turkish loan did not seem to be regarded as an attractive business undertaking in New York. Mr. Simon wrote, however, that Mr. C. K. G. Billings had shown much interest in the idea, and that, if I desired, Mr. Billings would come out in his yacht and discuss the matter with the Turkish Cabinet and with me. In a few days Mr. Billings had started for Constantinople.

The news of Mr. Billings's approach spread with great rapidity all over the Turkish capital; the fact that he was coming in his own private yacht seemed to magnify the importance and the glamour of the event. That a great American millionaire was prepared to reinforce the depleted Turkish Treasury and that this support was merely the preliminary step in the reorganization of Turkish finances by American capitalists, produced a tremendous flutter in the foreign embassies. So rapidly did the information spread, indeed, that I rather suspected that the Turkish Cabinet had taken no particular pains to keep it secret. This suspicion was strengthened by a visit which I received from the Chief Rabbi Nahoum, who informed me that he had come at the request of Talaat.

"There is a rumour," said the Chief Rabbi, "that Americans are about to make a loan to Turkey. Talaat would be greatly pleased if you would not contradict it."

Wangenheim. displayed an almost hysterical interest: the idea of America coming to the financial assistance of Turkey did not fall in with his plans at all, for in his eyes Turkey's poverty was chiefly valuable as a means of forcing the empire into Germany's hands. One day I showed Wangenheim a book containing etchings of Mr. Billings's homes, pictures, and horses; he showed a great interest, not only in the horses---Wangenheim was something of a horseman himself---but in this tangible evidence of great wealth. For the next few days several ambassadors and ministers filed into my office, each solemnly asking for a glimpse at this book! As the time approached for Mr. Billings's arrival, Talaat began making elaborate plans for his entertainment; he consulted me as to whom we should invite to the proposed dinners, lunches, and receptions. As usual Wangenheim got in ahead of the rest. He could not come to the dinner which we had planned and asked me to have him for lunch, and in this way he met Mr. Billings several hours before the other diplomats. Mr. Billings frankly told him that he was interested in Turkey and that it was not unlikely that he would make the loan.

In the evening we gave the Billings party a dinner, all the important members of the Turkish Cabinet being present. Before this dinner, Talaat, Mr. Billings, and myself had a long talk about the loan. Talaat informed us that the French bankers had accepted their terms that very day, and that they would, therefore, need no American money at that time. He was exceedingly gracious and grateful to Mr. Billings, and profuse in expressing his thanks. Indeed, he might well have been, for Mr. Billings's arrival enabled Turkey at last to close negotiations with the French bankers. His attempt to express his appreciation had one curious manifestation. Enver, the second man in the Cabinet, was celebrating his wedding when Mr. Billings arrived. The progress which Enver was making in the Turkish world is evidenced from the fact that, although Enver, as I have said, came of the humblest stock, his bride was a daughter of the Turkish Imperial House. Turkish weddings are prolonged affairs, lasting two or three days. The day following the Embassy dinner, Talaat gave the Billings party a luncheon at the Cercle d'Orient, and he insisted that Enver should leave his wedding ceremony long enough to attend this function. Enver, therefore, came to the luncheon, sat through all the speeches, and then returned to his bridal party.

I am convinced that Talaat did not regard this Billings episode as closed. As I look back upon this transaction, I see clearly -that he was seeking to extricate his country, and that the possibility that the United States would assist him in performing the rescue was ever present in his mind. He frequently spoke to me of Mr. "Beelings," as he called him, and even after Turkey had broken with France and England, and was depending on Germany for money, his mind still reverted to Mr. Billings's visit; perhaps he was thinking of our country as a financial haven of rest after he had carried out his plan of expelling the Germans. I am certain that the possibility of American help led him, in the days of the war, to do many things for me that he would not otherwise have done. "Remember me to Mr. Beelings" were almost the last words he said to me when I left Constantinople. This yachting visit, though it did not lack certain comedy elements at the time, I am sure ultimately saved many lives from starvation and massacre.

Chapter III - "The Personal Representative of the Kaiser" -Wangenheim Opposes the Sale of American Warships to Greece

But even in March, 1914, the Germans had pretty well tightened their hold on Turkey. Liman von Sanders, who had arrived in December, had become the predominant influence in the Turkish army. At first Von Sanders' appointment aroused no particular hostility, for German missions had been called in before to instruct the Turkish army, notably that of Von der Goltz, and an English naval mission, headed by Admiral Limpus, was even then in Turkey attempting the difficult task of reorganizing the Turkish navy. We soon discovered, however, that the Von Sanders military mission was something quite different from those which I have named. Even before Von Sanders' arrival it had been announced that he was to take command of the first Turkish army corps, and that General Bronssart von Schnellendorf was to become Chief of Staff. The appointments signified nothing less than that the Kaiser had almost completed his plans to annex the Turkish army to his own. To show the power which Von Sanders' appointment had given him, it is only necessary to say that the first army corps practically controlled Constantinople. These changes clearly showed to what an extent Enver Pasha had become a cog in the Prussian system.

Naturally the representatives of the Entente Powers could not tolerate such a usurpation by Germany. The British, French, and Russian Ambassadors immediately called upon the Grand Vizier and protested with more warmth than politeness over Von Sanders' elevation. The Turkish Cabinet hemmed and hawed in the usual way, protested that the change was not important, but finally it withdrew Von Sanders' appointment as head of the first army corps, and made him Inspector General. However, this did not greatly improve the situation, for this post really gave Von Sanders greater power than the one which he had held before. Thus, by January, 1914, seven months before the Great War began, Germany held this position in the Turkish army: a German general was Chief of Staff; another was Inspector General; scores of German officers held commands of the first importance, and the Turkish politician who was even then an outspoken champion of Germany, Enver Pasha, was Minister of War.

After securing this diplomatic triumph Wangenheim was granted a vacation---he had certainly earned it---and Giers, the Russian Ambassador, went off on a vacation at the same time. Baroness Wangenheim explained to me---I was ignorant at this time of all these subtleties of diplomacy---precisely what these vacations signified. Wangenheim's leave of absence, she said, meant that the German Foreign Office regarded the Von Sanders episode as closed---and closed with a German victory. Giers's furlough, she explained, meant that Russia declined to accept this point of view and that, so far as Russia was concerned, the Von Sanders affair had not ended. I remember writing to my family that, in this mysterious Near-Eastern diplomacy, the nations talked to each other with acts, not words, and I instanced Baroness Wangenheim's explanation of these diplomatic vacations as a case in point.

An incident which took place in my own house opened all our eyes to how seriously Von Sanders regarded this military mission. On February 18th, I gave my first diplomatic dinner; General Von Sanders and his two daughters attended, the General sitting next to my daughter Ruth. My daughter, however, did not have a very enjoyable time; this German field marshal, sitting there in his gorgeous uniform, his breast all sparkling with medals, hardly said a word throughout the whole meal. He ate his food silently and sulkily, all my daughter's attempts to enter into conversation evoking only an occasional surly monosyllable. The behaviour of this great military leader was that of a spoiled child.

At the end of the dinner Von Mutius, the German charg? d'affaires, came up to me in a high state of excitement. It was some time before he could sufficiently control his agitation to deliver his message.

"You have made a terrible mistake, Mr. Ambassador," he said.

"What is that?" I asked, naturally taken aback.

"You have greatly offended Field Marshal Von Sanders. You have placed him at the dinner lower in rank than the foreign ministers. He is the personal representative of the Kaiser and as such is entitled to equal rank with the ambassadors. He should have been placed ahead of the cabinet ministers and the foreign ministers."

So I had affronted the Emperor himself! This, then, was the explanation of Von Sanders' boorish behaviour. Fortunately, my position was an impregnable one. I had not arranged the seating precedence at this dinner; I had sent the list of my guests to the Marquis Pallavicini, the Austrian Ambassador and dean of the diplomatic corps, and the greatest authority in Constantinople on such delicate points as this. The Marquis had returned the list, marking in red ink against each name the order of precedence 1, 2, 3, 4, 5, etc. I still possess this document as it came from the Austrian Embassy, and General Von-Sanders' name appears with the numerals "13" against it. I must admit, however, that "the 13th chair" did bring him pretty well to the foot of the table.

I explained the situation to Von Mutius and asked M. Panfili, conseiller of the Austrian Embassy, who was a guest at the dinner, to come up and make everything clear to the outraged German diplomat. As the Austrians and Germans were allies, it was quite apparent that the slight, if slight there had been, was unintentional. Panfili said that he had been puzzled over the question of Von Sanders's position, and had submitted the question to the Marquis. The outcome was that the Austrian Ambassador had himself fixed Von Sanders' rank at number 13. But the German Embassy did not let the matter rest there, for afterward Wangenheim called on Pallavicini, and discussed the matter with considerable liveliness.

"If Liman von Sanders represents the Kaiser, whom do you represent?" Pallavicini asked Wangenheim. The argument was a good one, as the ambassador is always regarded as the alter ego of his sovereign.

"It is not customary," continued the Marquis, "for an emperor to have two representatives at the same court."

As the Marquis was unyielding, Wangenheim carried the question to the Grand Vizier. But Sa?d Halim refused to assume responsibility for so momentous a decision and referred the dispute to the Council of Ministers. This body solemnly sat upon the question and rendered this verdict: Von Sanders should rank ahead of the ministers of foreign countries, but below the members of the Turkish Cabinet. Then the foreign ministers lifted up their voices in protest. Von Sanders not only became exceedingly unpopular for raising this question, but the dictatorial and autocratic way in which he had done it aroused general disgust. The ministers declared that, if Von Sanders were ever given precedence at any function of this kind, they would leave the table in a body. The net result was that Von Sanders was never again invited to a diplomatic dinner. Sir Louis Mallet, the British Ambassador, took a sardonic interest in the episode. It was lucky, he said, that it had not happened at his Embassy; if it had, the newspapers would have had columns about the strained relations between England and Germany!

After all, this proceeding did have great international importance. Von Sanders's personal vanity had led him to betray a diplomatic secret; he was not merely a drill master who had been sent to instruct the Turkish army; he was precisely what he had claimed to be---the personal representative of the Kaiser. The Kaiser had selected him, just as he had selected Wangenheim, as an instrument for working his will in Turkey. Afterward Von Sanders told me, with all that pride which German aristocrats manifest when speaking of their imperial master, how the Kaiser had talked to him a couple of hours the day he had appointed him to this Constantinople mission, and how, the day that he had started, Wilhelm had spent another hour giving him final instructions. I reported this dinner incident to my government as indicating Germany's growing ascendancy in Turkey and I presume the other ambassadors likewise reported it to their governments. The American military attach?, Major John R. M. Taylor, who was present, attributed the utmost significance to it. A month after the occurrence he and Captain McCauley, commanding the Scorpion, the American stationnaire at Constantinople, had lunch at Cairo with Lord Kitchener. The luncheon was a small one, only the Americans, Lord Kitchener, his sister, and an aide making up the party. Major Taylor related this incident, and Kitchener displayed much interest.

"What do you think it signifies ?" asked Kitchener.

"I think it means," Major Taylor said, "that when the big war comes, Turkey will probably be the ally of Germany. If she is not in direct alliance, I think that she at least will mobilize on the line of the Caucasus and thus divert three Russian army corps from the European theatre of operations."

Kitchener thought for a moment and then said, "I agree with you."

And now for several months we had before our eyes this spectacle of the Turkish army actually under the control of Germany. German officers drilled the troops daily---all, I am now convinced, in preparation for the approaching war. Just what results had been accomplished appeared when, in July, there was a great military review. The occasion was a splendid and a gala affair. The Sultan attended in state; he sat under a beautifully decorated tent where he held a little court; and the Khedive of Egypt, the Crown Prince of Turkey, the princes of the imperial blood and the entire Cabinet were also on hand. We now saw that, in the preceding six months, the Turkish army had been completely Prussianized. What in January had been an undisciplined, ragged rabble was now parading with the goose step; the men were clad in German field gray, and they even wore a casque-shaped head covering, which slightly suggested the German pickelhaube. The German officers were immensely proud of the exhibition, and the transformation of the wretched Turkish soldiers of January into these neatly dressed, smartly stepping, splendidly manoeuvring troops was really a creditable military achievement. When the Sultan invited me to his tent I naturally congratulated him upon the excellent showing of his men. He did not manifest much enthusiasm; he said that he regretted the possibility of war; he was at heart a pacifist. I noticed certain conspicuous absences from this great German f?te, for the French, British, Russian, and Italian ambassadors had kept away. Bompard said that, he had received his ten tickets but that he did not regard that as an invitation. Wangenheim told me, with some satisfaction, that the other, ambassadors were jealous and that they did not care to see the progress which the Turkish army had made under German instruction. I did not have the slightest question that these ambassadors refused to attend because they had no desire to grace this German holiday; nor did I blame them.

Meanwhile, I had other evidences that Germany was playing her part in Turkish politics. In June the relations between Greece and Turkey approached the breaking-point. The Treaty of London (May 30, 1913) had left Greece in possession of the islands of Chios and Mitylene. A reference to the map discloses the strategic importance of these islands. They stand there in the Aegean Sea like guardians controlling the bay and the great port of Smyrna, and it is quite apparent that any strong military nation which permanently held these vantage points would ultimately control Smyrna and the whole Aegean coast of Asia Minor. The racial situation made the continued retention of these islands by Greece a constant military danger to Turkey. Their population was Greek and had been Greek since the days of Homer; the coast of Asia Minor itself was also Greek; more than half the population of Smyrna, Turkey's greatest Mediterranean seaport, was Greek; in its industries, its commerce, and its culture the city was so predominantly Greek that the Turks usually referred to it as giaour Ismir---"infidel Smyrna." Though this Greek population was nominally Ottoman in nationality it did not conceal its affection for the Greek fatherland, these Asiatic Greeks even making contributions to promote Greek national aims. The Aegean islands and the mainland, in fact, constituted Graecia Irredenta; and that Greece was determined to redeem them, precisely as she had recently redeemed Crete, was no diplomatic secret. Should the Greeks ever land an army on this Asia Minor coast, there was little question that the native Greek population would welcome it enthusiastically and cooperate with it.

Since Germany, however, had her own plans for Asia Minor, inevitably the Greeks in this region formed a barrier to Pan-German aspirations. As long as this region remained Greek, it formed a natural obstacle to Germany's road to the Persian Gulf, precisely as did Serbia. Any one who has read even cursorily the literature of Pan-Germania is familiar with the peculiar method which German publicists have advocated for dealing with populations that stand in Germany's way. That is by deportation. The violent shifting of whole peoples from one part of Europe to another, as though they were so many herds of cattle, has for years been part of the Kaiser's plans for German expansion. This is the treatment which, since the war began, she has applied to Belgium, to Poland, to Serbia; its most hideous manifestation, as I shall show, has been to Armenia. Acting under Germany's prompting, Turkey now began to apply this principle of deportation to her Greek subjects in Asia Minor. Three years afterward the German admiral, Usedom, who had been stationed in the Dardanelles during the bombardment, told me that it was the Germans "who urgently made the suggestion that the Greeks be moved from the seashore." The German motive, Admiral Usedom said, was purely military. Whether Talaat and his associates realized that they were playing the German game I am not sure, but there is no doubt that the Germans were constantly instigating them in this congenial task.

The events that followed foreshadowed the policy adopted in' the Armenian massacres. The Turkish officials pounced upon the Greeks, herded them in groups and marched them toward the ships. They gave them no time to settle their private affairs, and they took no pains to keep families together. The plan was to transport the Greeks to the wholly Greek islands in the Aegean. Naturally the Greeks rebelled against such treatment, and occasional massacres were the result, especially in Phocaea, where more than fifty people were murdered. The Turks demanded that all foreign establishments in Smyrna dismiss their Greek employees and replace them with Moslems. Among other American concerns, the Singer Manufacturing Company received such instructions, and though I interceded and obtained sixty days' delay, ultimately this American concern had to obey the mandate. An official boycott was established against all Christians, not only in Asia Minor, but in Constantinople, but this boycott did not discriminate against the Jews, who have always been more popular with the Turks than have the Christians. The officials particularly requested Jewish merchants. to put signs over their doors indicating their nationality and trade such signs as "Abraham the Jew, tailor," "Isaac the Jew, shoemaker," and the like. I looked upon this boycott as illustrating the topsy-turvy national organization of Turkey, for here we had a nation engaging in a commercial boycott against its own subjects.

This procedure against the Greeks not improperly aroused my indignation. I did not have the slightest suspicion at that time that the Germans had instigated these deportations, but I looked upon them merely as an outburst of Turkish ferocity and chauvinism. By this time I knew Talaat well; I saw him nearly every day, and he used to discuss practically every phase of international relations with me. I objected vigorously to his treatment of the Greeks; I told him that it would make the worst possible impression abroad and that it affected American interests. Talaat explained his national policy: these different blocs in the Turkish Empire, he said, had always conspired against Turkey; because of the hostility of these native populations, Turkey had lost province after province---Greece, Serbia, Rumania, Bulgaria, Bosnia, Herzegovina, Egypt, and Tripoli. In this way the Turkish Empire had dwindled almost to the vanishing point. If what was left of Turkey was to survive, added Talaat, he must get rid of these alien peoples. "Turkey for the Turks " was now Talaat's controlling idea. Therefore he proposed to Turkify Smyrna and the adjoining islands. Already 40,000 Greeks had left, and he asked me again to urge American business houses to employ only Turks. He said that the accounts of violence and murder had been greatly exaggerated and suggested that a commission be sent to investigate. "They want a commission to whitewash Turkey," Sir Louis Mallet, the British Ambassador, told me. True enough, when this commission did bring in its report, it exculpated Turkey.

The Greeks in Turkey had one great advantage over the Armenians, for there was such a thing as a Greek government, which naturally has a protecting interest in them. The Turks knew that these deportations would precipitate a war with Greece; in fact, they welcomed such a war and were preparing for it. So enthusiastic were the Turkish people that they had raised money by popular subscription and bad purchased a Brazilian dreadnaught which was then under construction in England. The government had ordered also a second dreadnaught in England, and several submarines and destroyers in France. The purpose of these naval preparations was no secret in Constantinople. As soon as they obtained these ships, or even the one dreadnaught which was nearing completion, Turkey intended to attack Greece and take back the islands. A single modern battleship like the Sultan Osman---this was the name the Turks had given the Brazilian vessel---could easily overpower the whole Greek navy and control the Aegean Sea. As this powerful vessel would be finished and commissioned in a few months, we all expected the Greco-Turkish war to break out in the fall. What could the Greek navy possibly do against this impending danger?

Such was the situation when, early in June, I received a most agitated visitor. This was Djemal Pasha, the Turkish Minister of Marine and one of the three men who then dominated the Turkish Empire. I have hardly ever seen a man who appeared more utterly worried than was Djemal on this occasion. As he began talking excitedly to my interpreter in French, his whiskers trembling with his emotions and his hands wildly gesticulating, he seemed to be almost beside himself. I knew enough French to understand what he was saying, and the news which he brought---this was the first I had heard of it---sufficiently explained his agitation. The American Government, he said, was negotiating with Greece for the sale of two battleships, the Idaho and the Mississippi. He urged that I should immediately move to prevent any such sale. His attitude was that of a suppliant; he begged, he implored that I should intervene. All along, he said, the Turks regarded the United States as their best friend; I had frequently expressed my desire to help them; well, here was the chance to show our good feeling. The fact that Greece and Turkey were practically on the verge of war, said Djemal, really made the sale of the ships an unneutral act. Still, if the transaction were purely a commercial one, Turkey would like a chance to bid. "We will pay more than Greece," he added. He ended with a powerful plea that I should at once cable my government about the matter, and this I promised to do.

Evidently the clever Greeks had turned the tables on their enemy. Turkey had rather too boldly advertised her intention of attacking Greece as soon as she had received her dreadnaughts. Both the ships for which Greece was now negotiating were immediately available for battle! The Idaho and Mississippi were not indispensable ships for the American navy; they could not take their place in the first line of battle; they were powerful enough, however, to drive the whole Turkish navy from the Aegean. Evidently the Greeks did not intend politely to postpone the impending war until the Turkish dreadnaughts had been finished, but to attack as soon as they received these American ships. Djemal's point, of course, had no legal validity. However great the threat of war might be, Turkey and Greece were still actually at peace. Clearly Greece had just as much right to purchase warships in the United States as Turkey had to purchase them in Brazil or England.

But Djemal was not the only statesman who attempted to prevent the sale; the German Ambassador displayed the keenest interest. Several days after Djemal's visit, Wangenheim and I were riding in the hills north of Constantinople; Wangenheim began to talk about the Greeks, to whom he displayed a violent antipathy, about the chances of war, and the projected sale of American warships. He made a long argument about the sale, his reasoning being precisely the same as Djemal's---a fact which aroused my suspicions that he had himself coached Djemal for his interview with me.

"Just look at the dangerous precedent you are establishing," said Wangenheim. "It is not unlikely that the United States may sometime find itself in a position like Turkey's to-day. Suppose that you were on the brink of war with Japan; then England could sell a fleet of dreadnaughts to Japan. How would the United States like that?"

And then he made a statement which indicated what really lay back of his protest. I have thought of it many times in the last three years. The scene is indelibly impressed on my mind. There we sat on our horses; the silent ancient forest of Belgrade lay around us, while in the distance the Black Sea glistened in the afternoon sun. Wangenheim suddenly became quiet and extremely earnest. He looked in my eyes and said:

"I don't think that the United States realizes what a serious matter this is. The sale of these ships might be the cause that would bring on a European war."

This conversation took place on June 13th; this was about six weeks before the conflagration broke out. Wangenheim. knew perfectly well that Germany was rushing preparations for this great conflict, and he also knew that preparations were not yet entirely complete. Like all the German ambassadors, Wangenheim, had received instructions not to let any crisis arise that would precipitate war until all these preparations had been finished. He had no objections to the expulsion of the Greeks, for that in itself was part of these preparations; he was much disturbed, however, over the prospect that the Greeks might succeed in arming themselves and disturbing existing conditions in the Balkans. At that moment the Balkans were a smouldering volcano; Europe had gone through two Balkan wars without becoming generally involved, and Wangenheim knew that another would set the whole continent ablaze. He knew that war was coming, but he did not want it just then. He was simply attempting to influence me at that moment to gain a little more time for Germany.

He went so far as to ask me to cable personally to the President, explain the seriousness of the situation, and to call his attention to the telegrams that had gone to the State Department on the proposed sale of the ships. I regarded his suggestion as an impertinent one and declined to act upon it.

To Djemal and the other Turkish officials who kept pressing me I suggested that their ambassador in Washington should take up the matter directly with the President. They acted on this advice, but the Greeks again got ahead of them. At two o'clock, June 22d, the Greek charg? d'affaires at Washington and Commander Tsouklas, of the Greek navy, called upon the President and arranged the sale. As they left the President's office, the Turkish Ambassador entered---just fifteen minutes too late!

I presume that Mr. Wilson consented to the sale because he knew that Turkey was preparing to attack Greece and believed that the Idaho and Mississippi would prevent such an attack and so preserve peace in the Balkans.

Acting under the authorization of Congress, the administration sold these ships on July 8, 1914, to Fred J. Gauntlett, for $12,535,276.98. Congress immediately voted the money realized from the sale to the construction of a great modern dreadnaught, the California. Mr. Gauntlett transferred the ships to the Greek Government. Rechristened the Kilkis and the Lemnos, those battleships immediately took their places as the most powerful vessels of the Greek Navy, and the enthusiasm of the Greeks in obtaining them was unbounded.

By this time we had moved from the Embassy to our summer home on the Bosphorus. All the summer embassies were located there, and a more beautiful spot I have never seen. Our house was a three-story building, something in the Venetian style; behind it the cliff rose abruptly, with several terraced gardens towering one above the other; the building stood so near the shore and the waters of the Bosphorus rushed by so rapidly that when we sat outside, especially on a moonlight night, we had almost a complete illusion that we were sitting on the deck of a fast sailing ship. In the daytime the Bosphorus, here little more than a mile wide, was alive with gaily coloured craft; I recall this animated scene with particular vividness because I retain in my mind the contrast it presented a few months afterward, when Turkey's entrance into the war had the immediate result of closing this strait. Day by day the huge Russian steamships, on their way from Black Sea ports to Smyrna, Alexandria, and other cities, made clear the importance of this little strip of water, and explained the bloody contests of the European nations, extending over a thousand years, for its possession. However, these early summer months were peaceful; all the ambassadors and ministers and their families were thrown constantly together; here daily gathered the representatives of all the powers that for the last four years have been grappling in history's bloodiest war, all then apparently friends, sitting around the same dining tables, walking arm in arm upon the porches. The ambassador of one power would most graciously escort to dinner the wife of another whose country was perhaps the most antagonistic to his own. Little groups would form after dinner; the Grand Vizier would hold an impromptu reception in one corner, cabinet ministers would be whispering in another; a group of ambassadors would discuss the Greek situation out on the porch; the Turkish officials would glance quizzically upon the animated scene and perhaps comment quietly in their own tongue; the Russian Ambassador would glide about the room, pick out someone whom he wished to talk to, lock arms and push him into a corner for a surreptitious t?te-?-t?te. Meanwhile, our sons and daughters, the junior members' of the diplomatic corps, and the officers of the several stationnaires, dancing and flirting, seemed to think that the whole proceeding had been arranged solely for their amusement. And to realize, while all this was going on, that neither the Grand Vizier, nor any of the other high Turkish officials, would leave the house without outriders and bodyguards to protect them from assassination---whatever other emotions such a vibrating atmosphere might arouse, it was certainly alive with interest. I felt also that there was something electric about it all; war was ever the favourite topic of conversation; everyone seemed to realize that this peaceful, frivolous life was transitory, and that at any moment might come the spark that was to set everything aflame.

Yet, when the crisis came, it produced no immediate sensation. On June 29th we heard of the assassination of the Grand Duke of Austria and his consort. Everybody received the news calmly, there was, indeed, a stunned feeling that something momentous had happened, but there was practically no excitement. A day or two after this tragedy I had a long talk with Talaat on diplomatic matters; he made no reference at all to this event. I think now that we were all affected by a kind of emotional paralysis---as we were nearer the centre than most people, we certainly realized the dangers in the situation. In a day or two our tongues seemed to have been loosened, for we began to talk and to talk war. When I saw Von Mutius, the German charg?, and Weitz, the diplomat-correspondent of the Frankfurter Zeitung, they also discussed the impending conflict, and again they gave their forecast a characteristically Germanic touch; when war came, they said, of course the United States would take advantage of it to get all the Mexican and South American trade!

When I called upon Pallavicini to express my condolences over the Grand Duke's death, he received me with the most stately solemnity. He was conscious that he was representing the imperial family, and his grief seemed to be personal; one would think that he had lost his own son. I expressed my abhorrence and that of my nation for the deed, and our sympathy with the aged emperor.

"Jab, Jab, es is sear schrecklich" (yes, yes, it is very terrible), he answered, almost in a whisper.

"Serbia will be condemned for her conduct," he added. " She will be compelled to make reparation."

A few days later, when Pallavicini called upon me, he spoke of the nationalistic societies that Serbia had permitted to exist and of her determination to annex Bosnia and Herzegovina. He said that his government would insist on the abandonment of these societies and these pretentions, and that probably a punitive expedition into Serbia would be necessary to prevent such outrages as the murder of the Grand Duke. Herein I had my first intimation of the famous ultimatum of July 22d.

The entire diplomatic corps attended the requiem mass for the Grand Duke and Duchess, celebrated at the Church of Sainte Marie on July 4th. The church is located in the Grande Rue de Pera, not far from the Austrian Embassy; to reach it we had to descend a flight of forty stone steps. At the top of these stairs representatives of the Austrian Embassy, dressed in full uniform, with cr?pe on the left arm, met us, and escorted us to our seats. All the ambassadors sat in the front pew; I recall this with strange emotions now, for it was the last time that we ever sat together. The service was dignified and beautiful; I remember it with especial vividness. because of the contrasting scene that immediately followed. When the stately, gorgeously robed priests had finished, we all shook hands with the Austrian Ambassador, returned to our automobiles, and started on our eight-mile ride along the Bosphorus to the American Embassy. For this day was not only the day when we paid our tribute to the murdered heir of this medieval autocracy; it was also the Fourth of July. The very setting of the two scenes symbolized these two national ideals. I always think of this ambassadorial group going down those stone steps to the church, to pay their respect to the Grand Duke, and then going up to the gaily decorated American Embassy, to pay their respect to the Declaration of Independence. All the station ships of the foreign countries lay out in the stream, decorated and dressed in honour of our national holiday, and the ambassadors and ministers called in full regalia. From the upper gardens we could see the place where Darius crossed from Asia with his Persian hosts 2,500 years before---one of those ancient autocrats the line of which is not yet entirely extinct. There also we could see magnificent Robert College, an institution that represented America's conception of the way to "penetrate" the Turkish Empire. At night our gardens were illuminated with Chinese lanterns; good old American fireworks, lighting up the surrounding hills and the Bosphorus, and the American flag flying at the front of the house, seemed almost to act as a challenge to the plentiful reminders of autocracy and oppression which we had had in the early part of the day. Not more than a mile across the water the dark and gloomy hills of Asia, for ages the birthplace of military despotisms, caught a faint and, I think, a prophetic glow from these illuminations.

In glancing at the ambassadorial group at the church and, afterward, at our reception, I was surprised to note that one familiar figure was missing. Wangenheim, Austria's ally, was not present. This somewhat puzzled me at the time, but afterward I had the explanation from Wangenheim's own lips. He had left some days before for Berlin. The Kaiser had summoned him to an imperial council, which met on July 5th, and which decided to plunge Europe into war.

Chapter IV - Germany Mobilizes the Turkish Army

In reading the August newspapers, which described the mobilizations in Europe, I was particularly struck with the emphasis which they laid upon the splendid spirit that was overnight changing the civilian populations into armies. At that time Turkey had not entered. the war and her political leaders were loudly protesting their intention of maintaining a strict neutrality. Despite these pacific statements, the occurrences in Constantinople were almost as warlike as those that were taking place in the European capitals. Though Turkey was at peace, her army was mobilizing, merely, we were told, as a precautionary measure. Yet the daily scenes which I witnessed in Constantinople bore few resemblances to those which were agitating every city of Europe. The martial patriotism of men, and the sublime patience and sacrifice of women, may sometimes give war an heroic aspect, but in Turkey the prospect was one of general listlessness and misery. Day by day the miscellaneous Ottoman hordes passed through the streets. Arabs, bootless and shoeless, dressed in their most gaily coloured garments, with long linen bags (containing the required five days' rations) thrown over their shoulders, shambling in their gait and bewildered in their manner, touched shoulders with equally dispirited Bedouins, evidently suddenly snatched from the desert.

A motley aggregation of Turks, Circassians, Greeks, Kurds, Armenians, and Jews, showing signs of having been summarily taken from their farms and shops, constantly jostled one another. Most were ragged and many looked half-starved; everything about them suggested hopelessness and a cattle-like submission to a fate which they knew that they could not avoid. There was no joy in approaching battle, no feeling that they were sacrificing themselves for a mighty cause; day by day they passed, the unwilling children of a tatterdemalion empire that was making one last despairing attempt to gird itself for action.

These wretched marchers little realized what was the power that was dragging them from the four corners of their country. Even we of the diplomatic group had not then clearly grasped the real situation. We learned afterward that the signal for this mobilization had not come originally from Enver or Talaat or the Turkish Cabinet, but from the General Staff in Berlin and its representatives in Constantinople. Liman von Sanders and Bronssart were really directing the complicated operation. There were unmistakable signs of German activity. As soon as the German armies crossed the Rhine, work was begun on a mammoth wireless station a few miles outside of Constantinople. The materials all came from Germany by way of Rumania, and the skilled mechanics, industriously working from daybreak to sunset, were unmistakably Germans. Of course, the neutrality laws would have prohibited the construction of a wireless station for a belligerent in a neutral country like Turkey; it was therefore officially announced that a German company was building this heaven-pointing structure for the Turkish Government and on the Sultan's own property. But this story deceived no one. Wangenheim, the German Ambassador, spoke of it freely and constantly as a German enterprise.

"Have you seen our wireless yet?" he would ask me. "Come on, let's ride up there and look it over."

He proudly told me that it was the most powerful in the world---powerful enough to catch all messages sent from the Eiffel Tower in Paris! He said that it would put him in constant communication with Berlin. So little did he attempt to conceal its German ownership that several times, when ordinary telegraphic communication was suspended, he offered to let me use it to send my telegrams.

This wireless plant was an outward symbol of the close though unacknowledged association which then existed between Turkey and Berlin. It. took some time to finish such an extensive station and in the interim Wangenheim was using the apparatus on the Corcovado, a German merchant ship which was lying in the Bosphorus opposite the German Embassy. For practical purposes, Wangenheim had a constant telephone connection with Berlin.

German officers were almost as active as the Turks themselves in this mobilization. They enjoyed it all immensely; indeed they gave every sign that they were having the time of their lives. Bronssart, Humann, and Lafferts were constantly at Enver's elbow, advising and directing the operations. German officers were rushing through the streets every day in huge automobiles, all requisitioned from the civilian population; they filled all the restaurants and amusement places at night, and celebrated their joy in the situation by consuming large quantities of champagne---also requisitioned. A particularly spectacular and noisy figure was that of Von der Goltz Pasha. He was constantly making a kind of vice-regal progress through the streets in a huge and madly dashing automobile, on both sides of which flaring German eagles were painted. A trumpeter on the front seat would blow loud, defiant blasts as the conveyance rushed along, and woe to any one, Turk or non-Turk, who happened to get in the way! The Germans made no attempt to conceal their conviction that they owned this town. Just as Wangenheim had established a little Wilhelmstrasse in his Embassy, so had the German military men established a sub-station of the Berlin General Staff. They even brought their wives and families from Germany; I heard Baroness Wangenheim remark that she was holding a little court at the German Embassy.

The Germans, however, were about the only people who were enjoying this proceeding. The requisitioning that accompanied the mobilization really amounted to a wholesale looting of the civilian population. The Turks took all the horses, mules, camels, sheep, cows, and other beasts that they could lay their hands on; Enver told me that they had gathered in 150,000 animals. They did it most unintelligently, making no provision for the continuance of the species; thus they would leave only two cows or two mares in many of the villages. This system of requisitioning, as I shall describe, had the inevitable result of destroying the nation's agriculture, and ultimately led to the starvation of hundreds of thousands of people. But the Turks, like the Germans, thought that the war was destined to be a very short one, and that they would quickly recuperate from the injuries which their methods of supplying an army were causing their peasant population. The Government showed precisely the same shamelessness and lack of intelligence in the way that they requisitioned materials from merchants and shopmen. These proceedings amounted to little less than conscious highwaymanship. But practically none of these merchants were Moslems; most of them were Christians, though there were a few Jews; and the Turkish officials therefore not only provided the needs of their army and incidentally lined their own pockets, but they found a religious joy in pillaging the infidel establishments. They would enter a retail shop, take practically all the merchandise on the shelves, and give merely a piece of paper in acknowledgment. As the Government had never paid for the supplies which it had taken in the Italian and Balkan wars, the merchants hardly expected that they would ever receive anything for these latest requisitions. Afterward many who understood officialdom, and were politically influential, did recover to the extent of 70 per cent what became of the remaining 30 per cent. is not a secret to those who have had experience with Turkish bureaucrats.

Thus for most of the population requisitioning simply meant financial ruin. That the process was merely pillaging is shown by many of the materials which the army took, ostensibly for the use of the soldiers. Thus the officers seized all the mohair they could find; on occasion they even carried off women's silk stockings, corsets, and baby's slippers, and I heard of one case in which they reinforced the Turkish commissary with caviar and other delicacies. They demanded blankets from one merchant who was a dealer in women's underwear; because he had no such stock, they seized what he had, and he afterward saw his appropriated goods reposing in rival establishments. The Turks did the same thing in many other cases. The prevailing system was to take movable property wherever available and convert it into cash; where the money ultimately went I do not know, but that many private fortunes were made I have little doubt. I told Enver that this ruthless method of mobilizing and requisitioning was destroying his country. Misery and starvation soon began to afflict the land. Out of a 4,000,000 adult male population more than 1,500,000 were ultimately enlisted and so about a million families were left without breadwinners, all of them in a condition of extreme destitution. The Turkish Government paid its soldiers 25 cents a month, and gave the families a separation allowance of $1.20 a month. As a result thousands were dying from lack of food and many more were enfeebled by malnutrition; I believe that the empire has lost a quarter of its Turkish population since the war started. I asked Enver why he permitted his people to be destroyed in this way. But sufferings like these did not distress him. He was much impressed by his success in raising a large army with practically no money --- something, he boasted, which no other nation had ever done before. In order to accomplish this, Enver had issued orders which stigmatized the evasion of military service as desertion and therefore punishable with the death penalty. He also adopted a scheme by which any Ottoman could obtain exemption by the payment of about $190. Still Enver regarded his accomplishment as a notable one. It was really his first taste of unlimited power and he enjoyed the experience greatly.

That the Germans directed this mobilization is not a matter of opinion but of proof. I need only mention that the Germans were requisitioning materials in their own name for their own uses. I have a photographic copy of such a requisition made by Humann, the German naval attach?, for a shipload of oil cake. This document is dated September 29, 1914. "The lot by the steamship Derindje which you mentioned in your letter of the 26th," this paper reads, "has been requisitioned by me for the German Government." This clearly shows that, a month before Turkey had entered the war, Germany was really exercising the powers of sovereignty at Constantinople.

Chapter V - Wangenheim Smuggles the "Goeben" and the "Breslau" Through The Dardanelles

On August 10th, I went out on a little launch to meet the Sicilia, a small Italian ship which had just arrived from Venice. I was especially interested in this vessel because she was bringing to Constantinople my son-in-law and daughter, Mr. and Mrs. Maurice Wertheim, and their three little daughters. The greeting proved even more interesting than I had expected. I found the passengers considerably excited, for they had witnessed, the day before, a naval engagement in the Ionian Sea.

"We were lunching yesterday on deck," my daughter told me, "when I saw two strange-looking vessels just above the horizon. I ran for the glasses and made out two large battleships, the first one with two queer, exotic-looking towers and the other one quite an ordinary-looking battleship. We watched and saw another ship coming up behind them and going very fast. She came nearer and nearer and then we heard guns booming. Pillars of water sprang up in the air and there were many little puffs of white smoke. It took me some time to realize what it was all about, and then it burst upon me that we were actually witnessing an engagement. The ships continually shifted their position but went on and on. The two big ones turned and rushed furiously for the little one, and then apparently they changed their minds and turned back. Then the little one turned around and calmly steamed in our direction. At first I was somewhat alarmed at this, but nothing happened. She circled around us with her tars excited and grinning and somewhat grimy. They signalled to our captain many questions, and then turned and finally disappeared. The captain told us that the two big ships were Germans which had been caught in the Mediterranean and which were trying to escape from the British fleet. He said that the British ships are chasing them all over the Mediterranean, and that the German ships are trying to get into Constantinople. Have you seen anything of them? Where do you suppose the British fleet is? "

A few hours afterward I happened to meet Wangenheim. When I told him what Mrs. Wertheim had seen, he displayed an agitated interest. Immediately after lunch he called at the American Embassy with Pallavicini, the Austrian Ambassador, and asked for an interview with my daughter. The two ambassadors solemnly planted themselves in chairs before Mrs. Wertheim and subjected her to a most minute, though very polite, cross examination. "I never felt so important in my life," she afterward told me. They would not permit her to leave out a single detail; they wished to know how many shots had been fired, what direction the German ships had taken, what everybody on board had said, and so on. The visit seemed to give these allied ambassadors immense relief and satisfaction, for they left the house in an almost jubilant mood, behaving as though a great weight had been taken off their minds. And certainly they had good reason for their elation. My daughter had been the means of giving them the news which they had desired to hear above everything else-that the Goeben and the Breslau had escaped the British fleet and were then steaming rapidly in the direction of the Dardanelles.

For it was those famous German ships, the Goeben and the Breslau, which my daughter had seen engaged in battle with a British scout ship!

The next day official business called me to the German Embassy. But Wangenheim's animated manner soon disclosed that he had no interest in routine matters. Never had I seen him so nervous and so excited. He could not rest in his chair more than a few minutes at a time; he was constantly jumping up, rushing to the window and looking anxiously out toward the Bosphorus, where his private wireless station, the Corcovado, lay about three quarters of a mile away. Wangenheim's face was flushed and his eyes were shining; he would stride up and down the room, speaking now of a recent German victory, now giving me a little forecast of Germany's plans--- and then he would stalk to the window again for another look at the Corcovado.

"Something is seriously distracting you," I said, rising. "I will go and come again some other time."

"No. not" the Ambassador almost shouted. "I want you to stay right where you are. This will be a great day for Germany! If you will only remain for a few minutes you will hear a great piece of news---something that has the utmost bearing upon Turkey's relation to the war."

Then he rushed out on the portico and leaned over the balustrade. At the same moment I saw a little launch put out from the Corcovado toward the Ambassador's dock. Wangenheim hurried down, seized an envelope from one of the sailors, and a moment afterward burst into the room again.

"We've got them!" he shouted to me.

"Got what?" I asked.

"The Goeben and the Breslau have passed through the Dardanelles!"

He was waving the wireless message with all the enthusiasm of a college boy whose football team has won a victory.

Then, momentarily checking his enthusiasm, he came up to me solemnly, humorously shook his forefinger, lifted his eyebrows, and said, "Of course, you understand that we have sold those ships to Turkey!

"And Admiral Souchon," he added with another wink, "will enter the Sultan's service!"

Wangenheim had more than patriotic reasons for this exultation; the arrival of these ships was the greatest day in his diplomatic career. It was really the first diplomatic victory which Germany had won. For years the chancellorship of the empire had been Wangenheim's laudable ambition, and he behaved now like a man who saw his prize within his grasp. The voyage of the Goeben and the Breslau was his personal triumph; he had arranged with the Turkish Cabinet for their passage through the Dardanelles, and he had directed their movements by wireless in the Mediterranean. By safely getting the Goeben and the Breslau into Constantinople, Wangenheim had definitely clinched Turkey as Germany's ally. All his intrigues and plottings for three years had now finally succeeded.

I doubt if any two ships have exercised a greater influence upon history than these two German cruisers. Few of us at that time realized their great importance, but subsequent developments have fully justified Wangenheim's exuberant satisfaction. The Goeben was a powerful battle cruiser of recent construction; the Breslau was not so large a ship, but she, like the Goeben, had the excessive speed that made her extremely serviceable in those waters. These ships had spent the few months preceding the war cruising in the Mediterranean, and when the declaration finally came they were taking on supplies at Messina. I have always regarded it as more than a coincidence that these two vessels, both of them having a greater speed than any French or English ships in the Mediterranean, should have been lying not far from Turkey when war broke out. The selection of the Goeben was particularly fortunate, as she had twice before visited Constantinople and her officers and men knew the Dardanelles perfectly. The behaviour of these crews, when the news of war was received, indicated the spirit with which the German navy began hostilities; the men broke into singing and shouting, lifted their Admiral upon their shoulders, and held a real German jollification. It is said that Admiral Souchon preserved, as a touching souvenir of this occasion, his white uniform bearing the finger prints of his grimy sailors!

For all their joy at the prospect of battle, the situation of these ships was still a precarious one. They formed no match for the large British and French naval forces which were roaming through the Mediterranean. The Goeben and the Breslau were far from their native bases; with the coaling problem such an acute one, and with England in possession of all important stations, where could they flee for safety? Several Italian destroyers were circling around the German ships at Messina, enforcing neutrality and occasionally reminding them that they could remain in port only twenty-four hours. England had ships stationed at the Gulf of Otranto, the head of the Adriatic, to cut them off in case they sought to escape into the Austrian port of Pola. The British navy also stood guard at Gibraltar and Suez, the only other exits that apparently offered the possibility of escape. There was only one other place in which the Goeben and the Breslau might find a safe and friendly reception. That was Constantinople. Apparently the British navy dismissed this as an impossibility. At that time, early in August, international law had not entirely disappeared as the guiding conduct of nations. Turkey was then a neutral country, and, despite the many evidences of German domination, she seemed likely to maintain her neutrality. The Treaty of Paris, which was signed in 1856, as well as the Treaty of London, signed in 1871, provided that war ships should not use the Dardanelles except by the special permission of the Sultan, which could be granted only in times of peace. In practice the government had seldom given this permission except for ceremonial occasions. Under the existing conditions it would have amounted virtually to an unfriendly act for the Sultan to have removed the ban against war vessels in the Dardanelles, and to permit the Goeben and the Breslau to remain in Turkish waters for more than twenty-four hours would have been nothing less than a declaration of war. It is perhaps not surprising that the British, in the early days of August, 1914, when Germany had not completely made clear her official opinion that "international law had ceased to exist," regarded these treaty stipulations as barring the German ships from the Dardanelles and Constantinople. Relying upon the sanctity of these international regulations, the British navy had shut off every point through which these German ships could have escaped to safety---except the entrance to the Dardanelles. Had England, immediately on the declaration of war, rushed a powerful squadron to this vital spot, how different the history of the last three years might have been!

"His Majesty expects the Goeben and the Breslau to succeed in breaking through!" Such was the, wireless that reached these vessels at Messina at five o'clock on the evening of August 4th. The twenty-four hours' stay permitted by the Italian Government had nearly expired. Outside, in the Strait of Otranto, lay the force of British battle cruisers, sending false radio messages to the Germans, instructing them to rush for Pola. With bands playing and flags flying, the officers and crews having had their spirits fired by oratory and drink, the two vessels started at full speed toward the awaiting British fleet. The little Gloucester, a scout boat, kept in touch, wiring constantly the German movements to the main squadron. Suddenly, when off Cape Spartivento, the Goeben and the Breslau let off into the atmosphere all the discordant vibrations which their wireless could command, jamming the air with such a hullabaloo that the Gloucester was unable to send any intelligible messages. Then the German cruisers turned southward and made for the Aegean Sea. The plucky little Gloucester kept close on their heels, and, as my daughter had related, once had even audaciously offered battle. A few hours behind the British squadron pursued, but uselessly, for the German ships, though far less powerful in battle, were much speedier. Even then the British admiral probably thought that he had spoiled the German plans. The German ships might get first to the Dardanelles, but at that point stood international law across the path, barring the entrance.

Meanwhile Wangenheim had accomplished his great diplomatic success. From the Corcovado wireless station in the Bosphorus he was sending the most agreeable news to Admiral Souchon. He was telling him to hoist the Turkish flag when he reached the Strait, for Admiral Souchon's cruisers had suddenly become parts of the Turkish navy, and, therefore, the usual international prohibitions did not apply. These cruisers were no longer the Goeben and the Breslau, for, like an oriental magician, Wangenheim had suddenly changed them into the Sultan Selim and the Medilli. The fact was that the German Ambassador had cleverly taken advantage of the existing situation to manufacture a "sale." As I have already told, Turkey had two dreadnaughts under construction in England when the war broke out. These ships were not exclusively governmental enterprises; their purchase represented what, on the surface, appeared to be a popular enthusiasm of the Turkish people. They were to be the agencies through which Turkey was to attack Greece and win back the islands of the Aegean, and the Turkish people had raised the money to build them by a so-called popular subscription. Agents had gone from house to house, painfully collecting- these small sums of money; there had been entertainments and fairs, and, in their eagerness for the cause, Turkish women had sold their hair for the benefit of the common fund. These two vessels thus represented a spectacular outburst of patriotism that was unusual in Turkey, so unusual, indeed, that many detected signs that the Government had stimulated it. At the very moment when the war began, Turkey had made her last payment to the English shipyards and the Turkish crews had arrived in England prepared to take the finished vessels home. Then, a few days before the time set to deliver them, the British Government stepped in and commandeered these dreadnaughts for the British navy.

There is not the slightest question that England had not only a legal but a moral right to do this; there is also no question that her action was a proper one, and that, had she been dealing with almost any other nation, such a proceeding would not have aroused any resentment. But the Turkish people cared nothing for distinctions of this sort; all they saw was that they had two ships in England, which they had greatly strained their resources to purchase, and that England had now stepped in and taken them. Even without external pressure they would have resented the act, but external pressure was exerted in plenty. The transaction gave Wangenheim the greatest opportunity of his life. Violent attacks upon England, all emanating from the German Embassy, began to fill the Turkish press. Wangenheim was constantly discoursing to the Turkish leaders on English perfidy and he now suggested that Germany, Turkey's good friend, was prepared to make compensation for England's "unlawful" seizure. He suggested that Turkey go through the form of "purchasing" the Goeben and the Breslau, which were then wandering around the Mediterranean, perhaps in anticipation of this very contingency, and incorporate them in the Turkish navy in place of the appropriated ships in England. The very day that these vessels passed through the Dardanelles, the Ikdam, a Turkish newspaper published in Constantinople, had a triumphant account of this "sale," with big headlines calling it a great success for the Imperial Government."

Thus Wangenheim's manoeuvre accomplished two purposes: it placed Germany before the populace as Turkey's friend, and it also provided a subterfuge for getting the ships through the Dardanelles, and enabling them to remain in Turkish waters. All this beguiled the more ignorant of the Turkish people, and gave the Cabinet a plausible ground for meeting the objection of Entente diplomats, but it did not deceive any intelligent person. The Goeben and Breslau might change their names, and the German sailors might adorn themselves with Turkish fezzes, but we all knew from the beginning that this sale was a sham. Those who understood the financial condition of Turkey could only be amused at the idea that she could purchase these modern vessels. Moreover, the ships were never incorporated in the Turkish navy; on the contrary, what really happened was that the Turkish navy was annexed to these German ships. A handful of Turkish sailors were placed on board at one time for appearance sake, but their German officers and German crews still retained active charge. Wangenheim, in his talks with me, never made any secret of the fact that the ships still remained German property. "I never expected to have such big checks to sign," he remarked one day, referring to his expenditures on the Goeben and the Breslau. He always called them "our" ships. Even Talaat told me in so many words that the cruisers did not belong to Turkey.

"The Germans say they belong to the Turks," he remarked, with his characteristic laugh. "At any rate, it's very comforting for us to have them here. After the war, if the Germans win, they will forget all about it and leave the ships to us. If the Germans lose, they won't be able to take them away from us!"

The German Government made no real pretension that the sale had been bona fide; at least when the Greek Minister at Berlin protested against the transaction as unfriendly to Greece,---na?vely forgetting the American ships which Greece bad recently purchased---the German officials soothed him by admitting, sotto voce, that the ownership still remained with Germany. Yet when the Entente ambassadors constantly protested against the presence of the German vessels, the Turkish officials blandly kept up the pretence that they were integral parts of the Turkish navy!

The German officers and crews greatly enjoyed this farcical pretence that the Goeben and the Breslau were Turkish ships. They took delight in putting on Turkish fezzes, thereby presenting to the world conclusive evidence that these loyal sailors of the Kaiser were now parts of the Sultan's navy. One day the Goeben sailed up the Bosphorus, halted in front of the Russian Embassy, and dropped anchor. Then the officers and men lined the deck in full view of the enemy embassy. All solemnly removed their Turkish fezzes and put on German caps. The band played "Deutschland ?ber Alles," the "Watch on the Rhine, "and other German songs, the German sailors singing loudly to the accompaniment. When they had spent an hour or more serenading the Russian Ambassador, the officers and crews removed their German caps and again put on their Turkish fezzes. The Goeben then picked up her anchor and started southward for her station, leaving in the ears of the Russian diplomat the gradually dying strains of German war songs as the cruiser disappeared down stream.

I have often speculated on what would have happened if the English battle cruisers, which pursued the Breslau and the Goeben up to the mouth of the Dardanelles, had not been too gentlemanly to violate international law. Suppose that they had entered the Strait, attacked the German cruisers in the Marmora, and sunk them. They could have done this, and, knowing all that we know now, such an action would have been justified. Not improbably the destruction would have kept Turkey out of the war. For the arrival of these cruisers made it inevitable that Turkey, when the proper moment came, should join her forces with Germany. With them the Turkish navy became stronger than the Russian Black Sea Fleet and thus made it certain that Russia could make no attack on Constantinople. The Goeben and the Breslau, therefore, practically gave the Ottoman and German naval forces control of the Black Sea. Moreover, these two ships could easily dominate Constantinople, and thus they furnished the means by which the German navy, if the occasion should arise, could terrorize the Turks. I am convinced that, when the judicious historian reviews this war and its consequences, he will say that the passage of the Strait by these German ships made it inevitable that Turkey should join Germany at the moment that Germany desired her assistance, and that it likewise sealed the doom of the Turkish Empire. There were men in the Turkish Cabinet who perceived this, even then. The story was told in Constantinople---though I do not vouch for it as authentic history---that the cabinet meeting at which this momentous decision had been made had not been altogether harmonious. The Grand Vizier and Djemal, it was said, objected to the fictitious "sale," and demanded that it should not be completed. When the discussion had reached its height Enver, who was playing Germany's game, announced that he had already practically completed the transaction. In the silence that followed his statement this young Napoleon pulled out his pistol and laid it on the table.

"If any one here wishes to question this purchase," he said quietly and icily, "I am ready to meet him."

A few weeks after the Goeben and the Breslau had taken up permanent headquarters in the Bosphorus, Djavid Bey, Minister of Finance, happened to meet a distinguished Belgian jurist, then in Constantinople.

"I have terrible news for you," said the sympathetic Turkish statesman. "The Germans have captured Brussels."

The Belgian, a huge figure, more than six feet high, put his arm soothingly upon the shoulder of the diminutive Turk.

"I have even more terrible news for you," he said, pointing out to the stream where the Goeben and the Breslau lay anchored. "The Germans have captured Turkey."

Chapter VI - Wangenheim Tells the American Ambassador How the Kaiser Started the War

But there was one quarter in which this transaction produced no appreciable gloom. That was the German Embassy. This great "success" fairly intoxicated the impressionable Wangenheim, and other happenings now aroused his furor Teutonicus to a fever heat. The Goeben and the Breslau arrived almost at the same time that the Germans captured Li?ge, Namur, and other Belgian towns. And now followed the German sweep into France and the apparently triumphant rush for Paris. In all these happenings Wangenheim, like the militant Prussian that he was, saw the fulfilment of a forty-years' dream. We were all still living in the summer embassies along the Bosphorus. Germany had a beautiful park, which the Sultan had personally presented to the Kaiser's government; yet for some reason Wangenheim did not seem to enjoy his headquarters during these summer days. A little guard house stood directly in front of his embassy, on the street, within twenty feet of the rushing Bosphorus, and in front of this was a stone bench. This bench was properly a resting place for the guard, but Wangenheim seemed to have a strong liking for it. I shall always keep in my mind the figure of this German diplomat, in those exciting days before the Marne, sitting out on this little bench, now and then jumping up for a stroll back and forth in front of his house. Everybody passing from Constantinople to the northern suburbs had to pass along this road, and even the Russian and French diplomats frequently went by, stiffly ignoring, of course, the triumphant ambassadorial figure on his stone bench. I sometimes think that Wangenheim. sat there for the express purpose of puffing his cigar smoke in their direction. It all reminded me of the scene in Schiller's Wilhelm Tell, where Tell sits in the mountain pass, with his bow and arrow at his side, waiting for his intended victim, Gessler, to go by:

"Here through this deep defile he needs must pass; There leads no other road to K?ssnacht."

Wangenheim would also buttonhole his friends, or those whom he regarded as his friends, and have his little jollifications over German victories. I noticed that he stationed himself there only when the German armies were winning; if news came of a reverse, Wangenheim was utterly invisible. This led me to remark that he reminded me of a toy weather prophet, which is always outside the box when the weather is fine but which retires within when storms are gathering. Wangenheim appreciated my little joke as keenly as the rest of the diplomatic set.

In those early days, however, the weather for the German Ambassador was distinctly favourable. The good fortune of the German armies so excited him that he was sometimes led into indiscretions, and his exuberance one day caused him to tell me certain facts which, I think will always have great historical value. He disclosed precisely how and when Germany had precipitated this war. To-day his revelation of this secret looks like a most monstrous indiscretion, but we must remember Wangenheim's state of mind at the time. The whole world then believed that Paris was doomed and Wangenheim reflected this attitude in his frequent declarations that the war would be over in two or three months. The whole German enterprise was evidently progressing according to programme.

I have already mentioned that the German Ambassador had left for Berlin soon after the assassination of the Grand Duke, and he now revealed the cause of his sudden disappearance. The Kaiser, he told me, had summoned him to Berlin for an imperial conference. This meeting took place at Potsdam on July 5th. The Kaiser presided and nearly all the important ambassadors attended. Wangenheim himself was summoned to give assurance about Turkey and enlighten his associates generally on the situation in Constantinople, which was then regarded as almost the pivotal point in the impending war. In telling me who attended this conference Wangenheim used no names, though he specifically said that among them were---the facts are so important that I quote his exact words in the German which he used---"die Haeupter des Generalstabs und der Marine"---(The heads of the general staff and of the navy) by which I have assumed that he meant Von Moltke and Von Tirpitz. The great bankers, railroad directors, and the captains of German industry, all of whom were as necessary to German war preparations as the army itself, also attended.

Wangenheim now told me that the Kaiser solemnly put the question to each man in turn: "Are you ready for war?" All replied "yes" except the financiers.

They said that they must have two weeks to sell their foreign securities and to make loans. At that time few people had looked upon the Sarajevo tragedy as something that would inevitably lead to war. This conference, Wangenheim told me, took all precautions that no such suspicion should be aroused. It decided to give the bankers time to readjust their finances for the coming war, and then the several members went quietly back to their work or started on vacations. The Kaiser went to Norway on his yacht, Von Bethmann-Hollweg left for a rest, and Wangenheim returned to Constantinople.

In telling me about this conference Wangenheim, of course, admitted that Germany had precipitated the war. I think that he was rather proud of the whole performance, proud that Germany had gone about the matter in so methodical and far-seeing a way, and especially proud that he himself had been invited to participate in so epoch-making a gathering. I have often wondered why he revealed to me so momentous a secret, and I think that perhaps the real reason was his excessive vanity---his desire to show me how close he stood to the inner counsels of his emperor and the part that he had played in bringing on this conflict. Whatever the motive, this indiscretion certainly had the effect of showing me who were really the guilty parties in this monstrous crime. The several blue, red, and yellow books which flooded Europe during the few months following the outbreak, and the hundreds of documents which were issued by German propagandists attempting to establish Germany's innocence, have never made the slightest impression on me. For my conclusions as to the responsibility are not based on suspicions or belief or the study of circumstantial data. I do not have to reason or argue about the matter. I know. The conspiracy that has caused this greatest of human tragedies was hatched by the Kaiser and his imperial crew at this Potsdam conference of July 5, 1914. One of the chief participants, flushed with his triumph at the. apparent success of the plot, told me the details with his own mouth. Whenever I hear people arguing about the responsibility for this war or read the clumsy and lying excuses put forth by Germany, I simply recall the burly figure of Wangenheim as he appeared that August afternoon, puffing away at a huge black cigar, and giving me his account of this historic meeting. Why waste any time discussing the matter after that?

This imperial conference took place July 5th and the Serbian ultimatum was sent on July 22d. That is just about the two weeks' interval which the financiers had demanded to complete their plans. All the great stock exchanges of the world show that the German bankers profitably used this interval. Their records disclose that stocks were being sold in large quantities and that prices declined rapidly. At that time the markets were somewhat puzzled at this movement but Wangenheim's explanation clears up any doubts that may still remain. Germany was changing her securities into cash for war purposes. If any one wishes to verify Wangenheim, I would suggest that he examine the quotations of the New York stock market for these two historic weeks. He will find that there were astonishing slumps in prices, especially on the stocks that had an international market. Between July 5th and July 22d, Union Pacific dropped from 155 ½ to 127 ½, Baltimore and Ohio from 91 ½ to 81, United States Steel from 61 to 50 ½, Canadian Pacific from 194 to 185 ½, and Northern Pacific from 111 3/8 to 108. At that time the high protectionists were blaming the Simmons-Underwood tariff act as responsible for this fall in values, while other critics of the Administration attributed it to the Federal Reserve Act-which had not yet been put into effect. How little the Wall Street brokers and the financial experts realized that an imperial conference, which had been held in Potsdam and presided over by the Kaiser, was the real force that was then depressing the market!

Wangenheim not only gave me the details of this Potsdam conference, but he disclosed the same secret to the Marquis Garroni, the Italian Ambassador at Constantinople. Italy was at that time technically Germany's ally.

The Austrian Ambassador, the Marquis Pallavicini, also practically admitted that the Central Powers had anticipated the war. On August 18th, Francis Joseph's birthday, I made the usual ambassadorial visit of congratulation. Quite naturally the conversation turned upon the Emperor, who had that day passed his 84th year. Pallavicini spoke about him with the utmost pride and veneration. He told me how keen-minded and clear-headed the aged emperor was, how he had the most complete understanding of international affairs, and how he gave everything his personal supervision. To illustrate the Austrian Kaiser's grasp of public events, Pallavicini instanced the present war. The previous May, Pallavicini had had an audience with Francis Joseph in Vienna. At that time, Pallavicini now told me, the Emperor had said that a European war was unavoidable. The Central Powers would not accept the Treaty of Bucharest as a settlement of the Balkan question, and only a general war, the Emperor had told Pallavicini, could ever settle that problem. The Treaty of Bucharest, I may recall, was the settlement that ended the second Balkan war. This divided the European dominions of Turkey, excepting Constantinople and a small piece of adjoining territory, among the Balkan nations, chiefly Serbia and Greece. That treaty strengthened Serbia greatly; so much did it increase Serbia's resources, indeed, that Austria feared that it had laid the beginning of a new European state, which might grow sufficiently strong to resist her own plans of aggrandizement. Austria held a large Serbian population under her yoke in Bosnia and Herzegovina, and these Serbians desired, above everything else, annexation to their own country. Moreover, the Pan-German plans in the East necessitated the destruction of Serbia, the state which, so long as it stood intact, blocked the Germanic road to the Orient. It had been the Austro-German expectation that the Balkan War would destroy Serbia as a nation---that Turkey would simply annihilate King Peter's forces. This was precisely what the Germanic plans demanded, and for this reason Austria and Germany did nothing to prevent the Balkan wars. But the result was exactly the reverse, for out of the conflict arose a stronger Serbia than ever, standing firm like a breakwater against the Germanic flood.

Most historians agree that the Treaty of Bucharest made inevitable this war. I have the Marquis Pallavicini's evidence that this was likewise the opinion of Francis Joseph himself. The audience at which the Emperor made this statement was held in May, more than a month before the assassination of the Grand Duke. Clearly, therefore, we have the Austrian Emperor's assurances that the war would have come irrespective of the assassination at Sarajevo. It is quite apparent that this crime merely served as the convenient pretext for the war upon which the Central Empires had already decided.

Chapter VII - Germany's Plans for New Territories, Coaling Stations, and Indemnities

All through that eventful August and September Wangenheim continued his almost irresponsible behaviour---now blandly boastful, now depressed, always nervous and high strung, ingratiating to an American like myself, spiteful and petty toward the representatives of the enemy powers. He was always displaying his anxiety and impatience by sitting on the bench, that he might be within two or three minutes' quicker access to the wireless communications that were sent him from Berlin via the Corcovado. He would never miss an opportunity to spread the news of victories; several times he adopted the unusual course of coming to my house unannounced, to tell me of the latest developments, and to read me extracts from messages which he had just received. He was always apparently frank, direct, and even indiscreet. I remember his great distress the day that England declared war. Wangenheim had always professed a great admiration for England and, especially, for America. "There are only three great countries," he would say over and over again, "Germany, England, and the United States. We three should get together; then we could rule the world." This enthusiasm for the British Empire now suddenly cooled when that power decided to defend her treaty pledges and declared war. Wangenheim had said that the conflict would be a short one and that Sedan Day would be celebrated in Paris. But on August 5th, I called at his embassy and found him more than usually agitated and serious. Baroness Wangenheim, a tall, handsome woman, was sitting in the room reading her mother's memoirs of the war of 1870. Both regarded the news from England as almost a personal grievance, and what impressed me most was Wangenheim's utter failure to understand England's motives. "It's mighty poor politics on her part! " he exclaimed over and over again. His attitude was precisely the same as that of Bethmann-Hollweg with the "scrap of paper."

I was out for a stroll on August 26th, and happened to meet the German Ambassador. He began to talk as usual about the German victories in France, repeating, as was now his habit, his prophecy that the German armies would be in Paris within a week. The deciding factor in this war., he added, would be the Krupp artillery. "And remember that this time," he said, "we are making war. And we shall make it ruecksichtslos (without any consideration), We shall not be hampered as we were in 1870. Then Queen Victoria, the Czar, and Francis Joseph interfered and persuaded us to spare Paris. But there is no one to interfere now. We shall move to Berlin all the Parisian art treasures that belong to the state, just as Napoleon took Italian art works to France."

It is quite evident that the battle of the Marne saved Paris from the fate of Louvain.

So confidently did Wangenheim expect an immediate victory that he began to discuss the terms of peace. Germany would demand of France, he said, after defeating her armies, that she completely demobilize and pay an indemnity. "France now," said Wangenheim, "can settle for $5,000,000,000; but if she persists in continuing the war, she will have to pay $20,000,000,000."

He told me that Germany would demand harbours and coaling stations "everywhere." At that time, judging from Wangenheim's statements, Germany was not looking so much for new territory as for great commercial advantages. She was determined to be the great merchant nation, and for this she must have free harbours, the Bagdad railroad, and extensive rights in South America and Africa. Wangenheim said that Germany did not desire any more territory in which the populations did not speak German, for they had had all of that kind of trouble they wanted in Alsace-Lorraine, Poland, and other non-German countries. This statement certainly sounds interesting now in view of recent happenings in Russia. He did not mention England in speaking of Germany's demand for coaling stations and harbours; he must have had England in mind, however, for what other nation could have given them to Germany "everywhere?"

All these conversations were as illuminating to me as Wangenheim's revelation of the conference of July 5th. That episode clearly proved that Germany had consciously started the war, while these grandiose schemes, as outlined by this very able but somewhat talkative ambassador, showed the reasons that had impelled her in this great enterprise. Wangenheim gave me a complete picture of the German Empire embarking on a great buccaneering expedition, in which the spoils of success were to be the accumulated riches of her neighbours and the world position which their skill and industry had built up through the centuries.

If England attempted to starve Germany, said Wangenheim, Germany's response would be a simple one: she would starve France. At that time, we must remember, Germany expected to have Paris within a week, and she believed that this would ultimately give her control of the whole country. It was evidently the German plan, as understood by Wangenheim, to hold this nation as a pawn for England's behaviour, a kind of hostage on a gigantic scale. In that case, should England gain any military advantage, Germany would attempt to counter-attack by torturing the whole French people. At that moment German soldiers were murdering innocent Belgians in return

46

for the alleged misbehaviour of other Belgians, and evidently Germany had planned to apply this principle to whole nations as well as to individuals.

All through this and other talks, Wangenheim showed the greatest animosity to Russia.

"We've got our foot on Russia's corn," he said, "and we propose to keep it there."

By this he must have meant that Germany bad sent the Goeben and the Breslau through the Dardanelles and that by that master-stroke she controlled Constantinople. The old Byzantine capital, said Wangenheim, was the prize which a victorious Russia would demand, and her lack of an all-the-year-round port in warm waters was Russia's tender spot---her "corn." At this time Wangenheim boasted that Germany had 174 German gunners at the Dardanelles, that the strait could be closed in less than thirty minutes, and that Souchon, the German admiral, had informed him that the strait was impregnable. "We shall not close the Dardanelles, however," he said, "unless England attacks them."

At that time England, although she had declared war on Germany, had played no conspicuous part in the military operations; her "contemptible little army" was making its heroic retreat from Mons. Wangenheim. entirely discounted England as an enemy. It was the German intention, he said, to place their big guns at Calais, and throw their shells across the English Channel to the English coast towns; that Germany would not have Calais within the next ten days did not occur to him as a possibility. In this and other conversations at about the same time Wangenheim laughed at the idea that England could create a large independent army. "The idea is preposterous," he said. "It takes generations of militarism to produce anything like the German army. We have been building it up for two hundred years. It takes thirty years of constant training to produce such generals as we have. Our army will always maintain its organization. We have 500,000 recruits reaching military age every year and we cannot possibly lose that number annually, so that our army will be kept intact."

A few weeks later civilization was outraged by the German bombardment of English coast towns, such as Scarborough and Hartlepool. This was no sudden German inspiration, but part of their carefully considered plans. Wangenheim told me, on September 6, 1914, that Germany intended to bombard all English harbours, so as to stop the food supply. It is also apparent that German ruthlessness against American sea trade was no sudden decision of Von Tirpitz, for, on this same date, the German Ambassador to Constantinople warned me that it would be very dangerous for the United States to send ships to England!

Chapter VIII - A Classic Instance of German Propaganda

In those August and September days Germany had no intention of precipitating Turkey immediately into the war. As I then had a deep interest in the welfare of the Turkish people and in maintaining peace, I telegraphed Washington asking if I might use my influence to keep Turkey neutral. I received a reply that I might do this provided that I made my representations unofficially and purely upon humanitarian grounds. As the English and the French ambassadors were exerting all their efforts to keep Turkey out of the war, I knew that my intervention in the same interest would not displease the British Government. Germany, however, might regard any interference on my part as an unneutral act, and I asked Wangenheim if there would be any objection from that source.

His reply somewhat surprised me, though I saw through it soon afterward. "Not at all," he said. "Germany desires, above all, that Turkey shall remain neutral."

Undoubtedly Turkey's policy at that moment precisely fitted in with German plans. Wangenheim was steadily increasing his ascendancy over the Turkish Cabinet, and Turkey was then pursuing the course that best served the German aims. Her policy was keeping the Entente on tenterhooks; it never knew from day to day where Turkey stood, whether she would remain neutral or enter the war on Germany's side. Because Turkey's attitude was so uncertain, Russia was compelled to keep large forces in the Caucasus, England was obliged to strengthen her forces in Egypt and India, and to maintain a considerable fleet at the mouth of the Dardanelles. All this worked in beautifully with Germany's plans, for these detached forces just so much weakened England and Russia on the European battle front. I am now speaking of the period just before the Marne, when Germany expected to defeat France and Russia with the aid of her ally, Austria,: and thus obtain a victory that would have enabled her to dictate the future of Europe. Should Turkey at that time be actually engaged in military operations, she could do no more toward bringing about this victory than she was doing now, by keeping considerable Russian and English forces away from the most important fronts. But should Germany win this easy victory, with Turkey's aid, she might find her new ally an embarrassment. Turkey would certainly demand compensation and she would not be particularly modest in her demands, which most likely would include the full control of Egypt and perhaps the return of Balkan territories. Such readjustments would have interfered with the Kaiser's plans. Thus he had no interest in having Turkey as an active ally, except in the event that he did not speedily win his anticipated triumph. But if Russia should make great progress against Austria, then Turkey's active alliance would have great value, especially if her entry should be so timed as to bring in Bulgaria and Rumania as allies. Meanwhile, Wangenheim was playing a waiting game, making Turkey a potential German ally, strengthening her army and her navy, and preparing to use her, whenever the moment arrived for using her to the best advantage. If Germany could not win the war without Turkey's aid, Germany was prepared to take her in as an ally; if she could win without Turkey, then she would not have to pay the Turk for his cooperation. Meanwhile, the sensible course was to keep her prepared in case the Turkish forces became essential to German success.

The duel that now took place between Germany and the Entente for Turkey's favour was a most unequal one. The fact was that Germany had won the victory when she smuggled the Goeben and the Breslau into the Sea of Marmora. The English, French, and Russian ambassadors well understood this, and they knew that they could not make Turkey an active ally of the Entente; they probably had no desire to do so, but they did hope that they might keep her neutral. To this end they now directed all their efforts. "You have had enough of war," they would tell Talaat and Enver. "You have fought two wars in the last four years; you will ruin your country absolutely if you get involved in this one." The Entente had only one consideration to offer Turkey for her neutrality, and this was an offer to guarantee the integrity of the Ottoman Empire. The Entente ambassadors showed their great desire to keep Turkey out of the war by their disinclination to press to the limit their case against the Breslau and the Goeben. It is true that they repeatedly protested against the continued presence of these ships, but every time the Turkish officials maintained that they were Turkish vessels.

"If that is so," Sir Louis Mallet would urge, and his argument was unassailable, "why don't you remove the German officers and crews?" That was the intention, the Grand Vizier would answer; the Turkish crews that had been sent to man the ships which had been built in England, he would say, were returning to Turkey and they would be put on board the Goeben and the Breslau as soon as they reached Constantinople. But days and weeks went by; these crews came home, and still Germany manned and officered the cruisers. These backings and fillings naturally did not deceive the British and French foreign offices. The presence of the Goeben and the Breslau was a standing casus belli, but the Entente ambassadors did not demand their passports, for such an act would have precipitated the very crisis which they were seeking to delay, and, if possible, to avoid---Turkey's entrance as Germany's ally. Unhappily the Entente's promise to guarantee Turkey's integrity did not win Turkey to their side.

"They promised that we should not be dismembered after the Balkan wars," Talaat would tell me, "and see what happened to European Turkey then."

Wangenheim constantly harped upon this fact. "You can't trust anything they say," he would tell Talaat and Enver, "didn't they all go back on you a year ago?" And then with great cleverness he would play upon the only emotion which really actuates the Turk. The descendants of Osman hardly resemble any people I have ever known. They do not hate, they do not love; they have no lasting animosities or affections. They only fear. And naturally they attribute to others the motives which regulate their own conduct. "How stupid you are," Wangenheim would tell Talaat and Enver, discussing the English attitude. "Don't you see why the English want you to keep out? It is because they fear you. Don't you see that, with the help of Germany, you have again become a great military power? No wonder England doesn't want to fight you! " He dinned this so continually in their ears that they finally believed it, for this argument not only completely explained to them the attitude of the Entente, but it flattered Turkish pride.

Whatever may have been the attitude of Enver and Talaat, I think that England and France were more popular with all classes in Turkey than was Germany. The Sultan was opposed to war; the heir apparent, Youssouff Isseddin, was openly pro-Ally; the Grand Vizier, Sa?d Halim, favoured England rather than Germany; Djemal, the third member of the ruling triumvirate, had the reputation of being a Francophile---he had recently returned from Paris, where the reception he had received had greatly flattered him; a majority of the Cabinet had no enthusiasm for Germany; and public opinion, so far as public opinion existed in Turkey, regarded England, not Germany, as Turkey's historic friend. Wangenheim, therefore, had much opposition to overcome, and the methods which he took to break it down form a classic illustration of German propaganda. He started a lavish publicity campaign against England, France, and Russia. I have described the feelings of the Turks at losing their ships in England. Wangenheim's agents now filled columns of purchased space in the newspapers with bitter attacks on England for taking over these vessels. The whole Turkish press rapidly passed under the control of Germany. Wangenheim purchased the Ikdam, one of the largest Turkish newspapers, which immediately began to sing the praises of Germany and to abuse the Entente. The Osmanischer Lloyd, published in French and German, became an organ of the German Embassy. Although the Turkish Constitution guaranteed a free press, a censorship was established in the interest of the Central Powers. All Turkish editors were ordered to write in Germany's favour and they obeyed instructions. The Jeune Turc, a pro-Entente newspaper, printed in French, was suppressed. The Turkish papers exaggerated German victories and completely manufactured others; they were constantly printing the news of Entente defeats, most of them wholly imaginary. In the evening Wangenheim and Pallavicini would show me official telegrams giving the details of military operations, but when, in the morning, I would look in the newspapers, I would find that this news had been twisted or falsified in Germany's favour. A certain Baron Oppenheim travelled all over Turkey manufacturing public opinion against England and France. Ostensibly he was an archaeologist, while in reality he opened offices everywhere from which issued streams of slander against the Entente. Huge maps were pasted on walls, showing all the territory which Turkey had lost in the course of a century. Russia was portrayed as the nation chiefly responsible for these "robberies," and attention was drawn to the fact that England had now become Russia's ally. Pictures were published, showing the grasping powers of the Entente as rapacious animals, snatching at poor Turkey. Enver was advertised as the "hero" who had recovered Adrianople; Germany was pictured as Turkey's friend; the Kaiser suddenly became "Hadji Wilhelm," the great protector of Islam, and stories were even printed that he had become a convert to Mohammedanism. The Turkish populace was informed that the Moslems of India and of Egypt were about to revolt and throw off their English "tyrants." The Turkish man-on-the-street was taught to say, "Gott Strafe England," and all the time the motive power of this infamous campaign was German money.

But Germany was doing more than poisoning the Turkish mind; she was appropriating Turkey's military resources. I have already described how, in January, 1914, the Kaiser had taken over the Turkish army and rehabilitated it in preparation for the European war. He now proceeded to do the same thing with the Turkish navy. In August, Wangenheim boasted to me that, " We now control both the Turkish army and navy." At the time the Goeben and Breslau arrived, an English mission, headed by Admiral Limpus, was hard at work restoring the Turkish navy. Soon afterward Limpus and his associates were unceremoniously dismissed; the manner of their going was really disgraceful, for not even the most ordinary courtesies were shown them. The English naval officers quietly and unobservedly left Constantinople for England---all except the Admiral himself, who had to remain longer because of his daughter's illness.

Night after night whole carloads of Germans landed at Constantinople from Berlin; the aggregations to the population finally amounted to 3,800 men, most of them sent to man the Turkish navy and to manufacture ammunition. They filled the caf?s every night, and they paraded the streets of Constantinople in the small hours of the morning, howling and singing German patriotic songs. Many of them were skilled mechanics, who immediately went to work repairing the destroyers and other ships and putting them in shape for war. The British firm of Armstrong & Vickers had a splendid dock in Constantinople, and this the Germans now appropriated. All day and night we could hear this work going on and we could hardly sleep because of the hubbub of riveting and hammering. Wangenheim, now found another opportunity for instilling more poison into the minds of Enver, Talaat, and Djemal. The German workers, he declared, had found that the Turkish ships were in a desperate state of disrepair, and for this he naturally blamed the English naval mission. He said that England had deliberately let the Turkish navy go to decay and he asserted that this was all a part of England's plot to ruin Turkey! "Look!" he would exclaim, "see what we Germans have done for the Turkish army, and see what the English have done for your ships!" As a matter of fact, all this was untrue, for Admiral Limpus had worked hard and conscientiously to improve the navy and had accomplished excellent results in that direction.

All this time the Germans were working at the Dardanelles, seeking to strengthen the fortifications, and preparing for a possible Allied attack. As September lengthened into October, the Sublime Porte practically ceased to be the headquarters of the Ottoman Empire. I really think that the most influential seat of authority at that time was a German merchant ship, the General. It was moored in the Golden Horn, at the Galata Bridge, and a permanent stairway had been built, leading to its deck. I knew well one of the most frequent visitors to this ship, an American who used to come to the embassy and entertain me with stories of what was going on.

The General, this American now informed me, was practically a German club or hotel. The officers of the Goeben and the Breslau and other German officers who had been sent to command the Turkish ships ate and slept on board. Admiral Souchon, who had brought the German cruisers to Constantinople, presided over these gatherings. Souchon was a man of French Huguenot extraction; he was a short, dapper, clean-cut sailor, very energetic and alert, and to the German passion for command and thoroughness he added much of the Gallic geniality and buoyancy. Naturally he gave much liveliness to the evening parties on the General, and the beer and champagne which were liberally dispensed on these occasions loosened the tongues of his fellow officers. Their conversation showed that they entertained no illusions as to who really controlled the Turkish navy. Night after night their impatience for action grew; they kept declaring that, if Turkey did not presently attack the Russians, they would force her to do so. They would relate how they had sent German ships into the Black Sea, in the hope of provoking the Russian fleet to some action that would make war inevitable. Toward the end of October my friend told me that hostilities could not much longer be avoided; the Turkish fleet had been fitted for action, everything was ready, and the impetuosity of these kriegslustige German officers could not much longer be restrained.

"They are just like a lot of boys with chips on their shoulders! They are simply spoiling for a fight!" he said.

Chapter IX - Germany Closes the Dardanelles and so Separates Russia From Her Allies

On September 27th, Sir Louis Mallet, the British Ambassador, entered my office in a considerably disturbed state of mind. The Khedive of Egypt had just left me, and I began to talk to Sir Louis about Egyptian matters.

"Let's discuss that some other time," he said. "I have something far more important to tell you. They have closed the Dardanelles."

By "they" he meant, of course, not the Turkish Government, the only power which had the legal right to take this drastic step, but the actual ruling powers in Turkey, the Germans. Sir Louis had good reason for bringing me this piece of news, since this was an outrage against the United States as well as against the Allies. He asked me to go with him and make a joint protest. I suggested, however, that it would be better for us to act separately and I immediately started for the house of the Grand Vizier.

When I arrived a cabinet conference was in session, and, as I sat in the anteroom, I could hear several voices in excited discussion. Among them all I could distinctly distinguish the familiar tones of Talaat, Enver, Djavid, the Minister of Finance, and other members of the Government. It was quite plain, from all that I could overhear through the thin partitions, that these nominal rulers of Turkey were almost as exasperated the closing as were Sir Louis Mallet and myself.

The Grand Vizier came out in answer to my request. He presented a pitiable sight. He was, in title at least, the most important official of the Turkish Government, the mouthpiece of the Sultan himself, yet now he presented a picture of abject helplessness and fear. His face was blanched and he was trembling from head to foot. He was so overcome by his emotions that he could hardly speak; when I asked him whether the news was true that the Dardanelles had been closed, he finally stammered out that it was.

"You know this means war," I said, and I protested as strongly as I could in the name of the United States.

All the time that we were talking I could hear the loud tones of Talaat and his associates in the interior apartment. The Grand Vizier excused himself and went back into the room. He then sent out Djavid to discuss the matter with me.

"It's all a surprise to us," were Djavid's first words---this statement being a complete admission that the Cabinet had had nothing to do with it. I repeated that the United States would not submit to closing the Dardanelles; Turkey was at peace, the Sultan had no legal right to shut the strait to merchant ships except in case of war. I said that an American ship, laden with supplies and stores for the American Embassy, was outside at that moment waiting to come in. Djavid suggested that I have this vessel unload her cargo at Smyrna: the Turkish Government, he obligingly added, would pay the cost of transporting it overland to Constantinople. This proposal, of course, was a ridiculous evasion of the issue and I brushed it aside.

Djavid then said that the Cabinet proposed to investigate the matter; that, in fact, they were discussing it at that moment. He told me how it had happened. A Turkish torpedo boat had passed through the Dardanelles and attempted to enter the Aegean. The British warships stationed outside hailed the ship, examined it, and found that there were German sailors on board. The English Admiral at once ordered the vessel to go back; this, under the circumstances, he had a right to do. Weber Pasha, the German general who was then in charge of the fortifications, did not consult the Turks but immediately gave orders to close the strait. Wangenheim had already boasted to me, as I have said, that the Dardanelles could be closed in thirty minutes and the Germans now made good his words. Down went the mines and the nets; the lights in the lighthouses were extinguished; signals were put up, notifying all ships that there was "no thoroughfare" and the deed, the most high-handed which the Germans had yet committed, was done. And here I found these Turkish statesmen, who alone had authority over this indispensable strip of water, trembling and stammering with fear, running hither and yon like a lot of frightened rabbits, appalled at the enormity of the German act, yet apparently powerless to take any decisive action. I certainly had a graphic picture of the extremities to which Teutonic bullying had reduced the present rulers of the Turkish Empire. And at the same moment before my mind rose the figure of the Sultan, whose signature was essential to close legally these waters, quietly dozing at his palace, entirely oblivious of the whole transaction.

Though Djavid informed me that the Cabinet might decide to reopen the Dardanelles, it did not do so. This great passageway has now remained closed for more than four years, from September 27, 1914. I saw, of course, precisely what this action signified. That month of September had been a disillusioning one for the Germans. The French had beaten back the invasion and had driven the German armies to entrenchments along the Aisne. The Russians were sweeping triumphantly through Galicia; already they had captured Lemberg and it seemed not improbable that they would soon cross the Carpathians into Austria-Hungary. In those days Pallavicini, the Austrian Ambassador, was a discouraged, lamentable figure. He confided to me his fears for the future, telling me that the German programme of a short, decisive war had clearly failed and that it was now quite evident that Germany could win, if she could win at all, which was exceedingly doubtful, only after a protracted struggle. I have described how Wangenheim, while preparing the Turkish army and navy for any eventualities, was simply holding Turkey in his hand, intending actively to use her forces only in case Germany failed to crush France and Russia in the first campaign. Now that that failure was manifest, Wangenheim was instructed to use the Turkish Empire as an active ally. Hitherto, this nation of 20,000,000 had been a passive partner, held back by Wangenheim until Germany had decided that it would be necessary to pay the price of letting her into the war as a real participant. The time had come when Germany needed the Turkish army, and the outward sign that the situation had changed was the closing of the Dardanelles. Thus Wangenheim had accomplished the task for which he had been working, and in this act had fittingly crowned his achievement of bringing in the Goeben and the Breslau. Few Americans realize, even to-day, what an overwhelming influence this act wielded upon future military operations. Yet the fact that the war has lasted for so many years is explained by this closing of the Dardanelles.

For this is the element in the situation that separated Russia from her allies, that, in less than a year, led to her defeat and collapse, which, in turn, was the reason why the Russian revolution became possible. The map discloses that this enormous land of Russia has just four ways of reaching the seas. One is by way of the Baltic, and this the German fleet had already closed. Another is Archangel, on the Arctic Ocean, a port which is frozen over several months in the year, and which connects with the heart of Russia only by a long, single-track railroad. Another is the Pacific port of Vladivostok, also ice bound for three months, which in connection with Russia only by the thin line of the Siberian railway, 5,000 miles long. The fourth passage was that of the Dardanelles; in fact, this was the only practicable one. This was the narrow gate through which the surplus products of 175,000,000 people reached Europe, and nine tenths of all Russian exports and imports had gone this way for years. By suddenly closing it, Germany destroyed Russia both as an economic and a military power. By shutting off the exports of Russian grain, she deprived Russia of the financial power essential to successful warfare. What was perhaps even more fatal, she prevented England and France from getting munitions to the Russian battle front in sufficient quantity to stem the German onslaught. As soon as the Dardanelles was closed, Russia had to fall back on Archangel and Vladivostok for such supplies as she could get from these ports. The cause of the military collapse of Russia in 1915 is now well known; the soldiers simply had no ammunition with which to fight. The first half of the year 1918 Germany spent in an unsuccessful attempt to drive a "wedge" between the French and English armies on the western front; to separate one ally from another and so obtain a position where she could attack each one separately. Yet the task of undoing the Franco-Russian treaty, and driving such a "wedge" between Russia and her western associates, proved to have been an easy one. It was simply a matter, as I have described, of controlling a corrupt and degenerate government, getting possession, while she was still at peace, of her main executives, her army, her navy, her resources, and then, at the proper moment, ignoring the nominal rulers and closing a little strip of water about twenty miles long and two or three wide! It did not cost a single human life or the firing of a single gun, yet, in a twinkling, Germany accomplished what probably three million men, opposed to a well-equipped Russian force, could not have brought to pass. It was one of the most dramatic military triumphs of the war, and it was all the work of German propaganda, German penetration, and German diplomacy.

In the days following this bottling up of Russia, the Bosphorus began to look like a harbour which has been suddenly stricken with the plague. Hundreds of ships arrived from Russia, Rumania, and Bulgaria, loaded with grain, lumber, and other products, only to discover that they could go no farther. There were not docks enough to accommodate them, and they had to swing out into the stream, drop anchor, and await developments. The waters were a cluster of masts and smoke stacks, and the crowded vessels became so dense that a motor boat had difficulty in picking its way through the tangled forest. The Turks held out hopes that they might reopen the water way, and for this reason these vessels, constantly increasing in number, waited patiently for a month or so. Then one by one they turned around, pointed their noses toward the Black Sea, and lugubriously started for their home ports. In a few weeks the Bosphorus and adjoining waters had become a desolate waste. What for years had been one of the most animated shipping ports in the world, was ruffled only by an occasional launch, or a tiny Turkish ca?que, or now and then a little sailing vessel. And for an accurate idea of what this meant, from a military standpoint, we need only call to mind the Russian battle front in the next year. There the peasants were fighting German artillery with their unprotected bodies, having few rifles and few heavy guns, while mountains of useless ammunition were piling up in their distant Arctic and Pacific ports, with no railroads to take them to the field of action.

Chapter X - Turkey's Abrogation of the Capitulations - Enver Living in a Palace, With Plenty of Money and an Imperial Bride

Another question, which had been under discussion for several months, now became involved in the Turkish international situation. That was the matter of the capitulations. These were the treaty rights which for centuries had regulated the position of foreigners in the Turkish Empire. Turkey had never been admitted to a complete equality with European nations, and in reality she had never been an independent sovereignty. The Sultan's laws and customs differed so radically from those of Europe and America that no non-Moslem country could think of submitting its citizens in Turkey to them. In many matters, therefore, the principle of exterritoriality had always prevailed in favour of all citizens or subjects of countries enjoying capitulatory rights. Almost all European countries, as well as the United States, for centuries had had their own consular courts and prisons in which they tried and punished crimes which their nationals committed in Turkey. We all had our schools, which were subject, not to Turkish law and protection, but to that of the country which maintained them. Thus Robert College and the Constantinople College for Women, those wonderful institutions which American philanthropy has erected on the Bosphorus, as well as hundreds of American religious, charitable, and educational institutions, practically stood on American territory and looked upon the American Embassy as their guardian. Several nations had their own post offices, as they did not care to submit their mail to the Ottoman postal service. Turkey likewise did not have unlimited power of taxation over foreigners. It could not even increase their customs taxes without the consent of the foreign powers. In 1914 it could impose only 11 per cent in tariff dues, and was attempting to secure the right to increase the amount to 14. We have always regarded England as the only free-trade country, overlooking the fact that this limitation in Turkey's customs dues had practically made the Ottoman Empire an unwilling follower of Cobden. Turkey was thus prohibited by the Powers from developing any industries of her own; instead, she was forced to take large quantities of inferior articles from Europe. Against these restrictions Turkish statesmen had protested for years, declaring that they constituted an insult to their pride as a nation and also interfered with their progress. However, the agreement was a bi-lateral one, and Turkey could not change it without the consent of all the contracting powers. Yet certainly the present moment, when both the Entente and the Central Powers were cultivating Turkey, served to furnish a valuable opportunity to make the change. And so, as soon as the Germans had begun their march toward Paris, the air was filled with reports that Turkey intended to abrogate the capitulations. Rumour said that Germany had consented, as part of the consideration for Turkish aid in the war, and that England had agreed to the abrogation, as part of her payment for Turkish neutrality. Neither of these reports was true.

What was manifest, however, was the panic which the mere suggestion of abrogation produced on the foreign population. The idea of becoming subject to the Turkish laws and perhaps being thrown into Turkish prisons made their flesh creep---and with good reason.

About this time I had a long conference with Enver. He asked me to call at his residence, as he was laid up with an infected toe, the result of a surgical operation. I thus had an illuminating glimpse of the Minister of War en famille. Certainly this humble man of the people had risen in the world. His house, which was in one of the quietest and most aristocratic parts of the city, was a splendid old building, very large and very elaborate. I was ushered through a series of four or five halls, and as I went by one door the Imperial Princess, Enver's wife, slightly opened it and peeked through at me. Farther on another Turkish lady opened her door and also obtained a fleeting glimpse of the Ambassadorial figure. I was finally escorted into a beautiful room in which Enver lay reclining on a semi-sofa. He had on a long silk dressing gown and his stockinged feet hung languidly over the edge of the divan. He looked much younger than in his uniform; he was an extremely neat and well-groomed object, with a pale, smooth face, made even more striking by his black hair, and with delicate white hands, and long, tapering fingers. He might easily have passed for under thirty, and, in fact, he was not much over that age. He had at hand a violin, and a piano near by also testified to his musical taste. The room was splendidly tapestried; perhaps its most conspicuous feature was a da s upon which stood a golden chair; this was the marriage throne of Enver's imperial wife. As I glanced around at all this luxury, I must admit that a few uncharitable thoughts came to mind and that I could not help pondering a question which was then being generally asked in Constantinople. Where did Enver get the money for this expensive establishment? He had no fortune of his own---his parents had been wretchedly poor, and his salary as a cabinet minister was only about $8,000. His wife had a moderate allowance as an imperial princess, but she had no private resources. Enver had never engaged in business, he had been a revolutionist, military leader, and politician all his life. But here he was living at a rate that demanded a very large income. In other ways Enver was giving evidences of great and sudden prosperity, and already I had heard much of his investments in real estate, which were the talk of the town.

Enver wished to discuss the capitulations. He practically said that the Cabinet had decided on the abrogation, and he wished to know the attitude of the United States. He added that certainly a country which had fought for its independence as we had would sympathize with Turkey's attempt to shake off these shackles. We had helped Japan free herself from similar burdens and wouldn't we now help Turkey? Certainly Turkey was as civilized a nation as Japan?

I answered that I thought that the United States might consent to abandon the capitulations in so far as they were economic. It was my opinion that Turkey should control her customs duties and be permitted to levy the same taxes on foreigners as on her own citizens. So long as the Turkish courts and Turkish prisons maintained their present standards, however, we could never agree to give up the judicial capitulations. Turkey should reform the abuses of her courts; then, after they had established European ideas in the administration of justice, the matter could be discussed. Enver replied that Turkey would be willing to have mixed tribunals and to have the United States designate some of the judges, but I suggested that, inasmuch as American judges did not know the Turkish language or Turkish law, his scheme involved great practical difficulties. I also told him that the American schools and colleges were very dear to Americans, and that we would never consent to subjecting them to Turkish jurisdiction.

Despite the protests of all the ambassadors, the Cabinet issued its notification that the capitulations would be abrogated on October 1st. This abrogation was all a part of the Young Turks' plan to free themselves from foreign tutelage and to create a new country on the basis of "Turkey for the Turks." It represented, as I shall show, what was the central point of Turkish policy, not only in the empire's relations to foreign powers, but to her subject peoples. England's position on this question was about the same as our own; the British Government would consent to the modification of the economic restrictions, but not the others. Wangenheim, was greatly disturbed, and I think that his foreign office reprimanded him for letting the abrogation take place, because he blandly asked me to announce that I was the responsible person! As October 1st approached, the foreigners in Turkey were in a high state of apprehension. The Dardanelles had been closed, shutting them off from Europe, and now they felt that they were to be left to the mercy of Turkish courts and Turkish prisons. Inasmuch as it was the habit in Turkish prisons to herd the innocent with the guilty, and to place in the same room with murderers, people who had been charged, with minor offenses, but not convicted of them, and to bastinado recalcitrant witnesses, the fears of the foreign residents may well be imagined. The educational institutions were also apprehensive, and in their interest I now appealed to Enver. He assured me that the Turks had no hostile intention toward Americans. I replied that he should show in unmistakable fashion that Americans would not be harmed.

"All right," he answered. "What would you suggest?"

"Why not ostentatiously visit Robert College on October 1st, the day the capitulations are abrogated?" I said.

The idea was rather a unique one, for in all the history of this institution an important Turkish official had never entered its doors. But I knew enough of the Turkish character to understand that an open, ceremonious visit by Enver would cause a public sensation. News of it would reach the farthest limits of the Turkish Empire, and it was certain that the Turks would interpret it as meaning that one of the two most powerful men in Turkey had taken this and other American institutions under his patronage. Such a visit would exercise a greater protective influence over American colleges and schools in Turkey than an army corps. I was therefore greatly pleased when Enver promptly adopted my suggestion.

On the day that the capitulations were abrogated, Enver appeared at the American Embassy with two autos, one for himself and me, and the other for his adjutants, all of whom were dressed in full uniform I was pleased that Enver had made the proceeding so spectacular, for I wished it to have the widest publicity. On the ride up to the college I told Enver all about these American institutions and what they were doing for Turkey. He really knew very little about them, and, like most Turks, he half suspected that they concealed a political purpose.

"We Americans are not looking for material advantages in Turkey," I said. "We merely demand that you treat kindly our children, these colleges, for which all the people in the United States have the warmest affection."

I told him that Mr. Cleveland H. Dodge, President of the trustees of Robert College, and Mr. Charles R. Crane, President of the trustees of the Women's College, were intimate friends of President Wilson. "These," I added, "represent what is best in America and the fine altruistic spirit which in our country accumulates wealth and then uses it to found colleges and schools. In establishing these institutions in Turkey they are trying, not to convert your people to Christianity, but to help train them in the sciences and arts and so prepare to make them better citizens. Americans feel that the Bible lands have given them their religion and they wish to repay with the best thing America has ---its education." I then told him about Mrs. Russell Sage and Miss Helen Gould, who had made large gifts to the Women's College.

"But where do these people get all the money for such benefactions?" Enver asked.

I then entertained him for an hour or so with a few pages from our own "American Nights." I told him how Jay Gould had arrived in New York, a penniless and ragged boy, with a mousetrap which he had invented, "and how he had died, almost thirty years afterward, leaving a fortune of about $100,000,000. I told him how Commodore Vanderbilt had started life as a ferryman and had become America's greatest railroad "magnate"; how Rockefeller had begun his career sitting on a high stool in a Cleveland commission house, earning six dollars a week, and had created the greatest fortune that had ever been accumulated by a single man in the world's history. I told him how the Dodges had become our great "copper kings" and the Cranes our great manufacturers of iron pipe. Enver found these stories more thrilling than any that had ever come out of Bagdad, and I found afterward that he had retold them so frequently that they had reached almost all the important people in Constantinople.

Enver was immensely impressed also by what I said about the American institutions. He went through all the buildings and expressed his enthusiasm at everything he saw, and he even suggested that he would like to send his brother there. He took tea with Mrs. Gates, wife of President Gates, discussed most intelligently the courses, and asked if we could not introduce the study of agriculture. The teachers he met seemed to be a great revelation.

"I expected to find these missionaries as they are pictured in the Berlin newspapers," he said, "with long hair and hanging jaws, and hands clasped constantly in a prayerful attitude. But here is Dr. Gates, talking Turkish like a native and acting like a man of the world. I am more than pleased, and thank you for bringing me."

We all saw Enver that afternoon in his most delightful aspect. My idea that this visit in itself would protect the colleges from disturbance proved to have been a happy one. The Turkish Empire has been a tumultuous place in the last four years, but the American colleges have had no difficulties, either with the Turkish Government or with the Turkish populace.

This visit was only an agreeable interlude in events of the most exciting character. Enver, amiable as he could be on occasion, had deliberately determined to put Turkey in the war on Germany's side. Germany had now reached the point where she no longer concealed her intentions. Once before, when I had interfered in the interest of peace, Wangenheim had encouraged my action. The reason, as I have indicated, was that, at that time, Germany had wished Turkey to keep out of the war, for the German General Staff expected to win without her help. But now Wangenheim wanted Turkey in. As I was not working in Germany's interest, but as I was anxious to protect

American institutions, I still kept urging Enver and Talaat to keep out. This made Wangenheim. angry. "I thought that you were a neutral?" he now exclaimed.

"I thought that you were---in Turkey," I answered.

Toward the end of October, Wangenheim. was leaving nothing undone to start hostilities; all he needed now was a favourable occasion.

Even after Germany had closed the Dardanelles, the German Ambassador's task was not an easy one. Talaat was not yet entirely convinced that his best policy was war, and, as I have already said, there was still plenty of pro-Ally sympathy in official quarters. It was Talaat's plan not to seize all the cabinet offices at once, but gradually to elbow his way into undisputed control. At this crisis the most popularly respected members of the Ministry were Djavid, Minister of Finance, a man who was Jewish by race, but a Mohammedan by religion; Mahmoud Pasha, Minister of Public Works, a Circassian; Bust?ny Effendi, Minister of Commerce and Agriculture, a Christian Arab; and Oskan Effendi, Minister of Posts and Telegraphs, an Armenian---and a Christian, of course. All these leaders, as well as the Grand Vizier, openly opposed war and all now informed Talaat and Enver that they would resign if Germany succeeded in her intrigues. Thus the atmosphere was exciting; how tense the situation was a single episode will show. Sir Louis Mallet, the British Ambassador, had accepted an invitation to dine at the American Embassy on October 20th, but he sent word at the last moment that he was ill and could not come. I called on the Ambassador an hour or two afterward and found him in his garden, apparently in the best of health. Sir Louis smiled and said that his illness had been purely political. He had received a letter telling him that he was to be assassinated that evening, this letter informing him of the precise spot where the tragedy was to take place, and the time. He therefore thought that he had better stay indoors. As I had no doubt that some such crime had been planned, I offered Sir Louis the protection of our Embassy. I gave him the key to the back gate of the garden; and, with Lord Wellesley, one of his secretaries---a descendant of the Duke of Wellington---I made all arrangements for his escape to our quarters in case a flight became necessary. Our two embassies were so located that, in the event of an attack, he might go unobserved from the back gate of his to the back gate of ours. "These people are relapsing into the Middle Ages," said Sir Louis, "when it was quite the thing to throw ambassadors into dungeons,", and I think that he anticipated that the present Turks might treat him in the same way. I at once went to the Grand Vizier and informed him of the situation, insisting that nothing less than a visit from Talaat to Sir Louis, assuring him of his safety, would undo the harm already done. I could make this demand with propriety, as we had already made arrangements to take over British interests when the break came. Within two hours Talaat made such a visit. Though one of the Turkish newspapers was printing scurrilous attacks on Sir Louis he was personally very popular with the Turks, and the Grand Vizier expressed his amazement and regret---and he was entirely sincere--- that such threats had been made.

Chapter XI - Germany Forces Turkey into The War

But we were all then in a highly nervous state, because we knew that Germany was working hard to produce a casus belli. Souchon frequently sent the Goeben and the Breslau to manoeuvre in the Black Sea, hoping that the Russian fleet would attack. There were several pending situations that might end in war. Turkish and Russian troops were having occasional skirmishes on the Persian and Caucasian frontier. On October 29th, Bedouin troops crossed the Egyptian border and had a little collision with British soldiers. On this same day I had a long talk with Talaat. I called in the interest of the British Ambassador, to tell him about the Bedouins crossing into Egypt. "I suppose," Sir Louis wrote me, "that this means war; you might mention this news to Talaat and impress upon him the possible results of this mad act." Already Sir Louis had had difficulties with Turkey over this matter. When he had protested to the Grand Vizier about the Turkish troops near the Egyptian frontier, the Turkish statesman had pointedly replied that Turkey recognized no such thing as an Egyptian frontier. By this he meant, of course, that Egypt itself was Turkish territory and that the English occupation was a temporary usurpation. When I brought this Egyptian situation to Talaat's attention he said that no Ottoman Bedouins had crossed into Egypt. The Turks had been building wells on the Sinai peninsula to use in case war broke out with England; England was destroying these wells and the Bedouins, said Talaat, had interfered to stop this destruction.

At this meeting Talaat frankly told me that Turkey had decided to side with the Germans and to sink or swim with them. He went again over the familiar grounds, and added that if Germany won---and Talaat said that he was convinced that Germany would win---the Kaiser would get his revenge on Turkey if Turkey had not helped him to obtain this victory. Talaat frankly admitted that fear---the motive, which, as I have said, is the one that chiefly inspires Turkish acts---was driving Turkey into a German alliance. He analyzed the whole situation most dispassionately; he said that nations could not afford such emotions as gratitude, or hate, or affection; the only guide to action should be cold-blooded policy.

"At this moment," said Talaat, "it is for our interest to side with Germany; if, a month from now, it is our interest to embrace France and England we shall do that just as readily."

"Russia is our greatest enemy," he continued; "and we are afraid of her. If now, while Germany is attacking Russia, we can give her a good strong kick, and so make her powerless to injure us for some time, it is Turkey's duty to administer that kick!"

And then turning to me with a half -melancholy, half-defiant smile, he summed up the whole situation.

"Ich mit die Deutschen," he said, in his broken German.

Because the Cabinet was so divided, however, the Germans themselves had to push Turkey over the precipice. The evening following my talk with Talaat, most fateful news came from Russia. Three Turkish torpedo boats had entered the harbour of Odessa, had sunk the Russian gunboat Donetz, killing a part of the crew, and had damaged two Russian dreadnaughts. They also sank the French ship Portugal, killing two of the crew and wounding two others. They then turned their shells on the town and destroyed a sugar factory, with some loss of life. German officers commanded these Turkish vessels; there were very few Turks on board, as the Turkish crews had been given a holiday for the Turkish religious festival of Bairam. The act was simply a wanton and unprovoked one; the Germans raided the town deliberately, in order to make war inevitable. The German officers on the General, as my friend had told me, were constantly threatening to commit some such act, if Turkey did not do so; well, now they had done it. When this news reached Constantinople, Djemal was playing cards at the Cercle d'Orient. As Djemal was Minister of Marine, this attack, had it been an official act of Turkey, could have been made only on his orders. When someone called him from the card table to tell him the news, Djemal was much excited. "I know nothing about it," he replied. "It has not been done by my orders." On the evening of the 29th I had another talk with Talaat. He told me that he had known nothing of this attack beforehand and that the whole responsibility rested with the German, Admiral Souchon.

Whether Djemal and Talaat were telling the truth in thus pleading ignorance I do not know; my opinion is that they were expecting some such outrage as this. But there is no question that the Grand Vizier, Sa?d Halim, was genuinely grieved. When M. Bompard and Sir Louis Mallet called on him and demanded their passports, he burst into tears. He begged them to delay; he was sure that the matter could be adjusted. The Grand Vizier was the only member of the Cabinet whom Enver and Talaat particularly wished to placate. As a prince of the royal house of Egypt and as an extremely rich nobleman, his presence in the Cabinet, as I have already said, gave it a certain standing. This probably explains the message which I now received. Talaat asked me to call upon the Russian Ambassador and ask what amends Turkey could make that would satisfy the Czar. There is little likelihood that Talaat sincerely wished me to patch up the difficulty; his purpose was merely to show the Grand Vizier that he was attempting to meet his wishes, and, in this way, to keep him in the Cabinet. I saw M. Giers, but found him in no submissive mood. He said that Turkey could make amends only by dismissing all the German officers in the Turkish army and navy; he had his instructions to leave at once and he intended to do so. However, he would wait long enough in Bulgaria to receive their reply, and, if they accepted his terms, he would come back.

"Russia, herself, will guarantee that the Turkish fleet does not again come into the Black Sea," said M. Giers, grimly. Talaat called on me in the afternoon, saying that he had just had lunch with Wangenheim. The Cabinet had the Russian reply under consideration, he said; the Grand Vizier wished to have M. Giers's terms put in writing; would I attempt to get it? By. this time Garroni, the Italian Ambassador, had taken charge of Russian affairs, and I told Talaat that such negotiations were out of my hands and that any further negotiations must be conducted through him.

"Why don't you drop your mask as messenger boy of the Grand Vizier and talk to me as Talaat? " I asked.

He laughed and said: "Well, Wangenheim, Enver, and I prefer that the war shall come now."

Bust?ny, Oskan, Mahmoud, and Djavid at once carried out their threats and resigned from the Cabinet, thus leaving the government in the hands of Moslem Turks. The Grand Vizier, although he had threatened to resign, did not do so; he was exceedingly pompous and vain, and enjoyed the dignities of his office so much that, when it came to the final decision, he could not surrender them. Thus the net result of Turkey's entrance into the war, so far as internal politics was concerned, was to put the nation entirely in the hands of the Committee of Union and Progress, which now controlled the Government in practically all its departments. Thus the idealistic organization which had come into existence to give Turkey the blessings of democracy had ended by becoming a tool of Prussian autocracy.

One final picture I have of these exciting days. On the evening of the 30th I called at the British Embassy. British residents were already streaming in large numbers to my office for protection, and fears of ill treatment, even the massacre of foreigners, filled everybody's mind. Amid all this tension I found one imperturbable figure. Sir Louis was sitting in the chancery, before a huge fireplace, with large piles of documents heaped about him in a semi-circle. Secretaries and clerks were constantly entering, their arms full of papers, which they added to the accumulations already surrounding the Ambassador. Sir Louis would take up document after document, glance through it and almost invariably drop it into the fire. These papers contained the embassy records for probably a hundred years. In them were written the great achievements of a long line of distinguished ambassadors. They contained the story of all the diplomatic triumphs in Turkey of Stratford de Redcliffe, the "Great Elchi," as the Turks called him, who, for the greater part of almost fifty years, from 1810 to 1858, practically ruled the Turkish Empire in the interest of England. The records of other great British ambassadors at the Sublime Porte now went, one by one, into Sir Louis Mallet's fire. The long story of British ascendency in Turkey had reached its close. The twenty-years' campaign of the Kaiser to destroy England's influence and to become England's successor had finally triumphed, and the blaze in Sir Louis's chancery was really the funeral pyre of England's vanished power in Turkey. As I looked upon this dignified and yet somewhat pensive diplomat, sitting there amid all the splendours of the British Embassy, I naturally thought of how once the sultans had bowed with fear and awe before the majesty of England, in the days when Prussia and Germany were little more than names. Yet the British Ambassador, as is usually the case with British diplomatic and military figures, was quiet and self-possessed. We sat there before his fire and discussed the details of his departure. He gave me a list of the English residents who were to leave and those who were to stay, and I made final arrangements with Sir Louis for taking over British interests. Distressing in many ways as was this collapse of British influence in Turkey, the honour of Great Britain and that of her ambassador was still secure. Sir Louis had not purchased Turkish officials with money, as had Wangenheim; he had not corrupted the Turkish press, trampled on every remaining vestige of international law, fraternized with a gang of political desperadoes, and conducted a ceaseless campaign of misrepresentations and lies against his enemy. The diplomatic game that had ended in England's defeat was one which English statesmen were not qualified to play. It called for talents such as only a Wangenheim possessed---it needed that German statecraft which, in accordance with Bismarck's maxim, was ready to sacrifice for the Fatherland "not only life but honour."

Chapter XII - The Turks Attempt to Treat Alien Enemies Decently But the Germans Insist on Persecuting Them

Soon after the bombardment of Odessa I was closeted with Enver, discussing the subject which was then uppermost in the minds of all the foreigners in Turkey. How would the Government treat its resident enemies? Would it intern them, establish concentration camps, pursue them with German malignity, and perhaps apply the favourite Turkish measure with Christians---torture and massacre? Thousands of enemy subjects were then living in the Ottoman Empire; many of them had spent their whole lives there; others had even been born on Ottoman soil. All these people, when Turkey entered the war, had every reason to expect the harshest kind of treatment. It is no exaggeration to say that most of them lived in constant fear of murder. The Dardanelles had been closed, so that there was little chance that outside help could reach these aliens; the capitulatory rights, under which they had lived for centuries, had been abrogated. There was really nothing between the foreign residents and destruction except the American flag. The state of war had now made me, as American Ambassador, the protector of all British, French, Serbian, and Belgian subjects. I realized from the beginning that my task would be a difficult one. On one hand were the Germans, urging their well-known ideas of repression and brutality, while on the other were the Turks, with their traditional hatred of Christians and their natural instinct to maltreat those who are helplessly placed in their power.

Yet I had certain strong arguments on my side and I now had called upon Enver for the purpose of laying them before him. Turkey desired the good opinion of the United States, and hoped, after the war, to find support among American financiers. At that time all the embassies in Constantinople took it for granted that the United States would be the peacemaker; if Turkey expected us to be her friend, I now told Enver, she would have to treat enemy foreigners in a civilized way.

"You hope to be reinstated as a world power," I said. "You must remember that the civilized world will carefully watch you; your future status will depend on how you conduct yourself in war." The ruling classes among the Turks, including Enver, realized that the outside world regarded them as a people who had no respect for the sacredness of human life or the finer emotions and they keenly resented this attitude. I now reminded Enver that Turkey had a splendid opportunity to disprove all these criticisms. "The world may say you are barbarians," I argued; "show by the way you treat these alien enemies that you are not. Only in this way can you be freed permanently from the ignominy of the capitulations. Prove that you are worthy of being emancipated from foreign tutelage. Be civilized, be modern!"

In view of what was happening in Belgium and northern France at that moment, my use of the word "modern," was a little unfortunate. Enver quickly saw the point. Up to this time he had maintained his usual attitude of erect and dignified composure, and his face, as always, had been attentive, imperturbable, almost expressionless. Now in a flash his whole bearing changed. His countenance broke into a cynical smile, he leaned over, brought his fist down on the table, and said:

"Modern! No; however Turkey shall wage war, at least we shall not be 'modern.' That is the most barbaric system of all. We shall simply try to be decent! "

Naturally I construed this as a promise; I understood the changeableness of the Turkish character well enough, however, to know that more than a promise was necessary. The Germans were constantly prodding the Turkish officials, persuading them to adopt the favourite German plan against enemy aliens. Germany has revived many of the principles of ancient and medieval warfare, one of her most barbaric resurrections from the past being this practice of keeping certain representatives of the population, preferably people of distinction and influence, as hostages for the "good behaviour " of others. At this moment the German military staff was urging the Turks to keep foreign residents for this purpose. Just as the Germans held noncombatants in Belgium as security for the "friendliness" of the Belgians, and placed Belgian women and children at the head of their advancing armies, so the Germans in Turkey were now planning to use French and British residents as part of their protective system against the Allied fleet. That this sinister influence was constantly at work I well knew; therefore it was necessary that I should meet it immediately, and, if possible, gain the upper hand at the very start. I decided that the departure of the Entente diplomats and residents from Constantinople would really put to the test my ability to protect the foreign residents. If all the French and English who really wished to leave could safely get out of Turkey, I believed that this demonstration would have a restraining influence, not only upon the Germans, but upon the underlings of the Turkish official world.

As soon as I arrived at the railroad station, the day following the break, I saw that my task was to be a difficult one. I had arranged with the Turkish authorities for two trains; one for the English and French residents, which was to leave at seven o'clock, and one for the diplomats and their staff, which was to go at nine. But the arrangement was not working according to schedule. The station was a surging mass of excited and frightened people; the police were there in full force, pushing the crowds back; the scene was an indescribable mixture of soldiers, gendarmes, diplomats, baggage, and Turkish functionaries.

One of the most conspicuous figures was Bedri Bey, prefect of police, a lawyer politician, who had recently been elevated to this position, and who keenly realized the importance of his new office. Bedri was an intimate friend and political subordinate of Talaat and one of his most valuable tools. He ranked high in the Committee of Union and Progress, and aspired ultimately to obtain a cabinet position. Perhaps his most impelling motive was his hatred of foreigners and foreign influence. In his eyes Turkey was the land exclusively of the Turks; he despised all the other elements in its population, and he particularly resented the control which the foreign embassies had for years exerted in the domestic concerns of his country. Indeed, there were few men in Turkey with whom the permanent abolition of the capitulations was such a serious matter. Naturally in the next few months I saw much of Bedri; he was constantly crossing my path, taking an almost malicious pleasure in interfering with every move which I made in the interest of the foreigners. His attitude was half provoking, half jocular; we were always trying to outwit each other---I attempting to protect the French and British, Bedri always turning up as an obstacle to my efforts; the fight for the foreigners, indeed, almost degenerated into a personal duel between the Prefect of Police and the American Embassy. Bedri was capable, well educated, very ag-

64

ile, and not particularly ill-natured, but he loved to toy with a helpless foreigner. Naturally, he found his occupation this evening a congenial one.

"What's all the trouble about?" I asked Bedri.

"We have changed our minds," he said, and his manner showed that the change had not been displeasing to him. "We shall let the train go that is to take the ambassadors and their staffs. But we have decided not to let the unofficial classes leave--- the train that was to take them will not go."

My staff and I had worked hard to get this safe passage for the enemy nationals. Now apparently some influence had negatived our efforts. This sudden change in plans was producing the utmost confusion and consternation. At the station there were two "groups of passengers, one of which could go and the other of which could not. The British and French ambassadors did not wish to leave their nationals behind, and the latter refused to believe that their train, which the Turkish officials had definitely promised, would not start sometime that evening. I immediately called up Enver, who substantiated Bedri's statement. Turkey had many subjects in Egypt, he said., whose situation was causing great anxiety. Before the French and English residents could leave Turkey, assurances must be given that the rights of Turkish subjects in these countries would be protected. I had no difficulty in arranging this detail, for Sir Louis Mallet immediately gave the necessary assurances. However, this did not settle the matter; indeed, it had been little more than a pretext. Bedri still refused to let the train start; the order holding it up, he said, could not be rescinded, for that would now disarrange the general schedule and might cause accidents. I recognized all this as mere Turkish evasion and I knew that the order had come from a higher source than Bedri; still nothing could be done at that moment. Moreover, Bedri would let no one get on the diplomatic train until I had personally identified him. So I had to stand at a little gate, and pass upon each applicant. Everyone, whether he belonged to the diplomatic corps or not, attempted to force himself through this narrow passageway, and we had an old-fashioned Brooklyn Bridge crush on a small scale. People were running in all directions, checking baggage, purchasing tickets, arguing with officials, consoling distracted women and frightened children, while Bedri, calm and collected, watched the whole pandemonium with an unsympathetic smile. Hats were knocked off, clothing was torn, and, to add to the confusion, Mallet, the British Ambassador, became involved in a set-to with an officious Turk---the Englishman winning first honours easily; and I caught a glimpse of Bompard, the French Ambassador, vigorously shaking a Turkish policeman. One lady dropped her baby in my arms, later another handed me a small boy, and still later, when I was standing at the gate, identifying Turkey's departing guests, one of the British secretaries made me the custodian of his dog. Meanwhile, Sir Louis Mallet became obstreperous and refused to leave.

"I shall stay here," he said, "until the last British subject leaves Turkey."

But I told him that he was no longer the protector of the British; that I, as American Ambassador, had assumed this responsibility; and that I could hardly assert myself in this capacity if he remained in Constantinople.

"Certainly," I said, "the Turks would not recognize me as in charge of British interests if you remain here."

Moreover, I suggested that he remain at Dedeagatch for a few days, and await the arrival of his fellow British. Sir Louis reluctantly accepted my point of view and boarded the train. As the train left the station I caught my final glimpse of the British Ambassador, sitting in a private car, almost buried in a mass of trunks, satchels, boxes, and diplomatic pouches, surrounded by his embassy staff, and sympathetically watched by his secretary's dog.

The unofficial foreigners remained in the station several hours, hoping that, at the last moment, they would be permitted to go. Bedri, however, was inexorable. Their position was almost desperate. They had given up their quarters in Constantinople, and now found themselves practically stranded. Some were taken in by friends for the night, others found accommodations in hotels. But their situation caused the utmost anxiety. Evidently, despite all official promises, Turkey was determined to keep these foreign residents as hostages. On the one hand were Enver and Talaat, telling me that they intended to conduct their war in a humane manner, and, on the other, were their underlings, such as Bedri, behaving in a fashion that negatived all these civilized pretensions. The fact was that the officials were quarrelling among themselves about the treatment of foreigners; and the German General Staff was telling the Cabinet that they were making a great mistake in showing any leniency to their enemy aliens. Finally, I succeeded in making arrangements for them to leave the following day. Bedri, in more complaisant mood, spent that afternoon at the embassy, vis?ing passports; we both went to the station in the evening and started the train safely toward Dedeagatch. I gave a box of candy---"Turkish Delights," to each one of the fifty women and children on the train; it altogether was a happy party and they made no attempt to hide their relief at leaving Turkey. At Dedeagatch they met the diplomatic corps, and the reunion that took place, I afterward learned, was extremely touching. I was made happy by receiving many testimonials of their gratitude, in particular a letter, signed by more than a hundred, expressing their thanks to Mrs. Morgenthau, the embassy staff, and myself.

There were still many who wished to go and next day I called on Talaat in their behalf. I found him in one of his most gracious moods. The Cabinet, he said, had carefully considered the whole matter of English and French residents in Turkey, and my arguments, he added, had greatly influenced them. They had reached the formal decision that enemy aliens could leave or remain, as they preferred. There would be no concentration camps, civilians could pursue their usual business in peace, and, so long as they behaved themselves, they would not be molested.

"We propose to show," said Talaat, "by our treatment of aliens, that we are not a race of barbarians."

In return for this promise he asked a favour of me: would I not see that Turkey was praised in the American and European press for this decision?

After returning to the embassy I immediately sent for Mr. Theron Damon, correspondent of the Associated Press, Doctor Lederer, correspondent of the Berliner Tageblatt, and Doctor Sandler, who represented the Paris Herald, and gave them interviews, praising the attitude of Turkey toward the foreign residents. I also cabled the news to Washington, London, and Paris and to all our consuls.

Hardly had I finished with the correspondents when I again received alarming news. I had arranged for another train that evening, and I now heard that the Turks were refusing to vis? the passports of those whose departure I had provided for. This news, coming right after Talaat's explicit promise, was naturally disturbing. I immediately started for the railroad station, and the sight which I saw there increased my anger at the Minister of the Interior. A mass of distracted people filled the inclosure; the women were weeping, and the children were screaming, while a platoon of Turkish soldiers, commanded by an undersized popinjay of a major, was driving everybody out of the station with the flat sides of their guns. Bedri, as usual, was there, and as usual, he was clearly enjoying the confusion; certain of the passengers, he told me, had not paid their income tax, and, for this reason, they would not be permitted to leave. I announced that I would be personally responsible for this payment.

"I can't get ahead of you, Mr. Ambassador, can I?" said Bedri, with a laugh. From this we all thought that my offer had settled the matter and that the train would leave according to schedule. But then suddenly, came another order holding it up again.

Since I had just had a promise from Talaat I decided to find that functionary and learn what all this meant. I jumped into my automobile and went to the Sublime Porte, where he usually had his headquarters. Finding no one there, I told the chauffeur to drive directly to Talaat's house. Sometime before I had visited Enver in his domestic surroundings and this occasion now gave me the opportunity to compare his manner of life with that of his more powerful associate. The contrast was a startling one. I had found Enver living in luxury, in one of the most aristocratic parts of the town, while now I was driving to one of the poorer sections. We came to a narrow street, bordered by little rough, unpainted wooden houses; only one thing distinguished this thoroughfare from all others in Constantinople and suggested that it was the abiding place of the most powerful man in the Turkish Empire. At either end stood a policeman, letting no one enter who could not give a satisfactory reason for doing so. Our auto, like all others, was stopped, but we were promptly permitted to pass when we explained who we were. As contrasted with Enver's palace, with its innumerable rooms and gorgeous furniture, Talaat's house was an old, rickety, wooden, three-story building. All this, I afterward learned, was part of the setting which Talaat had staged for his career. Like many an American politician, he had found his position as a man of "the people" a valuable political asset, and he knew that a sudden display of prosperity and ostentation would weaken his influence with the Union and Progress Committee, most of whose members, like himself, had risen from the lower walks of life. The contents of the house were quite in keeping with the exterior. There were no suggestions of Oriental magnificence. The furniture was cheap; a few coarse prints hung on the walls, and one or two well-worn rugs were scattered on the floor. On one side stood a wooden table, and on this rested a telegraph instrument---once Talaat's means of earning a living, and now a means by which he communicated with his associates. In the present troubled conditions in Turkey Talaat sometimes preferred to do his own telegraphing!

Amid these surroundings I awaited for a few minutes the entrance of the Big Boss of Turkey. In due time a door opened at the other end of the room, and a huge, lumbering, gaily-decorated figure entered. I was startled by the contrast which this Talaat presented to the one who had become such a familiar figure to me at the Sublime Porte. It was no longer the Talaat of the European clothes and the thin veneer of European manners; the man whom I now saw looked like a real Bulgarian gypsy. Talaat wore the usual red Turkish fez; the rest of his bulky form was clothed in thick gray pajamas; and from this combination protruded a rotund, smiling face. His mood was half genial, half deprecating; Talaat well understood what pressing business had led me to invade his domestic privacy, and his behaviour now resembled that of the unrepentant bad boy in school. He came and sat down with a good-natured grin, and began to make excuses. Quietly the door opened again, and a hesitating little girl was pushed into the room, bringing a tray of cigarettes and coffee. Presently I saw that a young woman, apparently about twenty-five years old, was standing back of the child, urging her to enter. Here, then, were Talaat's wife and adopted daughter; I had already discovered that, while Turkish women never enter society or act as hostesses, they are extremely inquisitive about their husbands' guests, and like to get surreptitious glimpses of them. Evidently Madame Talaat, on this occasion, was not satisfied with her preliminary view, for, a few minutes afterward, she appeared at a window directly opposite me, but entirely unseen by her husband, who was facing in the other direction, and there she remained very quiet and very observant for several minutes. As she was in the house, she was unveiled; her face was handsome and intelligent; and it was quite apparent that she enjoyed this close-range view of an American ambassador.

"Well, Talaat," I said, realizing that the time had come for plain speaking, "don't you know how foolishly you are acting? You told me a few hours ago that you had decided to treat the French and English decently and you asked me to publish this news in the American and foreign press. I at once called in the newspaper men and told them how splendidly you were behaving. And this at your own request! The whole world will be reading about it to-morrow. Now you are doing your best to counteract all my efforts in your behalf; here you have repudiated your first promise to be decent. Are you going to keep the promises you made me? Will you stick to them, or do you intend to keep changing your mind all the time? Now let's have a real understanding. The thing we Americans particularly pride ourselves on is keeping our word. We do it as individuals and as a nation. We refuse to deal with people as equals who do not do this. You might as well understand now that we can do no business with each other unless I can depend on your promises."

"Now, this isn't my fault," Talaat answered. "The Germans are to blame for stopping that train. The German Chief of Staff has just returned and is making a big fuss, saying that we are too easy with the French and English and that we must not let them go away. He says that we must keep them for hostages. It was his interference that did this."

That was precisely what I had suspected. Talaat had given me his promise, then Bronssart, head of the German Staff, had practically countermanded his orders. Talaat's admission gave me the opening which I had wished for. By this time my relations with Talaat had become so friendly that I could talk to him with the utmost frankness.

"Now, Talaat," I said, "you have got to have someone to advise you in your relations with foreigners. You must make up your mind whether you want me or the German Staff. Don't you think you will make a mistake if you place yourself entirely in the hands of the Germans? The time may come when you will need me against them."

"What do you mean by that?" he asked, watching for my answer with intense curiosity.

"The Germans are sure to ask you to do many things you don't want to do. If you can tell them that the American Ambassador objects, my support may prove useful to you. Besides, you know you all expect peace in a few months. You know that the

Germans really care nothing for Turkey, and certainly you have no claims on the Allies for assistance. There is only one nation in the world that you can look to as a disinterested friend and that is the United States."

This fact was so apparent that I hardly needed to argue it in any great detail. However, I had another argument that struck still nearer home. Already the struggle between the war department and the civil powers had started. I knew that Talaat, although he was Minister of the Interior, and a civilian, was determined not to sacrifice a tittle of his authority to Enver, the Germans, and the representatives of the military.

"If you let the Germans win this point to-day," I said, "you are practically in their power. You are now the head of affairs, but you are still a civilian. Are you going to let the military, represented by Enver and the German staff, overrule your orders? Apparently that is what has. happened to-day. If you submit to it, you will find that they will be running things from now on. The Germans will put this country under martial law; then where will you civilians be?"

I could see that this argument was having its effect on Talaat. He remained quiet for a few moments, evidently pondering my remarks. Then he said, with the utmost deliberation, "I am going to help you."

He turned around to his table and began working his telegraph instrument. I shall never forget the picture; this huge Turk, sitting there in his gray pajamas and his red fez, working industriously his own telegraph key, his young wife gazing at him through a little window and the late afternoon sun streaming into the room. Evidently the ruler of Turkey was having his troubles, and, as the argument went on over the telegraph, Talaat would bang his key with increasing irritation. He told me that the pompous major at the station insisted on having Enver's written orders---since orders over the wire might easily be counterfeited. It took Talaat some time to locate Enver, and then the dispute apparently started all over again. A piece of news which Talaat received at that moment over the wire almost ruined my case. After a prolonged thumping of his instrument, in the course of which Talaat's face lost its geniality and became almost savage, he turned to me and said:

"The English bombarded the Dardanelles this morning and killed two Turks!"

And then he added:

"We intend to kill three Christians for every Moslem killed!"

For a moment I thought that everything was lost. Talaat's face reflected only one emotion---hatred of the English. Afterward, when reading the Cromer report on the Dardanelles, I found that the British Committee stigmatized this early attack as a mistake, since it gave the Turks an early warning of their plans. I can testify that it was a mistake for another reason, for I now found that these few strange shots almost destroyed my plans to get the foreign residents out of Turkey. Talaat was enraged, and I had to go over much of the ground again, but finally I succeeded in pacifying him once more. I saw that he was vacillating between his desire to punish the English and his desire to assert his own authority over that of Enver and the Germans. Fortunately the latter motive gained the ascendancy. At all hazard, he was determined to show that he was boss.

We remained there more than two hours, my involuntary host pausing now and then in his telegraphing to entertain me with the latest political gossip. Djavid, the Minister of Finance, he said, had resigned, but had promised to work for them at home. The Grand Vizier, despite his threats, had been persuaded to retain his office.

Foreigners in the interior would not be molested unless Beirut, Alexandretta, or some unfortified port were bombarded, but, if such attacks were made, they would exact reprisals of the French and English. Talaat's conversation showed that he had no particular liking for the Germans. They were overbearing and insolent, he said, constantly interfering in military matters and treating the Turks with disdain.

Finally the train was arranged. Talaat had shown several moods in this interview; he had been by turns sulky, good-natured, savage, and complaisant. There is one phase of the Turkish character which Westerners do not comprehend and that is its keen sense of humour. Talaat himself greatly loved a joke and a funny story. Now that he had reestablished friendly relations and redeemed his promise, Talaat became jocular once more.

"Your people can go now," he said with a laugh. "It's time to buy your candies, Mr. Ambassador!"

This latter, of course, was a reference to the little gifts which I had made to the women and children the night before. We immediately returned to the station, where we found the disconsolate passengers sitting around waiting for a favourable word. When I told them that the train would leave that evening, their thanks and gratitude were overwhelming.

Chapter XIII - The Invasion of Notre Dame De Sion

Talaat's statement that the German Chief of Staff, Bronssart, had really held up this train, was a valuable piece of information. I decided to look into the matter further, and, with this idea in my mind, I called next day on Wangenheim. The Turkish authorities, I said, had solemnly promised that they would treat their enemies decently, and certainly I could not tolerate any interference in the matter from the German Chief of Staff. Wangenheim had repeatedly told me that the Germans were looking to President Wilson as the peacemaker and I therefore used the same argument with him that I had urged on Talaat. Proceedings of this sort would not help his country when the day of the final settlement came! Here, I said, we have a strange situation; a so-called barbarous country, like Turkey, attempting to make civilized warfare and treat their Christian enemies with decency and kindness, and, on the other hand, a supposedly cultured and Christian nation, like Germany, which is trying to persuade them to revert to barbarism. "What sort of an impression do you think that will make on the American people?" I asked Wangenheim. He expressed a willingness to help and suggested, as my consideration for such help, that I should try to persuade the United States to insist on free commerce with Germany, so that his country could receive plentiful cargoes of copper, wheat, and cotton. This was a subject to which, as I shall relate, Wangenheim constantly returned.

Despite Wangenheim's promise I had practically no support from the German Embassy in my attempt to protect the foreign residents from Turkish ill treatment. I realized that, owing to my religion, there might be a feeling in certain quarters that I was not exerting all my energies in behalf of these Christian peoples and religious organizations---hospitals, schools, monasteries, and convents---and I naturally thought that it would strengthen my influence with the Turks if I could have the support of my most powerful Christian colleagues. I had a long discussion on this matter with Pallavicini, himself a Catholic and the representative of the greatest Catholic power. Pallavicini frankly told me that Wangenheim would do nothing that would annoy the Turks. There was then a constant fear that the English and French fleets would force the Dardanelles, capture Constantinople, and hand it over to Russia, and only the Turkish forces, said Pallavicini, could prevent such a calamity. The Germans, therefore, believed that they were dependent on the good graces of the Turkish Government, and would do nothing to antagonize them. Evidently Pallavicini wished me to believe that Wangenheim and he really desired to help. Yet this plea was hardly frank, for I knew all the time that Turkey, if the Germans had not constantly interfered, would have behaved decently. I found that the evil spirit was not the Turkish Government, but Von Bronssart, the German Chief of Staff. The fact that certain members of the Turkish Cabinet, who represented European and Christian culture---men like Bust?ny and Oskan---had resigned as a protest against Turkey's action in entering the war, made the situation of foreigners even more dangerous. There was also much conflict of authority; a policy decided on one day would be reversed the next, the result being, that we never knew where we stood. The mere fact that the Government promised me that foreigners would not be maltreated by no means settled the matter, for some underling, like Bedri Bey, could frequently find an excuse for disregarding instructions. The situation, therefore, was one that called for constant vigilance; I had not only to get pledges from men like Talaat and Enver, but I had personally to see that these pledges were carried into action.

I awoke one November morning at four o'clock; I had been dreaming, or I had had a " presentiment," that all was not going well with the Sion Soeurs, a French sisterhood which had for many years conducted a school for girls in Constantinople. Madame Bompard, the wife of the French Ambassador, and several ladies of the French colony, had particularly requested us to keep a watchful eye on this institution. It was a splendidly conducted school; the daughters of many of the best families of all nationalities attended it, and when these girls were assembled, the Christians wearing silver crosses and the non-Christians silver stars, the sight was particularly beautiful and impressive. Naturally the thought of the brutal Turks breaking into such a community was enough to arouse the wrath of any properly constituted man. Though we had nothing more definite than an uneasy feeling that something might be wrong, Mrs. Morgenthau and I decided to go up immediately after breakfast. As we approached the building we noted nothing particularly suspicious; the place was quiet and the whole atmosphere was one of peace and sanctity. Just as we ascended the steps, however, five Turkish policemen followed on our heels. They crowded after us into the vestibule, much to the consternation of a few of the sisters, who happened to be in the waiting room. The mere fact that the American Ambassador came with the police in itself increased their alarm, though our arrival together was purely accidental.

"What do you want?" I asked, turning to the men. As they spoke only Turkish, naturally they did not understand me, and they started to push me aside. My own knowledge of Turkish was extremely limited, but I knew that the word "Elchi" meant "Ambassador." So, pointing to Myself, I said, "Elchi American."

This scrap of Turkish worked like magic. In Turkey an ambassador is a much-revered object, and these policemen immediately respected my authority. Meanwhile the sisters had sent for their superior, M?re Elvira. This lady was one of the most distinguished and influential personages in Constantinople. That morning, as she came in quietly and faced these Turkish policemen, showing not a sign of fear, and completely overawing them by the splendour and dignity of her bearing, she represented to my eyes almost a supernatural being. M?re Elvira was a daughter of one of the most aristocratic families of France; she was a woman of perhaps forty years of age, with black hair and shining black eyes, all accentuated by a pale face that radiated culture, character, and intelligence. I could not help thinking, as I looked at her that morning, that there was not a diplomatic circle in the world to which she would not have added grace and dignity. In a few seconds M?re Elvira had this present distracting situation completely under control. She sent for a sister who spoke Turkish and questioned the policemen. They said that they were acting under Bedri's orders. All the foreign schools were to be closed that morning, the Government intending to seize all their buildings. There were about seventy-two teachers and sisters in this convent; the police had orders to shut all these into two rooms, where they were to be held practically as prisoners. There were about two hundred girls; these were to be turned out into the streets, and left to shift for themselves. The fact that it was raining in torrents, and that the weather was extremely cold, accentuated the barbarity of this proceeding. Yet every enemy school and religious institution in Constantinople was undergoing a similar experience at this time. Clearly this was a situation which I could not handle alone, and I at once telephoned my Turkish-speaking legal adviser. Herein is another incident which may have an interest for those who believe in providential intervention. When I arrived in Constantinople telephones had been unknown, but, in the last few months, an English company had been introducing a system. The night before my experience with the Sion Soeurs, my legal adviser had called me up and proudly told me that his telephone had just been installed. I jotted down his number, and this memorandum I now found in my pocket. Without my interpreter I should have been hard pressed, and without this telephone I could not have immediately brought him to the spot.

While waiting for his arrival I delayed the operations of the policemen, and my wife, who fortunately speaks French, was obtaining all the details from the sisters. Mrs. Morgenthau understood the Turks well enough to know that they had other plans than the mere expulsion of the sisters and their charges. The Turks regard these institutions as repositories of treasure; the valuables which they contain are greatly exaggerated in the popular mind; and it was a safe assumption that, among other things, this expulsion was an industrious raiding expedition for tangible evidences of wealth.

"Have you any money and other valuables here?" Mrs. Morgenthau asked one of the sisters.

Yes, they had quite a large amount; it was kept in a safe upstairs. My wife told me to keep the policemen busy and then she and one of the sisters quietly disappeared from the scene. Upstairs the sister disclosed about a hundred square pieces of white flannel into each one of which had been sewed twenty gold coins. In all, the Sion Soeurs had in this liquid form about fifty thousand francs. They had been fearing expulsion for some time and had been getting together their money in this form, so that they could carry it away with them when forced to leave Turkey. Besides this, the sisters had several bundles of securities, and many valuable papers, such as the charter of their school. Certainly here was something that would appeal to Turkish cupidity. Mrs. Morgenthau knew that if the police once obtained control of the building there would be little likelihood that the Sion Soeurs would ever see their money again. With the aid of the sisters, my wife promptly concealed as much as she could on her person, descended the stairs, and marched through the line of gendarmes out into the rain. Mrs. Morgenthau told me afterward that her blood almost ran cold with fright as she passed by these guardians of the law; from all external signs, however, she was absolutely calm and collected. She stepped into the waiting auto, was driven to the American Embassy, placed the money in our vault, and promptly returned to the school. Again Mrs. Morgenthau solemnly ascended the stairs with the sisters. This time they took her to the gallery of the Cathedral, which stood behind the convent, but could be entered through it. One of the sisters lifted up a tile from a particular spot in the floor, and again disclosed a heap of gold coins. This was secreted on Mrs. Morgenthau's clothes, and once more she walked past the gendarmes, out into the rain, and was driven rapidly to the Embassy. In these two trips my wife succeeded in getting the money of the sisters to a place where it would be safe from the Turks.

Between Mrs. Morgenthau's trips Bedri had arrived. He told me that Talaat had himself given the order for closing all the institutions and that they had intended to have the entire job finished before nine o'clock. I have already said that the Turks have a sense of humour; but to this statement I should add that it sometimes manifests itself in a perverted form. Bedri now seemed to think that locking more than seventy Catholic sisters in two rooms and turning two hundred young and carefully nurtured girls into the streets of Constantinople was a great joke.

"We were going at it early in the morning and have it all over before you heard anything about it," he said with a laugh. "But you seem never to be asleep."

"You are very foolish to try to play such tricks on us," I said. "Don't you know that I am going to write a book? If you go on behaving this way, I shall put you in as the villain."

This remark was an inspiration of the moment; it was then that it first occurred to me that these experiences might prove sufficiently interesting for publication. Bedri took the statement seriously, and it seemed to have a sobering effect.

"'Do you really intend to write a book?" he asked, almost anxiously.

"Why not?" I rejoined. "General Lew Wallace was minister here---didn't he write a book? 'Sunset' Cox was also minister here---didn't he write one? Why shouldn't I? And you are such an important character that I shall have to give you a part. Why do you go on acting in a way that will make me describe you as a very bad man? These sisters here have always been your friends. They have never done you anything but good; they have educated many of your daughters; why do you treat them in this shameful fashion?"

This plea produced an effect; Bedri consented to postpone execution of the order until we could get Talaat on the wire. In a few minutes I heard Talaat laughing over the telephone.

"I tried to escape you," he said, "but you have caught me again. Why make such a row about this matter? Didn't the French themselves expel all their nuns and monks? Why shouldn't we do it? "

73

After I had remonstrated over this indecent haste Talaat told Bedri to suspend the order until we had had a chance to talk the matter over. Naturally this greatly relieved Mere Elvira and the sisters. Just as we were about to leave, Bedri suddenly had a new idea. There was one detail which he had apparently forgotten.

"'We'll leave the Sion sisters alone for the present," he said, "but we must get their money."

Reluctantly I acquiesced in his suggestion---knowing that all the valuables were safely reposing in the American Embassy. So I had the pleasure of standing by and watching Bedri and his associates search the whole establishment. All they turned up was a small tin box containing a few copper coins, a prize which was so trifling that the Turks disdained to take it. They were much puzzled and disappointed, and from that day to this they have never known what became of the money. If my Turkish friends do me the honour of reading these pages, they will find that I have explained here for the first time one of the many mysteries of those exciting days.

As some of the windows of the convent opened on the court of the Cathedral, which was Vatican property, we contended that the Turkish Government could not seize it. Such of the sisters as were neutrals were allowed to remain in possession of the part that faced the Vatican land, while the rest of the building was turned into an Engineers' School. We arranged that the French nuns should have ten days to leave for their own country; they all reached their destination safely, and most are at present engaged in charities and war work in France.

My jocular statement that I intended to write a book deeply impressed Bedri, and, in the next few weeks, he repeatedly referred to it. I kept banteringly telling him that, unless his behaviour improved, I should be forced to picture him as the villain. One day he asked me, in all seriousness, whether he could not do something that would justify me in portraying him in a more favourable light. This attitude gave me an opportunity I had been seeking for some time. Constantinople had for many years been a centre for the white-slave trade and a particularly vicious gang was then operating under cover of a fake synagogue. A committee, organized to fight this crew, had made me an honorary chairman. I told Bedri that he now had the chance to secure a reputation; because of the war, his powers as Prefect of Police had been greatly increased and a little vigorous action on his part would permanently rid the city of this disgrace. The enthusiasm with which Bedri adopted my suggestion and the thoroughness and ability with which he did the work entitle him to the gratitude of all decent people. In a few days every white-slave trader in Constantinople was scurrying for safety; most were arrested, a few made their escape; such as were foreigners, after serving terms in jail, were expelled from the country. Bedri furnished me photographs of all the culprits and they are now on file in our State Department. I was not writing a book at that time, but I felt obliged to secure some public recognition for Bedri's work. I therefore sent his photograph, with a few words about his achievement, to the New York Times, which published it in a Sunday edition. That a great American newspaper had recognized him in this way delighted Bedri beyond words. For months he carried in his pocket the page of the Times containing his picture, showing it to all his friends. This event ended my troubles with the Prefect of Police; for the rest of my stay we had very few serious clashes.

Chapter XIV - Wangenheim and the Bethlehem Steel Company - A Holy War That Was Made in Germany

All this time I was increasing my knowledge of the modern German character, as illustrated in Wangenheim and his associates. In the early days of the war, the Germans showed their most ingratiating side to Americans; as time went on, how ever, and it became apparent that public opinion in the United States almost unanimously supported the Allies, and that the Washington Administration would not disregard the neutrality laws in order to promote Germany's interest, this friendly attitude changed and became almost hostile.

The grievance to which the German Ambassador constantly returned with tiresome iteration was the old familiar one---the sale of American ammunition to the Allies. I hardly ever met him that he did not speak about it. He was constantly asking me to write to President Wilson, urging him to declare an embargo; of course, my contention that the commerce in munitions was entirely legitimate made no impression. As the struggle at the Dardanelles became more intense, Wangenheim's insistence on the subject of American ammunition grew. He asserted that most of the shells used at the Dardanelles had been made in America and that the United States was really waging war on Turkey.

One day, more angry than usual, he brought me a piece of shell. On it clearly appeared the inscription "B.S.Co."

"Look at that!" he said. "I suppose you know what 'B.S.Co.' means? That is the Bethlehem Steel Company! This will make the Turks furious. And remember that we are going to hold the United States responsible for it. We are getting more and more proof, and we are going to hold you to account for every death caused by American shells. If you would only write home and make them stop selling ammunition to our enemies, the war would be over very soon."

I made the usual defense, and called Wangenheim's attention to the fact that Germany had sold munitions to Spain in the Spanish War, but all this was to no purpose. All that Wangenheim saw was that American supplies formed an asset to his enemy; the legalities of the situation did not interest him. Of course I refused point blank to write to the President about the matter.

A few days afterward an article appeared in the Ikdam discussing Turkish and American relations. This contribution, for the greater part, was extremely complimentary to America; its real purpose, however, was to contrast the present with the past, and to point out that our action in furnishing ammunition to Turkey's enemies was hardly in accordance with the historic friendship between the two countries. The whole thing was evidently written merely to get before the Turkish people a statement almost parenthetically included in the final paragraph. "According to the report of correspondents at the Dardanelles it appears that most of the shells fired by the British and French during the last bombardment were made in America."

At this time the German Embassy controlled the Ikdam, and was conducting it entirely in the interest of German propaganda. A statement of this sort, instilled into the minds of impressionable and fanatical Turks, might have the most deplorable consequences. I therefore took the matter up immediately with the man whom I regarded as chiefly responsible for the attack---the German Ambassador.

At first Wangenheim asserted his innocence; he was as bland as a child in protesting his ignorance of the whole affair. I called his attention to the fact that the statements in the Ikdam were almost identically the same as those which he had made to me a few days before; that the language in certain spots, indeed, was almost a repetition of his own conversation.

"Either you wrote that article yourself," I said, or you called in the reporter and gave him the leading ideas."

Wangenheim saw that there was no use in further denying the authorship.

"Well," he said, throwing back his head, "what are you going to do about it? "

This Tweed-like attitude rather nettled me and I resented it on the spot.

"I'll tell you what I am going to do about it," I replied, "and you know that I will be able to carry out my threats. Either you stop stirring up anti-American feeling in Turkey or I shall start a campaign of anti-German sentiment here.

"You know, Baron," I added, "that you Germans are skating on very thin ice in this country. You know that the Turks don't love you any too well. In fact, you know that Americans are more popular here than you are. Supposing that I go out, tell the Turks how you are simply using them for your own benefit that you do not really regard them as your allies, but merely as pawns in the game which you are playing. Now, in stirring up anti-American feeling here you are touching my softest spot. You are exposing our educational and religious institutions to the attacks of the Turks. No one knows what they may do if they are persuaded that their relatives are being shot down by American bullets. You stop this at once, or in three weeks I will fill the whole of Turkey with animosity toward the Germans. It will be a battle between us, and I am ready for it."

Wangenheim's attitude changed at once. He turned around, put his arm on my shoulder, and assumed a most conciliatory, almost affectionate, manner.

"Come, let us be friends," he said. "I see that you are right about this. I see that such attacks might injure your friends, the missionaries. I promise you that they will be stopped."

From that day the Turkish press never made the slightest unfriendly allusion to the United States. The abruptness with which the attacks ceased showed me that the Germans had evidently extended to Turkey one of the most cherished expedients of the Fatherland ---absolute government control of the press. But when I think of the infamous plots which Wangenheim was instigating at that moment, his objection to the use of a few American shells by English battleships---if English battleships used any such shells, which I seriously doubt---seems almost grotesque. In the early days Wangenheim had explained to me one of Germany's main purposes in forcing Turkey into the conflict. He made this explanation quietly and nonchalantly, as though it had been quite the most ordinary matter in the world. Sitting in his office, puffing away at his big black German cigar, he unfolded Germany's scheme to arouse the whole fanatical Moslem world against the Christians. Germany had planned a real "holy war" as one means of destroying English and French influence in the world. "Turkey herself is not the really important matter," said Wangenheim. "Her army is a small one, and we do not expect it to do very much. For the most part it will act on the defensive. But the big thing is the Moslem world. If we can stir the Mohammedans up against the English and Russians, we can force them to make peace."

What Wangenheim evidently meant by the "Big thing" became apparent on November 13th, when the Sultan issued his declaration of war; this declaration was really an appeal for a Jihad, or a "Holy War" against the infidel. Soon afterward the Sheik-ul-Islam published his proclamation, summoning the whole Moslem world to arise and massacre their Christian oppressors. "Oh, Moslems!" concluded this document. "Ye who are smitten with happiness and are on the verge of sacrificing your life and your goods for the cause of right, and of braving perils, gather now around the Imperial throne, obey the commands of the Almighty, who, in the Koran, promises us bliss in this and in the next world; embrace ye the foot of the Caliph's throne and know ye that the state is at war with Russia, England, France, and their Allies, and that these are the enemies of Islam. The Chief of the believers, the Caliph, invites you all as Moslems to join in the Holy War!"

The religious leaders read this proclamation to their assembled congregations in the mosques; all the newspapers printed it conspicuously; it was spread broadcast in all the countries which had large Mohammedan populations---India, China, Persia, Egypt, Algiers, Tripoli, Morocco, and the like; in all these places it was read to the assembled multitudes and the populace was exhorted to obey the mandate. The Ikdam, the Turkish newspaper which had passed into German ownership, was constantly inciting the masses. "The deeds of our enemies," wrote this Turco-German editor, "have brought down the wrath of God. A gleam of hope has appeared. All Mohammedans, young and old, men, women, and children, must fulfil their duty so that the gleam may not fade away, but give light to us forever. How many great things can be accomplished by the arms of vigorous men, by the aid of others, of women and children! ... The time for action has come. We shall all have to fight with all our strength, with all our soul, with teeth and nails, with all the sinews of our bodies and of our spirits. If we do it, the deliverance of the subjected Mohammedan kingdoms is assured. Then, if God so wills, we shall march unashamed by the side of our friends who send their greetings to the Crescent. Allah is our aid and the Prophet is our support."

The Sultan's proclamation was an official public document, and dealt with the proposed Holy War only in a general way, but about this same time a secret pamphlet appeared which gave instructions to the faithful in more specific terms. This paper was not read in the mosques; it was distributed stealthily in all Mohammedan countries---India, Egypt, Morocco, Syria, and many others; and it was significantly printed in Arabic, the language of the Koran. It was a lengthy document---the English translation contains 10,000 words---full of quotations from the Koran, and its style was frenzied in its appeal to racial and religious hatred. It described a detailed plan of operations for the assassination and extermination of all Christians---except those of German nationality. A few extracts will fairly portray its spirit: "O people of the faith and O beloved Moslems, consider, even though but for a brief moment, the present condition of the Islamic world. For if you consider this but for a little you will weep long. You will behold a bewildering state of affairs which will cause the tear to fall and the fire of grief to blaze. You see the great country of India, which contains hundreds of millions of Moslems, fallen, because of religious divisions and weaknesses, into the grasp of the enemies of God, the infidel English. You see forty, millions of

Moslems in Java shackled by the chains of captivity and of affliction under the rule of the Dutch, although these infidels are much fewer in number than the faithful and do not enjoy a much higher civilization. You see Egypt, Morocco, Tunis, Algeria, and the Sudan suffering the extremes of pain and groaning in the grasp of the enemies of God and his apostle. You see the vast country of Siberia and Turkestan and Khiva and Bokhara and the Caucasus and the Crimea and Kazan and Ezferhan and Kosahastan, whose Moslem peoples believe in the unity of God, ground under the feet of their oppressors, who are the enemies already of our religion. You behold Persia being prepared for partition and you see the city of the Caliphate, which for ages has unceasingly fought breast to breast with the enemies of our religion, now become the target for oppression and violence. Thus wherever you look you see that the enemies of the true religion, particularly the English, the Russian, and the French, have oppressed Islam and invaded its rights in every possible way. We cannot enumerate the insults we have received at the hands of these nations who desire totally to destroy Islam and drive all Mohammedans off the face of the earth. This tyranny has passed all endurable limits; the cup of our oppression is full to overflowing. . . . In brief, the Moslems work and the infidels eat; the Moslems are hungry and suffer and the infidels gorge themselves and live in luxury. The world of Islam sinks down and goes backward, and the Christian world goes forward and is more and more exalted. The Moslems are enslaved and the infidels are the great rulers. This is all because the Moslems have abandoned the plan set forth in the Koran and ignored the Holy War which it commands. . . . But the time has now come for the Holy War, and by this the land of Islam shall be forever freed from the power of the infidels who oppress it. This holy war has now become a sacred duty. Know ye that the blood of infidels in the Islamic lands may be shed with impunity---except those to whom the Moslem power has promised security and who are allied with it. [Herein we find that Germans and Austrians are excepted from massacre.] The killing of -infidels who rule over Islam has become a sacred duty, whether you do it secretly or openly, as the Koran has decreed: 'Take them and kill them whenever you find them. Behold we have delivered them unto your hands and given you supreme power over them.' He who kills even one unbeliever of those who rule over us, whether he does it secretly or openly, shall be rewarded by God. And let every Moslem, in whatever part of the world he may be, swear a solemn oath to kill at least three or four of the infidels who rule over him, for they are the enemies of God and of the faith. Let every Moslem know that his reward for doing so shall be doubled by the God who created heaven and earth. A Moslem who does this shall be saved from the terrors of the day of Judgment, of the resurrection of the dead. Who is the man who can refuse such a recompense for such a small deed? . . . Yet the time has come that we should rise up as the rising of one man, in one hand a sword, in the other a gun, in his pocket balls of fire and death-dealing missiles, and in his heart the light of the faith, and that we should lift up our voices, saying India for the Indian Moslems, Java for the Javanese Moslems, Algeria for the Algerian Moslems, Morocco for the Moroccan Moslems, Tunis for the Tunisan Moslems, Egypt for the Egyptian Moslems, Iran for the Iranian Moslems, Turan for the Turanian Moslems, Bokhara for the Bokharan Moslems, Caucasus for the Caucasian Moslems, and the Ottoman Empire for the Ottoman Turks and Arabs."

Specific instructions for carrying out this holy purpose follow. There shall be a "heart war "---every follower of the Prophet, that is, shall constantly nourish in his spirit a hatred of the infidel; a "speech war" with tongue and pen every Moslem shall spread this same hatred wherever Mohammedans live; and a war of deed-fighting and killing the infidel wherever he shows his head. This latter conflict, says the pamphlet, is the "true war." There is to be a "little holy war" and a "great holy war"; the first describes the battle which every Mohammedan is to wage in his community against his Christian neighbours, and the second is the great world struggle which united Islam, in India, Arabia, Turkey, Africa, and other countries is to wage against the infidel oppressors. "The Holy War," says the pamphlet, " will be of three forms. First, the individual war, which consists of the individual personal deed. This may be carried on with cutting, killing instruments, like the holy war which one of the faithful made against Peter Galy, the infidel English governor, like the slaying of the English chief of police in India, and like the killing of one of the officials arriving in Mecca by Abi Busir (may God be pleased with him)." The document gives several other instances of assassination which the faithful are enjoined to imitate. Second, the believers are told to organize "bands," and to go forth and slay Christians. The most useful are those organized and operating in secret. "It is hoped that the Islamic world of to-day will profit very greatly from such secret bands." The third method is by "organized campaigns," that is, by trained armies.

In all parts of this incentive to murder and assassination there are indications that a German hand has exercised an editorial supervision. Only those infidels are to be slain, "who rule over us "---that is, those who have Mohammedan subjects. As Germany has no such subjects, this saving clause was expected to protect Germans from assault. The Germans, with their usual interest in their own well-being and their usual disregard of their ally, evidently overlooked the fact that Austria had many Mohammedan subjects in Bosnia and Herzegovina. Moslems are instructed that they should form armies, " even though it may be necessary to introduce some foreign elements "---that is, bring in German instructors and German officers. "You must remember "---this is evidently intended as a blanket protection to Germans everywhere—"that it is absolutely unlawful to oppose any of the peoples of other religions between whom and the Moslems there is a covenant or of those who have not manifested hostility to the seat of the Caliphate or those who have entered under the protection of the Moslems."

Even though I had not had Wangenheim's personal statement that the Germans intended to arouse the Mohammedans everywhere against England, France, and Russia, these interpolations would clearly enough have indicated the real inspiration of this amazing document. At the time Wangenheim discussed the matter with me, his chief idea seemed to be that a "holy war" of this sort would be the quickest means of forcing England to make peace. According to this point of view, it was really a great peace offensive. At that time Wangenheim reflected the conviction, which was prevalent in all official circles, that Germany had made a mistake in bringing England into the conflict, and it was evidently his idea now that if back fires could be started against England in India, Egypt, the Sudan, and other places, the British Empire would withdraw. Even if British Mohammedans refused to rise, Wangenheim believed that the mere threat of such an uprising would induce England to abandon Belgium and France to their fate. The danger of spreading such incendiary literature among a wildly fanatical people is apparent. I was not the only neutral diplomat who feared the most serious consequences. M. Tocheff, the Bulgarian Minister, one of the ablest members of the diplomatic corps, was much disturbed. At that time Bulgaria was neutral, and M. Tocheff used to tell me that his country hoped to maintain this neutrality. Each side, he said, expected that Bulgaria would become its ally, and it was Bulgaria's policy to keep each side in this expectant frame of mind. Should Germany succeed in starting a "Holy War " and should massacres result, Bulgaria, added M. Tocheff, would certainly join forces with the Entente.

We arranged that he should call upon Wangenheim and repeat this statement, and that I should bring similar pressure to bear upon Enver. From the first, however, the Holy War proved a failure. The Mohammedans of such countries as India, Egypt, Algiers, and Morocco knew that they were getting far better treatment than they could obtain under any other conceivable conditions. Moreover, the simple-minded Mohammedans could not understand why they should prosecute a holy war against Christians and at the same time have Christian nations, such as Germany and Austria, as their partners. This association made the whole proposition ridiculous. The Koran, it is true, commands the slaughter of Christians, but that sacred volume makes no exception in favour of the Germans and, in the mind of the fanatical Mohammedan, a German rayah is as much Christian dirt as an Englishman or a Frenchman, and his massacre is just as meritorious an act. The fine distinctions necessitated by European diplomacy he understands about as completely as he understands the law of gravitation or the nebular hypothesis. The German failure to take this into account is only another evidence of the fundamental German clumsiness and real ignorance of racial psychology. The only tangible fact that stands out clearly is the Kaiser's desire to let loose 300,000,000 Mohammedans in a gigantic St. Bartholomew massacre of Christians.

Was there then no "holy war" at all? Did Wangenheim's "Big Thing" really fail? Whenever I think of this burlesque Jihad a particular scene in the American Embassy comes to my mind. On one side of the table sits Enver, most peacefully sipping tea and eating cakes, and on the other side is myself, engaged in the same unwarlike occupation. It is November 14th, the day after the Sultan has declared his holy war; there have been meetings at the mosques and other places, at which the declaration has been read and fiery speeches made. Enver now assures me that absolutely no harm will come to Americans; in fact, that there will be no massacres anyway. While he is talking, one of my secretaries comes in and tells me that a little mob is making demonstrations against certain foreign establishments. It has assailed an Austrian shop which has unwisely kept up its sign saying that it has "English clothes" for sale. I ask Enver what this means; he answers that it is all a mistake; there is no intention of attacking anybody. A little while after he leaves I am informed that the mob has attacked the Bon March?, a French dry-goods store, and is heading directly for the British Embassy. I at once call Enver on the telephone; it is all right, he says, nothing will happen to the embassy. A minute or two after, the mob immediately wheels about and starts for Tokatlian's, the most important restaurant in Constantinople.

The fact that this is conducted by an Armenian makes it fair game. Six men who have poles, with hooks at the end, break all the mirrors and windows, others take the marble tops of the tables and smash them to bits. In a few minutes the place has been completely gutted.

This demonstration comprised the "Holy War," so far as Constantinople understood it. Such was the inglorious end of Germany's attempt to arouse 300,000,000 Mohammedans against the Christian world! Only one definite result did the Kaiser accomplish by spreading this inciting literature. It aroused in the Mohammedan soul all that intense animosity toward the Christian which is the fundamental fact in his strange emotional nature, and thus started passions aflame that afterward spent themselves in the massacres of the Armenians and other subject peoples.

Chapter XV - Djemal, a Troublesome Mark Antony

In early November, 1914, the railroad station at Haidar Pasha was the scene of a great demonstration. Djemal, the Minister of Marine, one of the three men who were then most powerful in the Turkish Empire, was leaving to take command of the Fourth Turkish Army, which had its headquarters in Syria. All the members of the Cabinet and other influential people in Constantinople assembled to give this departing satrap an enthusiastic farewell. They hailed him as the "Saviour of Egypt," and Djemal himself, just before his train started, made this public declaration:

"I shall not return to Constantinople until I have conquered Egypt!"

The whole performance seemed to me to be somewhat bombastic. Inevitably it called to mind the third member of another bloody triumvirate who, nearly two thousand years before, had left his native land to become the supreme dictator of the East. And Djemal had many characteristics in common with Mark Antony. Like his Roman predecessor, his private life was profligate; like Antony, he was an insatiate gambler, spending much of his leisure over the card table at the Cercle d'Orient. Another trait which he had in common with the great Roman orator was his enormous vanity. The Turkish world seemed to be disintegrating in Djemal's time, just as the Roman Republic was dissolving in the days of Antony; Djemal believed that he might himself become the heir of one or more of its provinces and possibly establish a dynasty. He expected that the military expedition on which he was now starting would make him not only the conqueror of Turkey's fairest province, but also one of the powerful figures of the world. Afterward, in Syria, he ruled as independently as a medieval robber baron---whom in other details he resembled; he became a kind of sub-sultan, holding his own court, having his own selamlik, issuing his own orders, dispensing freely his own kind of justice, and often disregarding the authorities at Constantinople.

The applause with which Djemal's associates were speeding his departure was not entirely disinterested. The fact was that most of them were exceedingly glad to see him go. He had been a thorn in the side of Talaat and Enver for some time, and they were perfectly content that he should exercise his imperious and stubborn nature against the Syrians, Armenians, and other non-Moslem elements in the Mediterranean provinces. Djemal was not a popular man in Constantinople. The other members of the triumvirate, in addition to their less desirable qualities, had certain attractive traits---Talaat, his rough virility and spontaneous good nature, Enver, his courage and personal graciousness---but there was little about Djemal that was pleasing. An American physician who had specialized in the study of physiognomy had found

Djemal a fascinating subject. He told me that he had never seen a face that so combined ferocity with great power and penetration. Enver, as his history showed, could be cruel and bloodthirsty, but he hid his more insidious qualities under a face that was bland, unruffled, and even agreeable. Djemal, however, did not disguise his tendencies, for his face clearly pictured the inner soul. His eyes were black and piercing; their sharpness, the rapidity and keenness with which they darted from one object to another, taking in apparently everything with a few lightning-like glances, signalized cunning, remorselessness, and selfishness to an extreme degree. Even his laugh, which disclosed all his white teeth, was unpleasant and animal-like. His black hair and black beard, contrasting with his pale face, only heightened this impression. At first Djemal's figure seemed somewhat insignificant---he was undersized, almost stumpy, and somewhat stoop-shouldered; as soon as he began to move, however, it was evident that his body was full of energy. Whenever he shook your hand, gripping you with a vise-like grasp and looking at you with those roving, penetrating eyes, the man's personal force became impressive.

Yet, after a momentary meeting, I was not surprised to hear that Djemal was a man with whom assassination and judicial murder were all part of the day's work. Like all the Young Turks his origin had been extremely humble. He had joined the Committee of Union and Progress in the early days, and his personal power, as well as his relentlessness, had rapidly made him one of the leaders. After the murder of Nazim, Djemal had become Military Governor of Constantinople, his chief duty in this post being to remove from the scene the opponents of the ruling powers. This congenial task he performed with great skill, and the reign of terror that resulted was largely Djemal's handiwork. Subsequently Djemal became a member of the Cabinet, but he could not work harmoniously with his associates; he was always a troublesome partner. In the days preceding the break with the Entente he was popularly regarded as a Francophile. Whatever feeling Djemal may have entertained toward the Entente, he made little attempt to conceal his detestation. of the Germans. It is said that he would swear at them in their presence---in Turkish, of course; and he was one of the few important Turkish officials who never came under their influence. The fact was that Djemal represented that tendency which was rapidly gaining the ascendancy in Turkish policy---Pan-Turkism. He despised the subject peoples of the Ottoman country--- Arabs, Greeks, Armenians, Circassians, Jews; it was his determination to Turkify the whole empire. His personal ambition brought him into frequent conflict with Enver and Talaat, who told me many times that they could not control him. It was for this reason that, as I have said, they were glad to see him go---not that they really expected him to capture the Suez Canal and drive the English out of Egypt. Incidentally, this appointment fairly indicated the incongruous organization that then existed in Turkey. As Minister of Marine, Djemal's real place was at the Navy Department; instead of working in his official field the head of the navy was sent to lead an army over the burning sands of Syria and Sinai.

Yet Djemal's expedition represented Turkey's most spectacular attempt to assert its military power against the Allies. As Djemal moved out of the station, the whole Turkish populace felt that an historic moment had arrived Turkey in less than a century had lost the greater part of her dominions, and nothing had more pained the national pride than the English occupation of Egypt. All during this occupation, Turkish suzerainty had been recognized; as soon as Turkey declared war on Great Britain, however, the British had ended this fiction and had formally taken over this great province. Djemal's expedition was Turkey's reply to this act of England. The real purpose of the war, the Turkish people had been told, was to restore the vanishing empire of the Osmans, and to this great undertaking the recovery of Egypt was merely the first step. The Turks also knew that, under English administration, Egypt had become a prosperous country and that it would, therefore, yield great treasure to the conqueror. It is no wonder that the huzzahs of the Turkish people followed the departing Djemal.

About the same time Enver left to take command of Turkey's other great military enterprise---the attack on Russia through the Caucasus. Here also were Turkish provinces to be "redeemed." After the war of 1878, Turkey had been compelled to cede to Russia certain rich territories between the Caspian and the Black seas, inhabited chiefly by Armenians, and it was this country which Enver now proposed to reconquer. But Enver had no ovation on his leaving. He went away quietly and unobserved. With the departure of these two men the war was now fairly on.

Despite these martial enterprises, other than warlike preparations were now under way in Constantinople. At that time---in the latter part of 1914---its external characteristics suggested nothing but war, yet now it suddenly became the great headquarters of peace. The English fleet was constantly threatening the Dardanelles and every day Turkish troops were passing through the streets. Yet these activities did not chiefly engage the attention of the German Embassy. Wangenheim was thinking of one thing and of one thing only; this fire-eating German had suddenly become a man of peace. For he now learned that the greatest service which a German ambassador could render his emperor would be to end the war on terms that would save Germany from exhaustion and even from ruin; to obtain a settlement that would reinstate his fatherland in the society of nations.

In November, Wangenheim began discussing this subject. It was part of Germany's system, he told me, not only to be completely prepared for war but also for peace. "A wise general, when he begins his campaign, always has at hand his plans for a retreat, in case he is defeated," said the German Ambassador. "This principle applies just the same to a nation beginning war. There is only one certainty about war---and that is that it must end some time. So, when we plan war, we must consider also a campaign for peace."

But Wangenheim was interested then in something more tangible than this philosophic principle. Germany had immediate reasons for desiring the end of hostilities, and Wangenheim discussed them frankly and cynically. He said that Germany had prepared for only a short war, because she had expected to crush France and Russia in two brief campaigns, lasting not longer than six months. Clearly this plan had failed and there was little likelihood that Germany would win the war; Wangenheim told me this in so many words. Germany, he added, would make a great mistake if she 'persisted in fighting to the point of exhaustion, for such a fight would mean the permanent loss of her colonies, her mercantile marine, and her whole-economic and commercial status. "If we don't get Paris in thirty days, we are beaten," Wangenheim had told me in August, and though his attitude changed somewhat after the battle of the Marne, he made no attempt to conceal the fact that the great rush campaign had collapsed, that all the Germans could now look forward to was a tedious, exhausting war, and that all they could obtain from the existing situation would be a drawn battle. "We have made a mistake this time," Wangenheim. said, "in not laying in supplies for a protracted struggle; it was an error, however, that we shall not repeat; next time we shall store up enough copper and cotton to last for five years."

Wangenheim had another reason for wishing an immediate peace, and it was a reason which shed much light upon the shamelessness of German diplomacy. The preparation which Turkey was making for the conquest of Egypt caused this German ambassador much annoyance and anxiety. The interest and energy which the Turks had manifested in this enterprise were particularly giving him concern. Naturally I thought at first that Wangenheim was worried that Turkey would lose; yet he confided to me that his real fear was that his ally might succeed. A victorious Turkish campaign in Egypt, Wangenheim explained, might seriously interfere with Germany's plans. Should Turkey conquer Egypt, naturally Turkey would insist at the peace table on retaining this great province and would expect Germany to support her in this claim. But Germany had no intention then of promoting the reestablishment of the Turkish Empire. At that time she hoped to reach an understanding with England, the basis of which was to be something in the nature of a division of interests in the East. Germany desired above all to obtain Mesopotamia as an indispensable part of her Hamburg-Bagdad scheme. In return for this, she was prepared to give her endorsement to England's annexation of Egypt. Thus it was Germany's plan at that time that she and England should divide Turkey's two fairest dominions. This was one of the proposals which Germany intended to bring forth in the peace conference which Wangenheim was now scheming for, and clearly Turkey's conquest of Egypt would have presented complications in the way of carrying out this plan. On the morality of Germany's attitude to her ally, Turkey, it is hardly necessary to comment. The whole thing was all of a piece with Germany's policy of "realism" in foreign relations.

Nearly all German classes, in the latter part of 1914 and the early part of 1915, were anxiously looking for peace and they turned to Constantinople as the most promising spot where peace negotiations might most favourably be started, The Germans took it for granted that President Wilson would be the peacemaker; indeed, they never for a moment thought of any one else in this capacity. The only point that remained for consideration was the best way to approach the President. Such negotiations would most likely be conducted through one of the American ambassadors in Europe. Obviously, Germany had no means of access to the American ambassadors in the great enemy capitals, and other circumstances induced the German statesmen to turn to the American Ambassador in Turkey.

At this time a German diplomat appeared in Constantinople who has figured much in recent history---Dr. Richard von K?hlmann, afterward Minister for Foreign Affairs. In the last five years Dr. Von K?hlmann has seemed to appear in that particular part of the world where important confidential diplomatic negotiations are being conducted by the German Empire. Prince Lichnowsky has described his activities in London in 1913 and 1914, and he figured even more conspicuously in the infamous peace treaty of Brest-Litovsk. Soon after the war started Dr. Von K?hlmann came to Constantinople as Conseiller of the German Embassy, succeeding Von Mutius, who had been called to the colours. For one reason his appointment was appropriate, for K?hlmann had been born in Constantinople, and had spent his early life there, his father having been president of the Anatolian railway. He therefore understood the Turks as only one can who has lived with them for many years. Personally, he proved to be an interesting addition to the diplomatic colony. He impressed me as not a particularly aggressive, but a very entertaining, man; he apparently wished to become friendly with the American Embassy and he possessed a certain attraction for us all as he had just come from the trenches and gave us many vivid pictures of life at the front. At that time we were all keenly interested in modern warfare, and K?hlmann's details of trench fighting held us spellbound many an afternoon and evening. His other favourite topic of conversation was Welt-Politik, and on all foreign matters he struck me as remarkably well informed. At that time we did not regard Von K?hlmann as an important man, yet the industry with which he attended to his business attracted everyone's attention even then. Soon, however, I began to have a feeling that he was exerting a powerful influence in a quiet, velvety kind of way. He said little, but I realized that he was listening to everything and storing all kinds of information away in his mind; he was apparently Wangenheim's closest confidant, and the man upon whom the Ambassador was depending for his contact with the German Foreign Office. About the middle of December, Von K?hlmann left for Berlin, where he stayed about two weeks. On his return, in the early part of January, 1915, there was a noticeable change in the atmosphere of the German Embassy. Up to that time Wangenheim had discussed peace negotiations more or less informally, but now he took up the matter specifically. I gathered that K?hlmann had been called to Berlin to receive all the latest details on this subject, and that he had come back with the definite instructions that Wangenheim should move at once. In all my talks with the German Ambassador on peace, K?hlmann. was always hovering in the background; at one most important conference he was present, though he participated hardly at all in the conversation, but his r?le, as usual, was that of a subordinate and quietly eager listener.

Wangenheim. now informed me that January, 1915, would be an excellent time to end the war. Italy had not yet entered, though there was every reason to believe that she would do so by spring. Bulgaria and Rumania were still holding aloof, though no one expected that their waiting attitude would last forever. France and England were preparing for the first of the 6 " spring offensives, " and the Germans had no assurance that it would not succeed; indeed, they much feared that the German armies would meet disaster. The British and French warships were gathering at the Dardanelles; and the German General Staff and practically all military and naval experts in Constantinople believed that the Allied fleets could force their way through and capture the city. Most Turks by this time were sick of the war, and Germany always had in mind that Turkey might make a separate peace. Afterward I discovered that whenever the military situation looked ominous to Germany, she was always thinking about peace, but that if the situation improved she would immediately become warlike again; it was a case of sick-devil, well-devil. Yet, badly as Wangenheim wanted peace in January, 1915, it was quite apparent that he was not thinking of a permanent peace. The greatest obstacle to peace at that time was the fact that Germany showed no signs that she regretted her crimes, and there was not the slightest evidence of the sackcloth in Wangenheim's attitude now. Germany had made a bad guess, that was all; what Wangenheim and the other Germans saw in the situation was that their stock of wheat, cotton, and copper was inadequate for a protracted struggle. In my notes of my conversations with Wangenheim I find him frequently using such phrases as the "next war," "next time," and, in confidently looking forward to another greater world cataclysm than the present, he merely reflected the attitude of the dominant junker-military class. The Germans apparently wanted a reconciliation---a kind of an armistice---that would give their generals and industrial leaders time to prepare for the next conflict. At that time, nearly four years ago, Germany was moving for practically the same kind of peace negotiations which she has suggested many times since and is suggesting now, Wangenheim's plan was that representatives of the warring powers should gather around a table and settle things on the principle of "give and take." He said that there was no sense in demanding that each side state its terms in advance. "For both sides to state their terms in advance would ruin the whole thing," he said. "What would we do? Germany, of course, would make claims which the other side would regard as ridiculously extravagant. The Entente would state terms which would put all Germany in a rage. As a result, both sides would get so angry that there would be no conference. No---if we really want to end this war we must have an armistice. Once we stop fighting, we shall not go at it again. History presents no instance in a great war where an armistice has not resulted in peace. It will be so in this case."

Yet, from Wangenheim's conversation I did obtain a slight inkling of Germany's terms. The matter of Egypt and Mesopotamia, set forth above, was one of them. Wangenheim. was quite insistent that Germany must have permanent naval bases in Belgium, with which her navy could at all times threaten England with blockade and so make sure "the freedom of the seas." Germany wanted coaling rights everywhere; this demand looks absurd because Germany has always possessed such rights in peace times. She might give France a piece of Lorraine and a part of Belgium---perhaps Brussels---in return for the payment of an indemnity.

Wangenheim requested that, I should place Germany's case before the American Government. My letter to Washington is dated January 11, 1915. It went fully into the internal situation which then prevailed and gave the reasons why Germany and Turkey desired peace.

A particularly interesting part of this incident was that Germany was apparently ignoring Austria. Pallavicini, the Austrian Ambassador, knew nothing of the pending negotiations until I myself informed him of them. In thus ignoring his ally, the German Ambassador meant no personal disrespect; he was merely treating him precisely as his Foreign Office was treating Vienna---not as an equal, but practically as a retainer. The world is familiar enough with Germany's military and diplomatic absorption of Austria-Hungary, but that Wangenheim should have made so important a move as to attempt peace negotiations and have left it to Pallavicini to learn about it through a third party shows that, as far back as January, 1915, the Austro-Hungarian Empire had ceased to be an independent nation.

Nothing came of this proposal, of course. Our Government declined to take action, evidently not regarding the time as opportune. Both Germany and Turkey, as I shall tell, recurred to this subject afterward. This particular negotiation ended in the latter part of March, when K?hlmann left Constantinople to become Minister at The Hague. He came and paid his farewell call at the American Embassy, as charming, as entertaining, and as debonair as ever. His last words, as he shook my hand and left the building, were---subsequent events have naturally caused me to remember them:

"We shall have peace within three months, Excellency!"

This little scene took place, and this happy forecast was made, in March, 1915!

Chapter XVI - The Turks Prepare to Flee From Constantinople and Establish a New Capital in Asia Minor

Probably one thing that stimulated this German desire for peace was the situation at the Dardanelles. In early January, when Wangenheim persuaded me to write my letter to Washington, Constantinople was in a state of the utmost excitement. It was reported that the Allies had assembled a fleet of forty warships at the mouth of the Dardanelles and that they intended to attempt the forcing of the straits. What made the situation particularly tense was the belief, which then generally prevailed in Constantinople, that such an attempt would succeed. Wangenheim. shared this belief, and so in a modified form, did Von der Goltz, who probably knew as much about the Dardanelles defenses as any other man, as he had for years been Turkey's military instructor. I find in my diary Von der Goltz's precise opinion on this point, as reported to me by Wangenheim, and I quote it exactly as written at that time: "Although he thought it was almost impossible to force the Dardanelles, still, if England thought it an important move of the general war, they could, by sacrificing ten ships, force the entrance, and do it very fast, and be up in the Marmora within ten hours from the time they forced it."

The very day that Wangenheim gave me this expert opinion of Von der Goltz, he asked me to store several cases of his valuables in the American Embassy. Evidently he was making preparations for his own departure.

Reading the Cromer report on the Dardanelles bombardment, I find that Admiral Sir John Fisher, then First Sea Lord, placed the price of success at twelve ships. Evidently Von der Goltz and Fisher did not differ materially in their estimates.

The situation of Turkey, when these first rumours of an allied bombardment reached us, was fairly desperate. On all sides there were. evidences of the fear and panic that had stricken not only the populace, but the official classes. Calamities from all sides were apparently closing in on the country. Up to January 1, 1915, Turkey had done nothing to justify her participation in the war; on the contrary, she had met defeat practically everywhere. Djemal, as already recorded, had left Constantinople as the prospective "Conqueror of Egypt," but his expedition had proved to be a bloody and humiliating failure. Enver's attempt to redeem the Caucasus from Russian rule had resulted in an even more frightful military disaster. He had ignored the advice of the Germans, which was to let the Russians advance to Sivas and make his stand there, and, instead, he had boldly attempted to gain Russian territory in the Caucasus. This army had been defeated at every point, but the military reverses did not end its sufferings. The Turks had a most inadequate medical and sanitary service; typhus and dysentery broke out in all-the camps, the deaths from these diseases reaching 100,000 men. Dreadful stories were constantly coming in, telling of the sufferings of these soldiers. That England was preparing for an invasion of Mesopotamia was well known, and no one at that time had any reason to believe that it would not succeed. Every day the Turks expected the news that the Bulgarians had declared war and were marching on Constantinople, and they knew that such an attack would necessarily bring in Rumania and Greece. It was no diplomatic secret that Italy was waiting only for the arrival of warm weather to join the Allies. At this moment the Russian fleet was bombarding Trebizond, on the Black Sea, and was daily expected at the entrance to the Bosphorus. Meanwhile, the domestic situation was deplorable: all over Turkey thousands of the populace were daily dying of starvation; practically all able-bodied men had been taken into the army, so that only a few were left to till the fields; the criminal requisitions had almost destroyed all business; the treasury was in a more exhausted state than normally, for the closing of the Dardanelles and the blockading of the Mediterranean ports had stopped all imports and customs dues; and the increasing wrath of the people seemed likely any day to break out against Taalat and his associates. And now, surrounded by increasing troubles on every hand, the Turks learned that this mighty armada of England and her allies was approaching, determined to destroy the defenses and capture the city. At that time there was no force which the Turks feared so greatly as they feared the British fleet. Its tradition of several centuries of uninterrupted victories had completely seized their imagination. It seemed to them superhuman---the one overwhelming power which it was hopeless to contest.

Wangenheim. and also nearly all of the German military and naval forces not only regarded the forcing of the Dardanelles as possible, but they believed it to be inevitable. The possibility of British success was one of the most familiar topics of discussion, and the weight of opinion, both lay and professional, inclined in favour of the Allied fleets. Talaat told me that an attempt to force the straits would succeed---it only depended on England's willingness to sacrifice a few ships. The real reason why Turkey had sent a force against Egypt, Talaat added, was to divert England from making an attack on the Gallipoli peninsula. The state of mind that existed is shown by the fact that, on January 1st, the Turkish Government had made preparations for two trains, one of which was to take the Sultan and his suite to Asia Minor, while the other was intended for Wangenheim, Pallavicini, and the rest of the diplomatic corps. On January 2d, I had an illuminating talk with Pallavicini. He showed me a certificate given him by Bedri, the Prefect of Police, passing him and his secretaries and servants on one of these emergency trains. He also had seat tickets for himself and all of his suite. He said that each train would have only three cars, so that it could make great speed; he had been told to have everything ready to start at an hour's notice. Wangenheim, made little attempt to conceal his apprehensions. He told me that he had made all preparations to send his wife to Berlin, and he invited Mrs. Morgenthau to accompany her, so that she, too, could be removed from the danger zone, Wangenheim showed the fear, which was then the prevailing one, that a successful bombardment would lead to fires and massacres in Constantinople as well as in the rest of Turkey. In anticipation of such disturbances he made a characteristic suggestion. Should the fleet pass the Dardanelles, he said, the life of no Englishman in Turkey would be safe---they would all be massacred. As it was so difficult to tell an Englishman from an American, he proposed that I should give the Americans a distinctive button to wear, which would protect them from Turkish violence. As I was convinced that Wangenheim's real purpose was to arrange some sure means of identifying the English and of so subjecting them to Turkish ill-treatment, I refused to act on this amiable suggestion.

Another incident illustrates the nervous tension which prevailed in those January days. I noticed that some shutters at the British Embassy were open, so Mrs. Morgenthau and I went up to investigate. In the early days we had sealed this building, which had been left in my charge, and this was the first time we had broken the seals to enter. About two hours after we returned from this tour of inspection, Wangenheim came into my office in one of his now familiar agitated moods. It had been reported, he said, that Mrs. Morgenthau and I had been up to the Embassy getting it ready for the British Admiral, who expected soon to take possession!

All this seems a little absurd now, for, in fact, the Allied fleets made no attack at that time. At the very moment when the whole of Constantinople was feverishly awaiting the British dreadnaughts, the British Cabinet in London was merely considering the advisability of such an enterprise. The record shows that Petrograd, on January 2d, telegraphed the British Government, asking that some kind of a demonstration be made against the Turks, who were pressing the Russians in the Caucasus. Though an encouraging reply was immediately sent to this request, it was not until January 28th that the British Cabinet definitely issued orders for an attack on the Dardanelles. It is no longer a secret that there was no unanimous confidence in the success of such an undertaking. Admiral Carden recorded his belief that the strait "could not be rushed, but that extended operations with a large number of ships might succeed." The penalty of failure, he added, would be the great loss that England would suffer, in prestige and influence in the East; how true this prophecy proved I shall have occasion to show. Up to this time one of the fundamental and generally accepted axioms of naval operations had been that warships should not attempt to attack fixed land fortifications. But the Germans had demonstrated the power of mobile guns against fortresses in their destruction of the emplacements at Li?ge and Namur, and there was a belief in some quarters of England that these events had modified this naval principle. Mr. Churchill, at that time the head of the Admiralty, placed great confidence in the destructive power of a new superdreadnaught which had just been finished---the Queen Elizabeth---and which was then on its way to join the Mediterranean fleet.

We in Constantinople knew nothing about these deliberations then, but the result became apparent in the latter part of February. On the afternoon of the nineteenth, Pallavicini, the Austrian Ambassador, came to me with important news. The Marquis was a man of great personal dignity, yet it was apparent that he was this day exceedingly nervous, and, indeed, he made no attempt to conceal his apprehension. The Allied fleets, he said, had reopened their attack on the Dardanelles, and this time their bombardment had been extremely ferocious. At that hour things were going badly for the Austrians; the Russian armies were advancing victoriously; Serbia had hurled the Austrians over the frontier, and the European press was filled with prognostications of the break up of the Austrian Empire, Pallavicini's attitude this afternoon was a perfect reflection of the dangers that were then encompassing his country. He was a sensitive and proud man; proud of his emperor and proud of what he regarded as the great Austro-Hungarian Empire; and he now appeared to be overburdened by the fear that this extensive Hapsburg fabric, which had withstood the assaults of so many centuries, was rapidly being overwhelmed with ruin. Like most human beings, Pallavicini yearned for sympathy; he could obtain none from Wangenheim, who seldom took him into his confidence and consistently treated him as the representative of a nation that was compelled to submit to the overlordship of Germany. Perhaps that was the reason why the Austrian Ambassador used to pour out his heart to me. And now this Allied bombardment of the Dardanelles came as the culmination of all his troubles. At this time the Central Powers believed that they had Russia bottled up; that they had sealed the Dardanelles, and that she could neither get her wheat to market nor import the munitions needed for carrying on the war. Germany and Austria thus had a stranglehold on their gigantic foe, and, if this condition could be maintained indefinitely, the collapse of Russia would be inevitable. At present, it is true, the Czar's forces wore making a victorious campaign, and this in itself was sufficiently alarming to Austria; but their present supplies of war materials would ultimately be exhausted and then their great superiority in men would help them little and they would inevitably go to pieces. But should Russia get Constantinople, with the control of the Dardanelles and the Bosphorus, she could obtain all the munitions needed for warfare on the largest scale, and the defeat of the Central Powers might immediately follow; and such a defeat, Pallavicini well understood, would be far more serious for Austria than for Germany. Wangenheim. had told me that it was Germany's plan, in case the Austro-Hungarian Empire disintegrated, to incorporate her 12,000,000 Germans in the Hohenzollern domain, and Pallavicini, of course, was familiar with this danger. The Allied attack on the Dardanelles thus meant to Pallavicini the extinction of his country, for if we are properly to understand his state of mind we must remember that he firmly believed, as did almost all the other important men in Constantinople, that such an attack would succeed.

Wangenheim's existence was made miserable by this same haunting conviction. As I have already shown, the bottling up of Russia was almost exclusively the German Ambassador's performance. He had brought the Goeben and the Breslau into Constantinople, and by this manoeuvre had precipitated Turkey into the war. The forcing of the strait would mean more than the transformation of Russia into a permanent and powerful participant in the war; it meant---and this was by no means an unimportant consideration with Wangenheim---the undoing of his great personal achievement. Yet Wangenheim, showed his apprehensions quite differently from Pallavicini. In true German fashion, he resorted to threats and bravado. He gave no external signs of depression, but his whole body tingled with rage. He was not deploring his fate; he was looking for ways of striking back. He would sit in my office, smoking with his usual energy, and tell me all the terrible things which he proposed to do to his enemy. The thing that particularly preyed upon Wangenheim's mind was the exposed position of the German Embassy. It stood on a high hill, one of the most conspicuous buildings in the town, a perfect target for an enterprising English admiral. Almost the first object the British fleet would sight, as it entered the harbour, would be this yellow monument of the Hohenzollerns, and the temptation to shell it might prove irresistible.

"Let them dare destroy my Embassy!" Wangenheim said. "I'll get even with them! If they fire a single shot at it, we'll blow up the French and the English embassies! Go tell the Admiral that, won't you? Tell him also that we have the dynamite all ready to do it!"

Wangenheim also showed great anxiety over the proposed removal of the Government to Eski-Shehr. In early January, when everyone was expecting the arrival of the Allied fleet, preparations had been made for moving the Government to Asia Minor; and now, at the first rumbling of the British and French guns, the special trains were prepared once more, Wangenheim and Pallavicini both told me of their unwillingness to accompany the Sultan and the Government to Asia Minor. Should the Allies capture Constantinople, the ambassadors of the Central Powers would find themselves cut off from their home countries and completely in the hands of the Turks. "The Turks could then hold us as hostages," said Wangenheim. They urged Talaat to establish the emergency government at Adrianople, from which town they could motor in and out of Constantinople, and then, in case the city were captured, they could make their escape home. The Turks, on the other hand, refused to adopt this suggestion because they feared an attack from Bulgaria. Wangenheim and Pallavicini now found themselves between two fires. If they stayed in Constantinople, they might become prisoners of the English and French; on the other hand, if they went to Eski-Shehr, it was not unlikely that they would become prisoners of the Turks. Many evidences of the flimsy basis on which rested the Germano-Turkish alliance had come to my attention, but this was about the most illuminating. Wangenheim knew, as did everybody else, that, in case the French and English captured Constantinople, the Turks would vent their rage not mainly against the Entente, but against the Germans who had enticed them into the war.

It all seems so strange now, this conviction that was uppermost in the minds of everybody then----that the success of the Allied fleets against the Dardanelles was inevitable and that the capture of Constantinople was a matter of only a few days. I recall an animated discussion that took place at the American Embassy on the afternoon of February 24th. The occasion was Mrs. Morgenthau's weekly reception---meetings which furnished almost the only opportunity in those days for the foregathering of the diplomats. Practically all were on hand this afternoon. The first great bombardment of the Dardanelles had taken place five days before; this had practically destroyed the fortifications at the mouth of the strait. There was naturally only one subject of discussion: Would the Allied fleets get through? What would happen if they did? Everybody expressed an opinion, Wangenheim, Pallavicini, Garroni, the Italian Ambassador; D'Anckarsvard, the Swedish Minister; Koloucheff, the Bulgarian Minister; K?hlmann; and Scharfenberg, First Secretary of the German Embassy, and it was the unanimous opinion that the Allied attack would succeed. I particularly remember K?hlmann's attitude. He discussed the capture of Constantinople almost as though it was something which had taken place already. The Persian Ambassador showed great anxiety; his embassy stood not far from the Sublime Porte; he told me that he feared that the latter building would be bombarded and that a few stray shots might easily set afire his own residence, and he asked if he might move his archives to the American Embassy. The wildest rumours were afloat; we were told that the Standard Oil agent at the Dardanelles had counted seventeen transports loaded with troops; that the warships had already fired 800 shots and had levelled all the hills at the entrance; and that Talaat's bodyguard had been shot-the implication being that the bullet had missed its intended victim. It was said that the whole Turkish populace was aflame with the fear that the English and the French, when they reached the city, would celebrate the event by a wholesale attack on Turkish women. The latter reports were, of course, absurd; they were merely characteristic rumours set afloat by the Germans and their Turkish associates. The fact is that the great mass of the people in Constantinople were probably praying that the Allied attack would succeed and so release them from the control of the political gang that then ruled the country.

And in all this excitement there was one lonely and despondent figure---this was Talaat. Whenever I saw him in those critical days, he was the picture of desolation and defeat. The Turks, like most primitive peoples, wear their emotions on the surface, and with them the transition from exultation to despair is a rapid one. The thunder of the British guns at the straits apparently spelled doom to Talaat. The letter carrier of Adrianople seemed to have reached the end of his career. He again confided to me his expectation that the English would capture the Turkish capital, and once more he said that he was sorry that Turkey had entered the war. Talaat well knew what would happen as soon as the Allied fleet entered the Sea of Marmora. According to the report of the Cromer Commission, Lord Kitchener, in giving his assent to a purely naval expedition, had relied upon a revolution in Turkey to make the enterprise successful. Lord Kitchener has been much criticized for his part in the Dardanelles attack; I owe it to his memory, however, to say that on this point he was absolutely right. Had the Allied fleets once passed the defenses at the straits, the administration of the Young Turks would have come to a bloody end. As soon as the guns began to fire, placards appeared on the hoardings, denouncing Talaat and his associates as responsible for all the woes that had come to Turkey. Bedri, the Prefect of Police, was busy collecting all the unemployed young men and sending them out of the city; his purpose was to free Constantinople of all who might start a revolution against the Young Turks. It was a common report that Bedri feared this revolution much more than he feared the British fleet. And this was the same Nemesis that was every moment now pursuing Talaat.

A single episode illustrates the nervous excitement that prevailed. Dr. Lederer, the correspondent of the Berliner Tageblatt, made a short visit to the Dardanelles, and, on his return, reported to certain ladies of the diplomatic circle that the German officers had told him that they were wearing their shrouds, as they expected any minute to be buried there. This statement went around the city like wild fire, and Dr. Lederer was threatened with arrest for making it. He appealed to me for help; I took him to Wangenheim, who refused to have anything to do with him; Lederer, he said, was an Austrian subject, although he represented a German newspaper. His anger at Lederer for this indiscretion was extreme. But I finally succeeded in getting the unpopular journalist into the Austrian Embassy, where he was harboured for the night. In a few days, Lederer had to leave town.

In the midst of all this excitement, there was one person who was apparently not at all disturbed. Though ambassadors, generals, and politicians might anticipate the worst calamities, Enver's voice was reassuring and quiet. The man's coolness and really courageous spirit never shone to better advantage. In late December and January, when the city had its first fright over the bombardment, Enver was fighting the Russians in the Caucasus. His experiences in this campaign, as already described, had been far from glorious. Enver had left Constantinople in November to join his army, an expectant conqueror; he returned, in the latter part of January, the commander of a thoroughly beaten and demoralized force. Such a disastrous experience would have utterly ruined almost any other military leader, and that Enver felt his reverses keenly was evident from the way in which he kept himself from public view. I had my first glimpse of him, after his return, at a concert, given for the benefit of the Red Crescent. At this affair Enver sat far back in a box, as though he intended to keep as much as possible out of sight; it was quite apparent that he was uncertain as to the cordiality of his reception by the public. All the important people in Constantinople, the Crown Prince, the members of the Cabinet, and the ambassadors attended this function, and, in accordance with the usual custom, the Crown Prince sent for these dignitaries, one after another, for a few words of greeting and congratulation. After that the visiting from box to box became general. The heir to the throne sent for Enver as well as the rest, and this recognition evidently gave him a new courage, for he began to mingle with the diplomats, who also treated him with the utmost cordiality and courtesy. Enver apparently regarded this favourable notice as having reestablished his standing, and now once more he assumed a leading part in the crisis. A few days afterward he discussed the situation with me. He was much astonished, he said, at the fear that so generally prevailed, and he was disgusted at the preparations that had been made to send away the Sultan and the Government and practically leave the city a prey to the English. He did not believe that the Allied fleets could force the Dardanelles; he had recently inspected all the fortifications and he had every confidence in their ability to resist successfully. Even though the ships did get through, he insisted that Constantinople should be defended to the last man.

Yet Enver's assurance did not satisfy his associates. They had made all their arrangements for the British fleet. If, in spite of the most heroic resistance the Turkish armies could make, it still seemed likely that the Allies were about to capture the city, the ruling powers had their final plans all prepared. They proposed to do to this great capital precisely what the Russians had done to Moscow, when Napoleon appeared before it.

"They will never capture an existing city," they told me, "only a heap of ashes." As a matter of fact, this was no idle threat. I was told that cans of petroleum had been already stored in all the police stations and other places, ready to fire the town at a moment's notice. As Constantinople is largely built of wood, this would have been no very difficult task. But they were determined to destroy more than these temporary structures; the plans aimed at the beautiful architectural monuments built by the Christians long before the Turkish occupation. The Turks had particularly marked for dynamiting the Mosque of Saint Sophia. This building, which had been a Christian church centuries before it became a Mohammedan mosque, is one of the most magnificent structures of the vanished Byzantine Empire. Naturally the suggestion of such an act of vandalism aroused us all, and I made a plea to Talaat that Saint Sophia should be spared. He treated the proposed destruction lightly.

"There are not six men in the Committee of Union and Progress," he told me, "who care for anything that is old. We all like new things!"

That was all the satisfaction I obtained in this matter at that time.

Enver's insistence that the Dardanelles could resist caused his associates to lose confidence in his judgment. About a year afterward, Bedri Bey, the Prefect of Police, gave me additional details. While Enver was still in the Caucasus, Bedri said, Talaat had called a conference, a kind of council of war, on the Dardanelles. This had been attended by Liman von Sanders, the German general who had reorganized the Turkish army; Usedom, the German admiral who was the inspector-general of the Ottoman coast defenses, Bronssart, the German Chief of Staff of the Turkish army, and several others. Every man present gave it as his opinion that the British and French fleets could force the straits; the only subject of dispute, said Bedri, was whether it would take the ships eight or twenty hours to reach Constantinople after they had destroyed the defenses. Enver's position was well understood, but this council decided to ignore him and to make the preparations without his knowledge---to eliminate the Minister of War, at least temporarily, from their deliberations.

In early March, Bedri and Djambolat, who was Director of Public Safety, came to see me. At that time the exodus from the capital had begun; Turkish women and children were being moved into the interior; all the banks had been compelled to send their gold into Asia Minor; the archives of the Sublime Porte had already been carried to Eski-Shehr; and practically all the ambassadors and their suites, as well as most of the government officials, had made their preparations to leave. The Director of the Museum, who was one of the six Turks to whom Talaat had referred as "liking old things" had buried many of Constantinople's finest works of art in cellars or covered them for protection. Bedri came to arrange the details of my departure. As ambassador I was personally accredited to the Sultan, and it would obviously be my duty, said Bedri, to go wherever the Sultan went. The train was all ready, he added; he wished to know how many people I intended to take, so that sufficient space could be reserved. To this proposal I entered a flat refusal. I informed Bedri that I thought that my responsibilities made it necessary for me to remain in Constantinople. Only a neutral ambassador, I said, could forestall massacres and the destruction of the city, and certainly I owed it to the civilized world to prevent, if I could, such calamities as these. If my position as ambassador made it inevitable that I should follow the Sultan, I would resign and become honorary Consul-General.

Both Bedri and Djambolat were much younger and less experienced men than I, and I therefore told them that they needed a man of maturer years to advise them in an international crisis of this kind. I was not only interested in protecting foreigners and American institutions, but I was also interested, on general humanitarian grounds, in safeguarding the Turkish population from the excesses that were generally expected. The several nationalities, many of them containing elements which were given to pillage and massacre, were causing great anxiety. I therefore proposed to Bedri and Djambolat that the three of us form a kind of a committee to take control in the approaching crisis.

They consented and the three of us sat down and decided on a course of action. We took a map of Constantinople and marked the districts which, under the existing rules of warfare, we agreed that the Allied fleet would have the right to bombard. Thus, we decided that the War Office, Marine Office, telegraph offices, railroad stations, and all public buildings could quite legitimately be made the targets for their guns. Then we marked out certain zones which we should insist on regarding as immune. The main residential section, and the part where all the embassies are located, is Pera, the district on the north shore of the Golden Horn. This we marked as not subject to attack. We also delimited certain residential areas of Stamboul and Galata, the Turkish sections. I telegraphed to Washington, asking the State Department to obtain a ratification of these plans and an agreement to respect these zones of safety from the British and French governments. I received a reply indorsing my action.

All preparations had thus been made. At the station stood the trains which were to take the Sultan and the Government and the ambassadors to Asia Minor. They had steam up, ready to move at a minute's notice. We were all awaiting the triumphant arrival of the Allied fleet.

Chapter XVII - Enver as the Man who Demonstrated "The Vulnerability of the British Fleet"

When the situation had reached this exciting stage, Enver asked me to visit the Dardanelles. He still insisted that the fortifications were impregnable and he could not understand, he said, the panic which was then raging in Constantinople. He had visited the Dardanelles himself, had inspected every gun and every emplacement, and he was entirely confident that his soldiers could hold off the Allied fleet indefinitely. He had taken Talaat down, and by doing so he had considerably eased that statesman's fears. It was Enver's conviction that, if I should visit the fortifications, I would be persuaded that the fleets could never get through, and that I would thus be able to give such assurances to the people that the prevailing excitement would subside. I disregarded certain natural doubts as to whether an ambassador should expose himself to the dangers of such a situation---the ships were bombarding nearly every day---and promptly accepted Enver's invitation.

On the morning of the 15th, we left Constantinople on the Yuruk. Enver himself accompanied us as far as Panderma, an Asiatic town on the Sea of Marmora. The party included several other notables: Ibrahim Bey, the Minister of Justice; Husni Pasha, the general who had commanded the army which had deposed Abdul Hamid in the Young Turk revolution; and Senator Cheriff Djafer Pasha, an Arab and a direct descendant of the Prophet. A particularly congenial companion was Fuad Pasha, an old field marshal, who had led an adventurous career; despite his age, he had an immense capacity for enjoyment, was a huge feeder and a capacious drinker, and had as many stories to tell of exile, battle, and hair breadth escapes as Othello. All of these men were much older than Enver, and all of them were descended from far more distinguished ancestors, yet they treated this stripling with the utmost deference.

Enver seemed particularly glad of this opportunity to discuss the situation. Immediately after breakfast, he took me aside, and together we went up to the deck.

The day was a beautiful sunny one, and the sky in the Marmora was that deep blue which we find only in this part of the world. What most impressed me was the intense quiet, the almost desolate inactivity of these silent waters. Our ship was almost the only one in sight, and this inland sea, which in ordinary times was one of the world's greatest commercial highways, was now practically a primeval waste. The whole scene was merely a reflection of the great triumph which German diplomacy had accomplished in the Near East. For nearly six months not a Russian merchant ship had passed through the straits. All the commerce of Rumania and Bulgaria, which had normally found its way to Europe across this inland sea, had long since disappeared. The ultimate significance of all this desolation was that Russia was blockaded and completely isolated from her allies. How much that one fact has meant in the history of the world for the last three years! And now England and France were seeking to overcome this disadvantage; to link up their own military resources with those of their great eastern ally, and to restore to the Dardanelles and the Marmora the thousands of ships that meant Russia's existence as a military and economic, and even, as subsequent events have shown, as a political power. We were approaching the scene of one of the great crises of the war.

Would England and her allies succeed in this enterprise? Would their ships at the Dardanelles smash the fortifications, break through, and again make Russia a permanent force in the war? That was the main subject which Enver and I discussed, as for nearly three hours we walked up and down the deck. Enver again referred to the "silly panic" that had seized nearly all classes in the capital. "Even though Bulgaria and Greece both turn against us," he said, "we shall defend Constantinople to the end. We have plenty of guns, plenty of ammunition, and we have these on terra firma, whereas the English and French batteries are floating ones. And the natural advantages of the straits are so great that the warships can make little progress against them. I do not care what other people may think. I have studied this problem more thoroughly than any of them, and I feel that I am right. As long as I am at the head of the War Department, we shall not give up. Indeed, I do not know just what these English and French battleships are driving at. Suppose that they rush the Dardanelles, get into the Marmora and reach Constantinople; what good will that do them? They can bombard and destroy the city, I admit; but they cannot capture it, as they have only a few troops to land. Unless they do bring a large army, they will really be caught in a trap. They can perhaps stay here for two or three weeks until their food and supplies are all exhausted and then they will have to go back----rush the straits again, and again run the risk of annihilation. In the meantime, we would have repaired the forts, brought in troops, and made ourselves ready for them. It seems to me to be a very foolish enterprise."

I have already told how Enver had taken Napoleon as his model, and in this Dardanelles expedition he now apparently saw a Napoleonic opportunity. As we were pacing the deck he stopped a moment, looked at me earnestly, and said:

"I shall go down in history as the man who demonstrated the vulnerability of England and her fleet. I shall show that her navy is not invincible. I was in England a few years before the war and discussed England's position with many of her leading men, such as Asquith, Churchill, Haldane. I told them that their course was wrong. Winston Churchill declared that England could defend herself with her navy alone, and that she needed no large army. I told Churchill that no great empire could last that did not have both an army and a navy. I found that Churchill's opinion was the one that prevailed everywhere in England. There was only one man I met who agreed with me, that was Lord Roberts. Well, Churchill has now sent his fleet down here---perhaps to show me that his navy can do all that he said it could do. Now we'll see."

Enver seemed to regard his naval expedition as a personal challenge from Mr. Churchill to himself---almost like a continuation of their argument in London.

"You, too, should have a large army," said Enver, referring to the United States.

"I do not believe," he went on, "that England is trying to force the Dardanelles because Russia has asked her to. When I was in England I discussed with Churchill the possibility of a general war. He asked me what Turkey would do in such a case, and said that, if we took Germany's side, the British fleet would force the Dardanelles and capture Constantinople. Churchill is not trying to help Russia---he is carrying out the threat made to me at that time."

Enver spoke with the utmost determination and conviction; he said that nearly all the damage inflicted on the outside forts had been repaired, and that the Turks had methods of defense the existence of which the enemy little suspected. He showed great bitterness against the English; he accused them of attempting to bribe Turkish officials and even said that they had instigated attempts upon his own life. On the other hand, he displayed no particular friendliness toward the Germans. Wangenheim's overbearing manners had caused him much irritation, and the Turks, he said, got on none too well with the German officers.

"The Turks and Germans," he added, "care nothing for each other. We are with them because it is our interest to be with them; they are with us because that is their interest. Germany will back Turkey just so long as that helps Germany; Turkey will back Germany just so long as that helps Turkey."

Enver seemed much impressed at the close of our interview with the intimate personal relations which we had established with each other. He apparently believed that he, the great Enver, the Napoleon of the Turkish Revolution, had unbended in discussing his nation's affairs with a mere ambassador.

"You know," he said, "that there is no one in Germany with whom the Emperor talks as intimately as I have talked with you to-day."

We reached Panderma about two o'clock. Here Enver and his auto were put ashore and our party started again, our boat arriving at Gallipoli late in the afternoon. We anchored in the harbour and spent the night on board. All the evening we could hear the guns bombarding the fortifications, but these reminders of war and death did not affect the spirits of my Turkish hosts. The occasion was for them a great lark; they had spent several months in hard, exacting work, and now they behaved like boys suddenly let out for a vacation. They cracked jokes, told stories, sang the queerest kinds of songs, and played childish pranks upon one another. The venerable Fuad, despite his nearly ninety years, developed great qualities as an entertainer, and the fact that his associates made him the butt of most of their horse-play apparently only added to his enjoyment of the occasion. The amusement reached its height when one of his friends surreptitiously poured him a glass of eau-de-cologne. The old gentleman looked at the new drink a moment and then diluted it with water. I was told that the proper way of testing raki, the popular Turkish tipple, is by mixing it with water; if it turns white under this treatment, it is the real thing and may be safely drunk. Apparently water has the same effect upon eau-de-cologne, for the contents of Fuad's glass, after this test, turned white. The old gentleman, therefore, poured the whole thing down his throat without a grimace----much to the hilarious entertainment of his tormentors.

In the morning we started again. We now had fairly arrived in the Dardanelles, and from Gallipoli we had a sail of nearly twenty-five miles to Tchanak Kale. For the most part this section of the strait is uninteresting and, from a military point of view, it is unimportant. The stream is about two miles wide, both sides are low-lying and marshy, and only a few scrambling villages show any signs of life. I was told that there were a few ancient fortifications, their rusty guns pointing toward the Marmora, the emplacements having been erected there in the early part of the nineteenth century for the purpose of preventing hostile ships entering from the north. These fortifications, however, were so inconspicuous that I could not see them; my hosts informed me that they had no fighting power, and that, indeed, there was nothing in the northern part of the straits, from Point Nagara to the Marmora, that could offer resistance to any modern fleet. The chief interest which I found in this part of the Dardanelles was purely historic and legendary. The ancient town of Lampsacus appeared in the modern Lapsaki, just across from Gallipoli, and Nagara Point is the site of the ancient Abydos, from which village Leander used to swim nightly across the Hellespont to Hero---a feat which was repeated about one hundred years ago by Lord Byron. Here also Xerxes crossed from Asia to Greece on a bridge of boats, embarking on that famous expedition which was to make him master of mankind. The spirit of Xerxes, I thought, as I passed the scene of his exploit, is still quite active in the world! The Germans and Turks had found a less romantic use for this, the narrowest part of the Dardanelles, for here they had stretched a cable and anti-submarine barrage of mines and nets---a device, which, as I shall describe, did not keep the English and French underwater boats out of the Marmora and the Bosphorus. It was not until we rounded this historic point of Nagara that the dull monotony of flat shores gave place to a more diversified landscape. On the European side the cliffs now began to descend precipitously to the water, reminding me of our own Palisades along the Hudson, and I obtained glimpses of the hills and mountain ridges that afterward proved such tragical stumbling blocks to the valiant Allied armies. The configuration of the land south of Nagara, with its many hills and ridges, made it plain why the military engineers had selected this stretch of the Dardanelles as the section best adapted to defense. Our boat was now approaching what was perhaps the most commanding point in the whole strait---the city Tchanak, or, to give it its modem European name, Dardanelles. In normal times this was a thriving port of 16,000 people, its houses built of wood, the headquarters of a considerable trade in wool and other products, and for centuries it had been an important military station. Now, excepting for the soldiers, it was deserted, the large civilian population having been moved into Anatolia. The British fleet , we were told, had bombarded this city; yet this statement seemed hardly probable, for I saw only a single house that had been hit, evidently by a stray shell which had been aimed at the near-by fortifications.

Djevad Pasha, the Turkish Commander-in-Chief at the Dardanelles, met us and escorted our party to headquarters. Djevad was a man of culture and of pleasing and cordial manners; as he spoke excellent German I had no need of an interpreter. I was much impressed by the deference with which the German officers treated him; that he was the Commander-in-Chief in this theatre of war, and that the generals of the Kaiser were his subordinates, was made plainly apparent. As we passed into his office, Djevad stopped in front of a piece of a torpedo, mounted in the middle of the hall, evidently as a souvenir.

"There is the great criminal!" he said, calling my attention to the relic.

About this time the newspapers were hailing the exploit of an English submarine, which had sailed from England to the Dardanelles, passed under the mine field, and torpedoed the Turkish warship Mesudi?.

"That's the torpedo that did it!" said Djevad. "You'll see the wreck of the ship when you go down."

The first fortification I visited was that of Anadolu Hamidi? (that is, Asiatic Hamidi?) located on the water's edge just outside of Tchanak. My first impression was that I was in Germany. The officers were practically all Germans and everywhere Germans were building buttresses with sacks of sand and in other ways strengthening the emplacements. Here German, not Turkish, was the language heard on every side. Colonel Wehrle, who conducted me over these batteries, took the greatest delight in showing them. He had the simple pride of the artist in his work, and told me of the happiness that had come into his days when Germany had at last found herself at war. All his life, he said, he had spent in military practices, and, like most Germans, he had become tired of manoeuvres, sham battles, and other forms of mimic hostilities. Yet he was approaching fifty, he had become a colonel, and he was fearful that his career would close without actual military experience---and then the splendid thing had happened and here he was, fighting a real English enemy, firing real guns and shells! There was nothing brutal about Wehrle's manners; he was a "gem?tlich" gentleman from Baden, and thoroughly likable; yet he was all aglow with the spirit of "Der Tag." His attitude was simply that of a man who had spent his lifetime learning a trade and who now rejoiced at the chance of exercising it. But he furnished an illuminating light on the German military character and the forces that had really caused the war.

Feeling myself so completely in German country, I asked Colonel Wehrle why there were so few Turks on this side of the strait. "You won't ask me that question this afternoon," he said, smiling, "when you go over to the other side."

The location of Anadolu Hamidi? seemed ideal. It stands right at the water's edge, and consists---or it did then---of ten guns, every one completely sweeping the Dardanelles. Walking upon the parapet, I had a clear view of the strait, and Kum Kale, at the entrance, about fifteen miles away, stood out conspicuously. No warship could enter these waters without immediately coming within complete sight of her gunners. Yet the fortress itself, to an unprofessional eye like my own, was not particularly impressive. The parapet and traverses were merely mounds of earth, and stand to-day practically as they were finished by their French constructors in 1837. There is a general belief that the Germans had completely modernized the Dardanelles defenses, but this was not true at that time. The guns defending Fort Anadolu Hamidi? were more than thirty years old, all being the Krupp model of 1885, and the rusted exteriors of some of them gave evidences of their age. Their extreme range was only about nine miles, while the range of the battleships opposing them was about ten miles, and that of the Queen Elizabeth was not far from eleven. The figures which I have given for Anadolu Hamidi? apply also to practically all the guns at the other effective fortifications. So far as the advantage of range was concerned, therefore., the Allied fleet had a decided superiority, the Queen Elizabeth alone having them all practically at her mercy. Nor did the fortifications contain very considerable supplies of ammunition. At that time the European and American papers were printing stories that train loads of shells and guns were coming by way of Rumania from Germany to the Dardanelles. From facts which I learned on this trip and subsequently I am convinced that these reports were pure fiction. A small number of "red heads"---that is, non-armour-piercing projectiles useful only for fighting landing parties---had been brought from Adrianople and were reposing in Hamidi? at the time of my visit, but these were small in quantity and of no value in fighting ships. I lay this stress upon Hamidi? because this was the most import ant fortification in the Dardanelles. Throughout the whole bombardment it attracted more of the Allied fire than any other position, and it inflicted at least 60 percent of all the damage that was done to the attacking ships. It was Anadolu Hamidi? which, in the great bombardment of March 18th, sank the Bouvet, the French battleship, and which in the course of the whole attack disabled several other units. All its officers were Germans and eighty-five per cent. of the men on duty came from the crews of the Goeben and the Breslau. Getting into the automobile, we sped along the military road to Dardanos, passing on the way the wreck of the Mesudi?. The Dardanos battery was as completely Turkish as the Hamidi? was German. The guns at Dardanos were somewhat more modern than those at Hamidi?---they were the Krupp model of 1905. Here also was stationed the only new battery which the Germans had established up to the time of my visit; it consisted of several guns which they had taken from the German and Turkish warships then lying in the Bosphorus. A few days before our inspection the Allied fleet had entered the Bay of Erenkeui and had submitted Dardanos to a terrific bombardment, the evidences of which I saw on every hand. The land for nearly half a mile about seemed to have been completely churned up; it looked like photographs I had seen of the battlefields in France. The strange thing was that, despite all this punishment, the batteries themselves remained intact; not a single gun, my guides told me, had been destroyed.

"After the war is over," said General Mertens, "we are going to establish a big tourist resort here, build a hotel, and sell relics to you Americans. We shall not have to do much excavating to find them---the British fleet is doing that for us now."

This sounded like a passing joke, yet the statement was literally true. Dardanos, where this emplacement is located, was one of the famous cities of the ancient world; in Homeric times it was part of the principality of Priam. Fragments of capitals and columns are still visible. And the shells from the Allied fleet were now ploughing up many relics which had been buried for thousands of years. One of my friends picked up a water jug which had perhaps been used in the days of Troy. The effectiveness of modern gunfire in excavating these evidences of a long lost civilization was striking---though unfortunately the relics did not always come to the surface intact.

The Turkish generals were extremely proud of the fight which this Dardanos battery had made against the British ships. They would lead me to the guns that had done particularly good service and pat them affectionately. For my benefit Djevad called out Lieutenant Hassan, the Turkish officer who had defended this position. He was a little fellow, with jetblack hair, black eyes, extremely modest and almost shrinking in the presence of these great generals. Djevad patted Hassan on both cheeks, while another high Turkish officer stroked his hair; one would have thought that he was a faithful dog who had just performed some meritorious service.

"It is men like you of whom great heroes are made," said General Djevad. He asked Hassan to describe the attack and the way it had been met. The embarrassed lieutenant quietly told his story, though he was moved almost to tears by the appreciation of his exalted chiefs.

"There is a great future for you in the army," said General Djevad, as we parted from this hero.

Poor Hassan's "future" came two days afterward when the Allied fleet made its greatest attack. One of the shells struck his dugout, which caved in, killing the young man. Yet his behaviour on the day I visited his battery showed that he regarded the praise of his general as sufficient compensation for all that he had suffered or all that he might suffer.

I was much puzzled by the fact that the Allied fleet, despite its large expenditures of ammunition, had not been able to hit this Dardanos emplacement. I naturally thought at first that such a failure indicated poor marksmanship, but my German guides said that this was not the case. All this misfire merely illustrated once more the familiar fact that a rapidly manoeuvring battleship is under a great disadvantage in shooting at a fixed fortification. But there was another point involved in the Dardanos battery. My hosts called my attention to its location; it was perched on the top of the hill, in full view of the ships, forming itself a part of the skyline. Dardanos was merely five steel turrets, each armed with a gun, approached by a winding trench.

That," they said, "is the most difficult thing in the world to hit. It is so distinct that it looks easy, but the whole thing is an illusion."

I do not understand completely the optics of the situation; but it seems that the skyline creates a kind of mirage, so that it is practically impossible to hit anything at that point, except by accident. The gunner might get what was apparently a perfect sight, yet his shell would go wild. The record of Dardanos had been little short of marvellous. Up to March 18th, the ships had fired at it about 4,000 shells. One turret had been hit by a splinter, which had also scratched the paint, another had been hit and slightly bent in, and another had been hit near the base and a piece about the size of a man's hand had been knocked out. But not a single gun had been even slightly damaged. Eight men had been killed, including Lieutenant Hassan, and about forty had been wounded. That was the extent of the destruction.

"It was the optical illusion that saved Dardanos," one of the Germans remarked.

Chapter XVIII - The Allied Armada Sails Away, Though on the Brink of Victory

Again getting into the automobile, we rode along the shore, my host calling my attention to the mine fields, which stretched from Tchanak southward about seven miles. In this area the Germans and Turks had scattered nearly 400 mines. They told me with a good deal of gusto that the Russians had furnished a considerable number of these destructive engines. Day after day Russian destroyers sowed mines at the Black Sea entrance to the Bosphorus, hoping that they would float down stream and fulfil their appointed task. Every morning Turkish and German mine sweepers would go up, fish out these mines, and place them in the Dardanelles.

The battery at Erenkeui had also been subjected to a heavy bombardment, but it had suffered little. Unlike Dardanos, it was situated back of a hill, completely shut out from view. In order to fortify this spot, I was told, the Turks had been compelled practically to dismantle the fortifications of the inner straits---that section of the stream which extends from Tchanak to Point Nagara. This was the reason why this latter part of the Dardanelles was now practically unfortified. The guns that had been moved for this purpose were old-style Krupp pieces of the model of 1885.

South of Erenkeui, on the hills bordering the road the Germans had introduced an innovation. They had found several Krupp howitzers left over from the Bulgarian war and had installed them on concrete foundations. Each battery had four or five of these emplacements so that, as I approached them, I found several substantial bases that apparently had no guns. I was mystified further at the sight of a herd of buffaloes---I think I Counted sixteen engaged in the operation---hauling one of these howitzers from one emplacement to another. This, it seems, was part of the plan of defense. As soon as the dropping shells indicated that the fleet had obtained the range, the howitzer would be moved, with the aid of buffalo-teams, to another concrete emplacement.

"We have even a better trick than that," remarked one of the officers. They called out a sergeant, and recounted his achievement. This soldier was the custodian of a contraption which, at a distance, looked like a real gun, but which, when I examined it near at hand, was apparently an elongated section of sewer pipe. Back of a hill, entirely hidden from the fleet, was placed the gun with which this sergeant had cooperated. The two were connected by telephone. When the command came to fire, the gunner in charge of the howitzer would discharge his shell, while the man in charge of the sewer pipe would burn several pounds of black powder and send forth a conspicuous cloud of inky smoke. Not unnaturally the Englishmen and Frenchmen on the ships would assume that the shells speeding in their direction came from the visible smoke cloud and would proceed to centre all their ,attention upon that spot. The space around this burlesque gun was pock-marked with shell holes; the sergeant in charge, I was told, had attracted more than 500 shots, while the real artillery piece still remained intact and undetected.

From Erenkeui we motored back to General Djevad's headquarters, where we had lunch. Djevad took me up to an observation post, and there before my eyes I had the beautiful blue expanse of the Aegean. I could see the entrances to the Dardanelles, Sedd-ul-Bahr and Kum Kale standing like the guardians of a gateway, with the rippling sunny waters stretching between. Far out I saw the majestic ships of England and France sailing across the entrance, and still farther away, I caught a glimpse of the island of Tenedos, behind which we knew that a still larger fleet lay concealed. Naturally this prospect brought to mind a thousand historic and legendary associations, for there is probably no single spot in the world more crowded with poetry and romance. Evidently my Turkish escort, General Djevad, felt the spell, for he took a telescope, and pointed at a bleak expanse, perhaps six miles away.

"Look at that spot," he said, handing me the glass. "Do you know what that is?"

I looked but could not identify this sandy beach.

"Those are the Plains of Troy," he said And the river that you see winding in and out," he added, "we Turks call it the Mendere, but Romer knew it as the Scamander. Back of us, only a few miles distant, is Mount Ida."

Then he turned his glass out to sea, swept the field where the British ships lay, and again asked me to look at an indicated spot. I immediately brought within view a magnificent English warship, all stripped for battle, quietly steaming along like a man walking on patrol duty.

"That," said General Djevad, "is the Agamemnon"!

"Shall I fire a shot at her?" he asked me.

"Yes, if you'll promise me not to hit her," I answered.

We lunched at headquarters, where we were joined by Admiral Usedom, General Mertens, and General Pomiankowsky, the Austrian Military Attach? at Constantinople. The chief note in the conversation was one of absolute confidence in the future. Whatever the diplomats and politicians in Constantinople may have thought, these men, Turks and Germans, had no expectation---at least their conversation betrayed none ---that the Allied fleets would pass their defenses. What they seemed to hope for above everything was that their enemies would make another attack.

"If we could only get a chance at the Queen Elizabeth! " said one eager German, referring to the greatest ship in the British navy, then lying off the entrance.

As the Rhein wine began to disappear, their eagerness for the combat increased.

"If the damn fools would only make a landing!" exclaimed one---I quote his exact words.

The Turkish and German officers, indeed, seemed to vie with each other in expressing their readiness for the fray. Probably a good deal of this was bravado, intended for my consumption---indeed, I had private information that their exact estimate of the situation was much less reassuring. Now, however, they declared that the war had presented no real opportunity for the German and English navies to measure swords, and for this reason the Germans at the Dardanelles welcomed this chance to try the issue.

Having visited all the important places on the Anatolian side, we took a launch and sailed over to the Gallipoli peninsula. We almost had a disastrous experience on this trip. As we approached the Gallipoli shore, our helmsman was asked if he knew the location of the minefield, and if he could steer through the channel. He said "yes" and then steered directly for the mines! Fortunately the other men noticed the mistake in time, and so we arrived safely at Kilid-ul-Bahr. The batteries here were of about the same character as those on the other side; they formed one of the main defenses of the straits. Here everything, so far as a layman could judge, was in excellent condition, barring the fact that the artillery pieces were of old design and the ammunition not at all plentiful.

The batteries showed signs of a heavy bombardment. None had been destroyed, but shell holes surrounded the fortifications. My Turkish and German escorts looked at these evidences of destruction rather seriously and they were outspoken in their admiration for the accuracy of the allied fire.

"How do they ever get the range?" This was the question they were asking each other. What made the shooting so remarkable was the fact that it came, not from Allied ships in the straits, but from ships stationed in the Aegean Sea, on the other side of the Gallipoli peninsula. The gunners had never seen their target, but, had had to fire at a distance of nearly ten miles, over high hills, and yet many of their shells had barely missed the batteries at Kilid-ul-Bahr.

When I was there, however, the place was quiet, for no fighting was going on that day. For my particular benefit the officers put one of their gun crews through a drill, so that I could obtain a perfect picture of the behaviour of the Turks in action. In their mind's eye these artillerists now saw the English ships advancing within range, all their guns pointed to destroy the followers of the Prophet. The bugleman blew his horn, and the whole company rushed to their appointed places. Some were bringing shells, others were opening the breeches, others were taking the ranges, others were straining at pulleys, and others were putting the charges into place. Everything was eagerness and activity; evidently the Germans had been excellent instructors, but there was more to it than German military precision, for the men's faces lighted up with all that fanaticism which supplies the morale of Turkish soldiers. These gunners momentarily imagined that they were shooting once more at the infidel English, and the exercise was a congenial one. Above the shouts of all I could hear the singsong chant of the leader, intoning the prayer with which the Moslem has rushed to battle for thirteen centuries.

"Allah is great, there is but one God, and Mohammed is his Prophet!"

When I looked upon these frenzied men, and saw so plainly written in their faces their uncontrollable hatred of the unbeliever, I called to mind what the Germans had said in the morning about the wisdom of not putting Turkish and German soldiers together. I am quite sure that, had this been done, here at least the "Holy War" would have proved a success, and that the Turks would have vented their hatred of Christians on those who happened to be nearest at hand, for the moment overlooking the fact that they were allies.

I returned to Constantinople that evening, and two days afterward, on March 18th, the Allied fleet made its greatest attack. As all the world knows, that attack proved disastrous to the Allies. The outcome was the sinking of the Bouvet, the Ocean, and the Irresistible and the serious crippling of four other vessels. Of the sixteen ships engaged in this battle of the 18th, seven were thus put temporarily or permanently out of action. Naturally the Germans and Turks rejoiced over this victory. The police went around, and ordered each householder to display a prescribed number of flags in honour of the event. The Turkish people have so little spontaneous patriotism or enthusiasm of any kind that they would never decorate their establishments without such definite orders. As a matter of fact, neither Germans nor Turks regarded this celebration too seriously, for they were not yet persuaded that they had really won a victory. Most still believed that the Allied fleets would succeed in forcing their way through. The only question, they said, was whether the Entente was ready to sacrifice the necessary number of ships. Neither Wangenheim, nor Pallavicini believed that the disastrous experience of the 18th would end the naval attack, and for days they anxiously waited for the fleet to return. The high tension lasted for days and weeks after the repulse of the 18th. We were still momentarily expecting the renewal of the attack. But the great armada never returned.

Should it have come back? Could the Allied ships really have captured Constantinople? I am constantly asked this question. As a layman my own opinion can have little value, but I have quoted the opinions of the German generals and admirals, and of the Turks---practically all of whom, except Enver, believed that the enterprise would succeed, and I am half inclined to believe that Enver's attitude was merely a case of graveyard whistling; in what I now have to say on this point, therefore, I wish it understood that I am giving not my own views, but merely those of the officials then in Turkey who were best qualified to judge.

Enver had told me, in our talk on the deck of the Yuruk, that he had "plenty of guns---plenty of ammunition." But this statement was not true. A glimpse at the map will show why Turkey was not receiving munitions from Germany or Austria at that time. The fact was that Turkey was just as completely isolated from her allies then as was Russia. There were two railroad lines leading from Constantinople to Germany. One went by way of Bulgaria and Serbia. Bulgaria was then not an ally; even though she had winked at the passage of guns and shells, this line could not have been used, since Serbia, which controlled the vital link extending from Nish to Belgrade, was still intact. The other railroad line went through Rumania, by way of, Bucharest. This route was independent of Serbia, and, had the Rumanian Government consented, it would have formed a clear route from the Krupps to the Dardanelles. The fact that munitions could be sent with the connivance of the Rumanian Government perhaps accounts for the suspicion that guns and shells were going by that route. Day after day the French and British ministers protested at Bucharest against this alleged violation of neutrality, only to be met with angry denials that the Germans were using this line. There is no doubt now that the Rumanian Government was perfectly honourable in making these denials. It is not unlikely that the Germans themselves started all these stories, merely to fool the Allied fleet into the belief that their supplies were inexhaustible.

Let us suppose that the Allies had returned, say on the morning of the nineteenth, what would have happened? The one overwhelming fact is that the fortifications were very short of ammunition. They had almost reached the limit of their resisting power when the British fleet passed out on the afternoon of the 18th. I had secured permission for Mr. George A. Schreiner, the well-known American correspondent of the Associated Press, to visit the Dardanelles on this occasion. On the night of the 18th, this correspondent discussed the situation with General Mertens, who was the chief technical officer at the straits. General Mertens admitted that the outlook was very discouraging !or the defense.

"We expect that the British will come back early tomorrow morning," he said, " and if they do, we may be able to hold out for a few hours."

General Mertens did not declare in so many words that the ammunition was practically exhausted, but Mr. Schreiner discovered that such was the case. The fact was that Fort Hamidi?, the most powerful defense on the Asiatic side, had just seventeen armour-piercing shells left, while at Kilid-ul-Bahr, which was the main defense on the European side, there were precisely ten.

"I should advise you to get up at six o'clock tomorrow morning," said General Mertens, "and take to the Anatolian hills. That's what we are going to do."

The troops at all the fortifications had their orders to man the guns until the last shell had been fired and then to abandon the forts.

Once these defenses became helpless, the problem of the Allied fleet would have been a simple one. The only bar to their progress would have been the minefield, which stretched from a point about two miles north of Erenkeui to Kilid-ul-Bahr. But the Allied fleet had plenty of mine-sweepers, which could have made a channel in a few hours. North of Tchanak, as I have already explained, there were a few guns, but they were of the 1878 model, and could not discharge projectiles that could pierce modern armour plate. North of Point Nagara there were only two batteries, and both dated from 1835! Thus, once having silenced the outer straits, there was nothing to bar the passage to Constantinople except the German and Turkish warships. The Goeben was the only first-class fighting ship in either fleet, and it would not have lasted long against the Queen Elizabeth. The disproportion in the strength of the opposing fleets, indeed, was so enormous that it is doubtful whether there would ever have been an engagement.

Thus the Allied fleet would have appeared before Constantinople on the morning of the twentieth. What would have happened then? We have heard much discussion as to whether this purely naval attack was justified. Enver, in his conversation with me, had laid much stress on the absurdity of sending a fleet to Constantinople, supported by no adequate landing force, and much of the criticism since passed upon the Dardanelles expedition has centred on that point. Yet it is my opinion that this exclusively naval attack was justified. I base this judgment purely upon the political situation which then existed in Turkey. Under ordinary circumstances such an enterprise would probably have been a foolish one, but the political conditions in Constantinople then were not ordinary. There was no solidly established government in Turkey at that time. A political committee, not exceeding forty members, headed by Talaat, Enver, and Djemal, controlled the Central Government, but their authority throughout the empire was exceedingly tenuous. As a matter of fact, the whole Ottoman state, on that eighteenth day of March, 1915, when the Allied fleet abandoned the attack, was on the brink of dissolution. All over Turkey ambitious chieftains had arisen, who were momentarily expecting its fall, and who were looking for the opportunity to seize their parts of the inheritance. As previously described, Djemal had already organized practically an independent government in Syria. In Smyrna Rahmi Bey, the Governor-General, had often disregarded the authorities at the capital. In Adrianople Hadji Adil, one of the most courageous Turks of the time, was believed to be plotting to set up his own government. Arabia had already become practically an independent nation. Among the subject races the spirit of revolt was rapidly spreading. The Greeks and the Armenians would also have welcomed an opportunity to strengthen the hands of the Allies. The existing financial and industrial conditions seemed to make revolution inevitable. Many farmers went on strike; they had no seeds and would not accept them as a free gift from the Government because, they said, as soon as their crops should be garnered the armies, would immediately requisition them. As for Constantinople, the populace there and the best elements among the Turks, far from opposing the arrival of the Allied fleet, would have welcomed it with joy. The Turks themselves were praying that the British and French would take their city, for this would relieve them of the controlling gang, emancipate them from the hated Germans, bring about peace, and end their miseries.

No one understood this better than Talaat. He was taking no chances on making an expeditious retreat, in case the Allied fleet appeared before the city. For several months the Turkish leaders had been casting envious glances at a Minerva automobile that had been reposing in the Belgian legation ever since Turkey's declaration of war. Talaat finally obtained possession of the coveted prize. He had obtained somewhere another automobile, which he had loaded with extra tires, gasolene, and all the other essentials of a protracted journey. This was evidently intended to accompany the more pretentious machine as a kind of "mother ship." Talaat stationed these automobiles on the Asiatic side of the city with chauffeurs constantly at hand. Everything was prepared to leave for the interior of Asia Minor at a moment's notice.

But the great Allied armada never returned to the attack.

About a week after this momentous defeat, I happened to drop in at the German Embassy. Wangenheim had a distinguished visitor whom he asked me to meet. I went into his private office and there was Von der Goltz Pasha, recently returned from Belgium, where he had served as governor. I must admit that, meeting Goltz thus informally, I had difficulty in reconciling his personality with all the stories that were then coming out of Belgium. That morning this mild-mannered, spectacled gentleman seemed sufficiently quiet and harmless. Nor did he look his age---he was then about seventy-four; his hair was only streaked with gray, and his face was almost unwrinkled; I should not have taken him for more than sixty-five. The austerity and brusqueness and ponderous dignity which are assumed by most highly-placed Germans were not apparent. His voice was deep, musical, and pleasing, and his manners were altogether friendly and ingratiating. The only evidence of pomp in his bearing was his uniform; he was dressed as a field marshal, his chest blazing with decorations and gold braid. Von der Goltz explained and half apologized for his regalia by saying that he had just returned from an audience with the Sultan. He had come to Constantinople to present his majesty a medal from the Kaiser, and was taking back to Berlin a similar mark of consideration from the Sultan to the Kaiser, besides an imperial present of 10,000 cigarettes.

The three of us sat there for some time, drinking coffee, eating German cakes, and smoking German cigars. I did not do much of the talking, but the conversation of Von der Goltz and Wangenheim, seemed to me to shed much light upon the German mind, and especially on the trustworthiness of German military reports. The aspect of the Dardanelles fight that interested them most at that time was England's complete frankness in publishing her losses. That the British Government should issue an official statement, saying that three ships had been sunk and that four others had been badly damaged, struck them as most remarkable. In this announcement I merely saw a manifestation of the usual British desire to make public the worst---the policy which we Americans also believe to be the best in war times. But no such obvious explanation could satisfy these wise and solemn Teutons. No, England had some deep purpose in telling the truth so unblushingly; what could it be?

"Es ist ausserordentlich!" (It is extraordinary) said Von der Goltz, referring to England's public acknowledgment of defeat.

"Es ist unerh?rt!" (It is unheard of) declared the equally astonished Wangenheim.

These master diplomatists canvassed one explanation after another, and finally reached a conclusion that satisfied the higher strategy. England, they agreed, really had had no enthusiasm for this attack, because, in the event of success, she would have had to hand Constantinople over to Russia---something which England really did not intend to do. By publishing the losses, England showed Russia the enormous difficulties of the task; she had demonstrated, indeed, that the enterprise was impossible. After such losses, England intended Russia to understand that she had made a sincere attempt to gain this great prize of war and expected her not to insist on further sacrifices.

The sequel to this great episode in the war came in the winter of 1915-16. By this time Bulgaria had joined the Central Powers, Serbia had been overwhelmed, and the Germans had obtained a complete, unobstructed railroad line from Constantinople to Austria and Germany. Huge Krupp guns now began to come over this line---all destined for the Dardanelles. Sixteen great batteries, of the latest model, were emplaced near the entrance, completely controlling Sedd-ul-Bahr. The Germans lent the Turks 500,000,000 marks, much of which was spent defending this indispensable highway. The thinly fortified straits through which I passed in March, 1915, is now as impregnably fortified as Heligoland. It is doubtful if all the fleets in the world could force the Dardanelles to-day.

Chapter XIX - A Fight for Three Thousand Civilians

On the second of May, 1915, Enver sent his aide to the American Embassy, bringing a message which he requested me to transmit to the French and British governments. About a week before this visit the Allies had landed on the Gallipoli peninsula. They had evidently concluded that a naval attack by itself could not destroy the defenses and open the road to Constantinople, and they had now adopted the alternative plan of despatching large bodies of troops, to be supported by the guns of their warships. Already many thousands of Australians and New Zealanders had entrenched themselves at the tip of the peninsula, and the excitement that prevailed in Constantinople was almost as great as that which had been caused by the appearance of the fleet two months before.

Enver now informed me that the Allied ships were bombarding in reckless fashion, and ignoring the well-established international rule that such bombardments should be directed only against fortified places; British and French shells, he said, were falling everywhere, destroying unprotected Moslem villages and killing hundreds of innocent non-combatants. Enver asked me to inform the Allied governments that such activities must immediately cease. He had decided to collect all the British and French citizens who were then living in Constantinople, take them down to the Gallipoli peninsula and scatter them in Moslem villages and towns. The Allied fleets would then be throwing their projectiles not only against peaceful and unprotected Moslems, but against their own countrymen. It was Enver's idea that this threat, communicated by the American Ambassador to the British and French governments, would soon put an end to "atrocities" of this kind. I was given a few days' respite to get the information to London and Paris.

At that time about 3,000 British and French citizens were living in Constantinople. The great majority belonged to the class known as Levantines; nearly all had been born in Turkey and in many cases their families had been domiciled in that country for two or more generations. The retention of their European citizenship is almost their only contact with the nation from which they have sprung. Not uncommonly we meet in the larger cities of Turkey men and women who are English by race and nationality, but who speak no English, French being the usual language of the Levantine. The great majority have never set foot in England, or any other European country; they have only one home, and that is Turkey. The fact that the Levantine usually retains citizenship in the nation of his origin was now apparently making him a fitting object for Turkish vengeance. Besides these Levantines, a large number of English and French were then living in Constantinople, as teachers in the schools, as missionaries, and as important business men and merchants. The Ottoman Government now proposed to assemble all these residents, both those who were immediately and those who were remotely connected with Great Britain and France, and to place them in exposed positions on the Gallipoli peninsula as targets for the Allied fleet.

Naturally my first question when I received this startling information was whether the warships were really bombarding defenseless towns. If they were murdering non-combatant men, women, and children in this reckless fashion, such an act of reprisal as Enver now proposed would probably have had some justification. It seemed to me incredible, however, that the English and French could commit such barbarities. I had already received many complaints of this kind from Turkish officials which, on investigation, had turned out to be untrue. Only a little while before Dr. Meyer, the first assistant to Suleyman Nouman, the Chief of the Medical Staff, had notified me that the British fleet had bombarded a Turkish hospital and killed 1,000 invalids. When I looked into the matter, I found that the building had been but slightly damaged, and only one man killed. I now naturally suspected that this latest tale of Allied barbarity rested on a similarly flimsy foundation. I soon discovered, indeed, that this was the case. The Allied fleet was not bombarding Moslem villages at all. A number of British warships had been stationed in the Gulf of Saros, an indentation of the Aegean Sea, on the western side of the peninsula, and from this vantage point they were throwing shells into the city of Gallipoli. All the "bombarding" of towns in which they were now engaging was limited to this one city. In doing this the British navy was not violating the rules of civilized warfare, for Gallipoli had long since been evacuated of its civilian population, and the Turks had established military head-quarters in several of the houses, which had properly become the object of the Allied attack. I certainly knew of no rule of warfare which prohibited an attack upon a military headquarters. As to the stories of murdered civilians, men, women, and children, these proved to be gross exaggerations; as almost the entire civilian population had long since left, any casualties resulting from the bombardment must have been confined to the armed forces of the empire.

I now discussed the situation for some time with Mr. Ernest Weyl, who was generally recognized as the leading French citizen in Constantinople, and with Mr. Hoffman Philip, the Conseiller of the Embassy, and then decided that I would go immediately to the Sublime Porte and protest to Enver.

The Council of Ministers was sitting at the time, but Enver came out. His manner was more demonstrative than usual. As he described the attack of the British fleet, he became extremely angry; it was not the imperturbable Enver with whom I had become so familiar. "These cowardly English! " he exclaimed." They tried for a long time to get through the Dardanelles, and we were too much for them! And see what kind of a revenge they are taking. Their ships sneak up into the outer bay, where our guns cannot reach them, and shoot over the hills at our little villages, killing harmless old men, women, and children, and bombarding our hospitals. Do you think we are going to let them do that? And what can we do? Our guns don't reach over the hills, so that we cannot meet them in battle. If we could, we would drive them off, just as we did at the straits a month ago. We have no fleet to send to England to bombard their unfortified towns as they are bombarding ours. So we have decided to move all the English and French we can find to Gallipoli. Let them kill their own people as well as ours."

I told him that, granted that the circumstances were as he had stated them, he had grounds for indignation. But I called his attention to the fact that he was wrong; that he was accusing the Allies of crimes which they were not committing.

"This is about the most barbarous thing that you have ever contemplated," I said. "The British have a perfect right to attack a military headquarters like Gallipoli."

But my argument did not move Enver. I became convinced that he had not decided on this step as a reprisal to protect his own countrymen, but that he and his associates were blindly venting their rage. The fact that the Australians and New Zealanders had successfully effected a landing had aroused their most barbarous instincts. Enver referred to this landing in our talk; though he professed to regard it lightly, and said that he would soon push the French and English into the sea, I saw that it was causing him much concern. The Turk, as I have said before, is psychologically primitive; to answer the British landing at Gallipoli by murdering hundreds of helpless British who were in his power would strike him as perfectly logical. As a result of this talk I gained only a few concessions. Enver agreed to postpone the deportation until Thursday---it was then Sunday; to exclude women and children from the order, and to take none of the British and French who were then connected with American institutions.

"All the rest will have to go," was his final word. "Moreover," he added, "we don't purpose to have the enemy submarines in the Marmora torpedo the transports we are sending to the Dardanelles. In the future we shall put a few Englishmen and Frenchmen on every ship we send down there as a protection to our own soldiers."

When I returned to our embassy I found that the news of the proposed deportation had been published. The amazement and despair that immediately resulted were unparalleled, even in that city of constant sensations. Europeans, by living for many years in the Levant, seem to acquire its emotions, particularly its susceptibility to fear and horror, and now, no longer having the protection of their embassies, these fears were intensified. A stream of frenzied people began to pour into the Embassy. From their tears and cries one would have thought that they were immediately to be taken out and shot, and that there was any possibility of being saved seemed hardly to occur to them. Yet all the time they insisted that I should get individual exemptions. One could not go because he had a dependent family; another had a sick child; another was ill himself. My ante-room was full of frantic mothers, asking me to secure exemption for their sons, and of wives, who sought special treatment for their husbands. They made all kinds of impossible suggestions: I should resign my ambassadorship as a protest; I should even threaten Turkey with war by the United States! They constantly besieged my wife, who spent hours listening to their stories and comforting them. In all this exciting mass there were many who faced the situation with more courage.

The day after my talk with Enver, Bedri, the Prefect of Police, began to arrest some of the victims.

The next morning one of my callers made what would ordinarily have seemed to be an obvious suggestion. This visitor was a German. He told me that Germany would suffer greatly in reputation if the Turks carried out their plan; the world would not possibly be convinced that Germans had not devised the whole scheme. He said that I should call upon the German and Austrian ambassadors; he was sure that they would support me in my pleas for decent treatment. As I had made appeals to Wangenheim several times before in behalf of foreigners, without success, I had hardly thought it worth while to ask his cooperation in this instance. Moreover, the plan of using non-combatants as a protective screen in warfare was such a familiar German device that I was not at all sure that the German Staff had not instigated the Turks. I decided, however, to adopt the advice of my German visitor and seek Wangenheim's assistance. I must admit that I did this as a forlorn hope, but at least I thought it only fair to Wangenheim. to give him a chance to help.

I called upon him in the evening at ten o'clock and stayed with him until eleven. I spent the larger part of this hour in a fruitless attempt to interest him in the plight of these non-combatants. Wangenheim said point blank that he would not assist me. "It is perfectly proper," he maintained, "for the Turks to establish a concentration camp at Gallipoli. It is also proper for them to put non-combatant English and French on their transports and thus insure them against attack. As I made repeated attempts to argue the matter, Wangenheim would deftly shift the conversation to other topics.

According to my record of this talk, written out at the time, the German Ambassador discussed almost every subject except the one upon which I had called.

"This act of the Turks will greatly injure Germany," I would begin.

"Do you know that the English soldiers at Gaba Tepe are without food and drink?" he would reply. " They made an attack to capture a well and were repulsed. The English have taken their ships away so as to prevent their soldiers from retreating---"

" But about this Gallipoli business," I interrupted. "Germans themselves here in Constantinople have said that Germany should stop it---"

"The Allies landed 45,000 men on the peninsula," Wangenheim answered, "and of these 10,000 were killed. In a few days we shall attack the rest and destroy them."

When I attempted to approach the subject from another angle, this master diplomatist would begin discussing Rumania and the possibility of obtaining ammunition by way of that country.

"Your Secretary Bryan,"' he said, "has just issued a statement showing that it would be unneutral for the United States to refuse to sell ammunition to the Allies. So we have used this same argument with the Rumanians; if it is unneutral not to sell ammunition, it is certainly unneutral to refuse to-transport it!"

The humorous aspects of this argument appealed to Wangenheim, but I reminded him that I was there to discuss the lives of between 2,000 and 3,000 non-combatants. As I touched upon this subject again, Wangenheim replied that the United States would not be acceptable to Germany as a peacemaker now, because we were so friendly to the Entente. He insisted on giving me all the details of recent German successes in the Carpathians and the latest news on the Italian situation.

"We would rather fight Italy than have her for our ally," he said.

At another time all this would have greatly entertained me, but not then. It was quite apparent that Wangenheim would not discuss the proposed deportation further than to say that the Turks were justified. His statement that it was planned to establish a "concentration camp" at Gallipoli unfolded his whole attitude. Up to this time the Turks had not established concentration camps for enemy aliens anywhere. I had earnestly advised them not to establish such camps, thus far with success. On the other hand, the Germans were protesting that Turkey was "too lenient" and urging the establishment of such camps in the interior. Wangenheim's use of the words "concentration camps in Gallipoli" showed that the German view was at last prevailing and that I was losing my battle for the foreigners. An internment camp is a distressing place under the most favourable circumstances, but who, except a German or a Turk, ever conceived of establishing one right in the field of battle? Let us suppose that the English and the French should assemble all their enemy aliens, march them to the front, and place them in a camp in No Man's Land, directly in the fire of both armies. That was precisely the kind of a "concentration camp" which the Turks and Germans now intended to establish for the resident aliens of Constantinople--- for my talk with Wangenheim left no doubt in my mind that the Germans were parties to the plot.

They feared that the land attack on the Dardanelles would succeed, just as they had feared that the naval attack would succeed, and they were prepared to use any weapon, even the lives of several thousand non-combatants, in their efforts to make it a failure.

My talk with Wangenheim produced no results, so far as enlisting his support was concerned, but it stiffened my determination to defeat this enterprise. I also called upon Pallavicini, the Austrian Ambassador. He at once declared that the proposed deportation was "inhuman."

"I will take up the matter with the Grand Vizier," he said, "and see if I can't stop it."

"But you know that is perfectly useless," I answered. "The Grand Vizier has no power---he is only a figurehead. Only one man can stop this, that is Enver."

Pallavicini had far finer sensibilities and a tenderer conscience than Wangenheim, and I had no doubt that he was entirely sincere in his desire to prevent this crime. But he was a diplomat of the old Austrian school. Nothing in his eyes was so important as diplomatic etiquette. As the representative of his emperor, propriety demanded that he should conduct all his negotiations with the Grand Vizier, who was also at that time Minister for Foreign Affairs. He never discussed state matters with Talaat and Enver---indeed, he had only limited official relations with these men, the real rulers of Turkey. And now the saving of 3,000 lives was not, in Pallavicini's eyes, any reason why he should disregard the traditional routine of diplomatic intercourse.

"I must go strictly according to rules in this matter," he said. And, in the goodness of his heart, he did speak to Sa?d Halim. Following this example Wangenheim also spoke to the Grand Vizier. In Wangenheim's case, however, the protest was merely intended for the official record.

"You may fool some people," I told the German Ambassador, "but you know that speaking to the Grand Vizier in this matter is of about as much use as shouting in the air."

However, there was one member of the diplomatic corps who worked wholeheartedly in behalf of the threatened foreigners. This was M. Koloucheff, the Bulgarian Minister. As soon as he heard of this latest Turco-German outrage, he immediately came to me with offers of assistance. He did not propose to waste his time by a protest to the Grand Vizier, but announced his intention of going immediately to the source of authority, Enver himself. Koloucheff was an extremely important man at that particular time, for Bulgaria was then neutral and both sides were angling for her support.

Meanwhile, Bedri and his minions were busy arresting some of the doomed English and French. The deportation was arranged to take place Thursday morning. On Wednesday, the excitement reached the hysterical stage. It seemed as if the whole foreign population of Constantinople had gathered at the American Embassy. Scores of weeping women and haggard men assembled in front and at the side of the building; more than three hundred gained personal access to my office, hanging desperately upon the Ambassador and his staff. Many almost seemed to think that I personally held their fates in my hand; in their agony of spirit some even denounced me, insisting that I was not exerting all my powers in their behalf. Whenever I left my office and passed into the hall I was almost mobbed by scores of terror-stricken and dishevelled mothers and wives. The nervous tension was frightful; I seized the telephone, called up Enver, and demanded an interview.

He replied that he would be happy to receive me on Thursday. By this time, however, the prisoners would already have been on their way to Gallipoli.

"No," I replied, "I must see you this afternoon."

Enver made all kinds of excuses; he was busy, he had appointments scheduled for the whole day.

"I presume you want to see me about the English and French," he said. "If that is so, I can tell you now that it will be useless. Our minds are made up. Orders have been issued to the police to gather them all by to-night and to ship them down to-morrow morning."

I still insisted that I must see him that afternoon and he still attempted to dodge the interview.

"My time is all taken," he said. "The Council of Ministers sits at four o'clock and the meeting is to be a very important one. I can't absent myself."

Emboldened by the thought of the crowds of women that were flooding the whole Embassy I decided on an altogether unprecedented move.

"I shall not be denied an interview," I replied. "I shall come up to the cabinet room at four o'clock. If you refuse to receive me then, I shall insist on going into the council room and discussing the matter with the whole Cabinet. I shall be interested to learn whether the Turkish Cabinet will refuse to receive the American Ambassador."

It seemed to me that I could almost hear Enver gasp over the telephone. I presume few responsible ministers of any country have ever had such an astounding proposition made to them.

"If you will meet me at the Sublime Porte at 3:30," he answered, after a considerable pause, "I shall arrange to see you."

When I reached the Sublime Porte I was told that the Bulgarian Minister was having a protracted conference with Enver. Naturally I was willing to wait, for I knew what the two men were discussing. Presently M. Koloucheff came out; his face was tense and anxious, clearly revealing the ordeal through which he had just passed.

"It is perfectly hopeless," he said to me. "Nothing will move Enver: he is absolutely determined that this thing shall go through. I cannot wish you good luck, for you will have none."

The meeting which followed between Enver and myself was the most momentous I had had up to that time. We discussed the fate of the foreigners for nearly an hour. I found Enver in one of his most polite but most unyielding moods. He told me before I began that it was useless to talk---that the matter was a closed issue. But I insisted on telling him what a splendid impression Turkey's treatment of her enemies had made on the outside world. "Your record in this matter is better than that of any other belligerent country," I said. "You have not put them into concentration camps, you have let them stay here and continue their ordinary business, just as before. You have done this in spite of strong pressure to act otherwise. Why do you destroy all the good effect this has produced by now making such a fatal mistake as you, propose?

But Enver insisted that the Allied fleets were bombarding unfortified towns, killing women, children, and wounded men.

"We have warned them through you that they must not do this," he said, "but they don't stop."

This statement, of course, was not true, but I could not persuade Enver that he was wrong. He expressed great appreciation for all that I had done, and regretted for my sake that he could not accept my advice. I told him that the foreigners had suggested that I threaten to give up the care of British and French interests.

"Nothing would suit us better," he quickly replied.

The only difficulty we have with you is when you come around and bother us with English and French affairs."

I asked him if I had ever given him any advice that had led them into trouble. He graciously replied that they had never yet made a mistake by following my suggestions.

"Very well, take my advice in this case, too," I replied. "You will find later that you have made no mistake by doing so. I tell you that it is my positive opinion that your cabinet is committing a terrible error by taking this step."

"But I have given orders to this effect," Enver answered. "I cannot countermand them. If I did, my whole influence with the army would go. Once having given an order I never change it. My own wife asked me to have her servants exempted from military service and I refused. The Grand Vizier asked exemption for his secretary, and I refused him, because I had given orders. I never revoke orders and I shall not do it in this case. If you can show me some way in which this order can be carried out and your prot?g?s still saved, I shall be glad to listen."

I had already discovered one of the most conspicuous traits in the Turkish character: its tendency to compromise and to bargain. Enver's request for a suggestion now gave me an opportunity to play on this characteristic.

"All right," I said. "I think I can. I should think you could still carry out your orders without sending all the French and English residents down. If you would send only a few, you would still win your point. You could still maintain discipline in the army, and these few would be as strong a deterrent to the Allied fleet as sending all."

It seemed to me that Enver almost eagerly seized upon this suggestion as a way out of his dilemma.

"How many will you let me send?" he asked quickly. The moment he put this question I knew that I had carried my point.

"I would suggest that you take twenty English and twenty French---forty in all."

"Let me have fifty," he said.

"All right---we won't haggle over ten," I answered. "But you must make another concession. Let me pick out the fifty who are to go."

This agreement had relieved the tension, and now the gracious side of Enver's nature began to show itself again.

"No, Mr. Ambassador," he replied. "You have prevented me from making a mistake this afternoon; now let me prevent you from making one. If you select the fifty men who are to go, you will simply make fifty enemies. I think too much of you to let you do that. I will prove to you that I am your real friend. Can't you make some other suggestion?"

"Why not take the youngest? They can stand the fatigue best."

"That is fair," answered Enver. He said that Bedri, who was in the building at that moment, would select the "victims." This caused me some uneasiness; I knew that Enver's modification of his order would displease Bedri, whose hatred of the foreigners had shown itself on many occasions, and that the head of the police would do his best to find some way of evading it. So I asked Enver to send for Bedri and give him his new orders in my presence. Bedri came in, and, as I had suspected, he did not like the new arrangement at all. As soon as he heard that he was to take only fifty and the youngest he threw up his hands and began to walk up and down the room.

"No, no, this will never do!" he said. "I don't want the youngest, I must have notables! "

But Enver stuck to the arrangement and gave Bedri orders to take only the youngest men. It was quite apparent that Bedri needed humouring, so I asked him to ride with me to the American Embassy, where we would have tea and arrange all the details. This invitation had an instantaneous effect which the American mind will have difficulty in comprehending. An American would regard it as nothing wonderful to be seen publicly riding with an ambassador, or to take tea at an embassy. But this is a distinction which never comes to a minor functionary, such as a Prefect of Police, in the Turkish capital. Possibly I lowered the dignity of my office in extending this invitation to Bedri; Pallavicini would probably have thought so; but it certainly paid, for it made Bedri more pliable than he would otherwise have been.

When we reached the Embassy, we found the crowds stiff there, awaiting the results of my intercession. When I told the besiegers that only fifty had to go and these the youngest, they seemed momentarily stupefied. They could not understand it at first; they believed that I might obtain some modification of the order, but nothing like this. Then, as the truth dawned upon them, I found myself in the centre of a crowd that had apparently gone momentarily insane, this time not from grief, but from joy. Women, the tears streaming down their faces, insisted on throwing themselves on their knees, seizing both my hands, and covering them with kisses. Mature men, despite my violent protestations, persisted in hugging me and kissing me on both cheeks. For several minutes I struggled with this crowd, embarrassed by its demonstrations of gratitude, but finally I succeeded in breaking away and secreting myself and Bedri in an inner room.

"Can't I have a few notables? " he asked.

"I'll give you just one," I replied.

"Can't I have three? " he asked again.

"You can have all who are under fifty," I answered.

But that did not satisfy him, as there was not a solitary person of distinction under that-age limit. Bedri really had his eye on Messieurs Weyl, Rey, and Dr. Frew. But I had one "notable" up my sleeve whom I was willing to concede. Dr. Wigram, an Anglican clergyman, one of the most prominent men in the foreign colony, had pleaded with me, asking that he might be permitted to go with the hostages and furnish them such consolation as religion could give them. I knew that nothing would delight Dr. Wigram, more than to be thrown as a sop to Bedri's passion for "notables."

"Dr. Wigram is the only notable you can have," I said to Bedri. So he accepted him as the best that he could do in that line.

Mr. Hoffman Philip, the Conseiller of the American Embassy---now American Minister to Colombia---had already expressed a desire to accompany the hostages, so that he might minister to their comfort. This manifestation of a fine humanitarian spirit was nothing new in Mr. Philip. Although not in good health, he had returned to Constantinople after Turkey had entered the war, in order that he might assist me in the work of caring for the foreign residents. Through all that arduous period he constantly displayed that sympathy for the unfortunate, the sick, and the poor, which is innate in his character. Though it was somewhat irregular for a representative of the Embassy to engage in such a hazardous enterprise as this one, Mr. Philip pleaded so earnestly that finally I reluctantly gave my consent. I also obtained permission for

Air. Arthur Ruhl of Collier's and Mr. Henry West Suydam, of the Brooklyn Eagle, to accompany the party.

At the end Bedri had to have his little joke. Though the fifty were informed that the boat for Gallipoli would leave the next morning at six o'clock, he, with his police, visited their houses at midnight, and routed them all out of bed. The crowd that assembled at the dock the next morning looked somewhat weather-beaten and worse for wear. Bedri was there, superintending the whole proceeding, and when he came up to me, he good-naturedly reproached me again for letting him have only one "notable." In the main, he behaved very decently, though he could not refrain from telling the hostages that the British airplanes were dropping bombs on Gallipoli! Of the twenty-five "Englishmen" assembled there were only two who had been born in England, and of the twenty-five "Frenchmen" only two who had been born in France. They carried satchels containing food and other essentials, their assembled relatives had additional bundles, and Mrs. Morgenthau. sent several large cases of food to the ship. The parting of these young men with their families was affecting, but they all stood it bravely.

I returned to the Embassy, somewhat wearied by the excitement of the last few days and in no particularly gracious humour for the honour which now awaited me. For I had been there only a few minutes when His Excellency, the German Ambassador, was announced. Wangenheim discussed commonplaces for a few minutes and then approached the real object of his call. He asked me to telegraph to Washington that he had been "helpful" in getting the number of the Gallipoli hostages reduced to fifty! In view of the actual happenings this request was so preposterous that I could scarcely maintain my composure. I had known that, in going through the form of speaking to the Grand Vizier, Wangenheim had been manufacturing his protest for future use, but I had not expected him to fall back upon it so soon.

"Well," said Wangenheim, "at least telegraph your government that I didn't 'hetz' the Turks in this matter."

The German verb "hetzen" means about the same as the English "sic," in the sense of inciting a dog. I was in no mood to give Wangenheim. a clean bill of health, and told him so. In fact, I specifically reported to Washington that he had refused to help me. A day or two afterward Wangenheim called me on the telephone and began to talk in an excited and angry tone. His government had wired him about my telegram to Washington. I told him that if he desired credit for assistance in matters of this kind, he should really exert himself and do something.

The hostages had an uncomfortable time at Gallipoli; they were put into two wooden houses with no beds and no food except that which they had brought themselves. The days and nights were made wretched by the abundant vermin that is a commonplace in Turkey. Had Mr. Philip not gone with them, they would have suffered seriously. After the unfortunates had been there for a few days I began work with Enver again to get them back. Sir Edward Grey, then British Secretary for Foreign Affairs, had requested our State Department to send me a message with the request that I present it to Enver and his fellow ministers; its purport was that the British Government would hold them personally responsible for any injury to the hostages. I presented this message to Enver on May 9th. I had seen Enver in many moods, but the unbridled rage which Sir Edward's admonition now caused was something entirely new. As I read the telegram his face became livid, and he absolutely lost control of himself. The European polish which Enver had sedulously acquired dropped like a mask; I now saw him for what he really was---a savage, bloodthirsty Turk.

"They will not come back!" he shouted. "I shall let them stay there until they rot! "

"I would like to see those English touch me!" he continued.

I saw that the method which I had always used with Enver, that of persuasion., was the only possible way of handling him. I tried to soothe the Minister now, and, after a while, he quieted down.

"But don't ever threaten me again!" he said.

After spending a week at Gallipoli, the party returned. The Turks had moved their military headquarters from Gallipoli and the English fleet, therefore, ceased to bombard it. All came back in good condition and were welcomed home with great enthusiasm.

Chapter XX - More Adventures of the Foreign Residents

The Gallipoli deportation gives some idea of my difficulties in attempting to fulfil my duty as the representative of Allied interests in the Ottoman Empire. Yet, despite these occasional out bursts of hatred, in the main the Turkish officials themselves behaved very well. They had promised me at the beginning that they would treat their alien enemies decently, and would permit them either to remain in Turkey, and follow their accustomed occupations, or to leave the empire. They apparently believed that the world would judge them, after the war was over, not by the way they treated their own subject peoples but by the way they treated the subjects of the enemy powers. The result was that a Frenchman, an Englishman, or an Italian enjoyed far greater security in Turkey than an Armenian, a Greek, or a Jew. Yet against this disposition to be decent a persistent malevolent force was constantly manifesting itself. In a letter to the State Department, I described the influence that was working against foreigners in Turkey. "The German Ambassador," I wrote on May 14,1915, "keeps pressing on the Turks the advisability both of repressive measures and of detaining as hostages the subjects of the belligerent powers. I have had to encounter the persistent opposition of my German colleague in endeavouring to obtain permission for the departure of the subjects of the nationalities under our protection."

Now and then the Turkish officials would retaliate upon one of their enemy aliens, usually in reprisal for some injury, or fancied injury, inflicted on their own subjects in enemy countries. Such acts gave rise to many exciting episodes, some tragical, some farcical, all illuminating in the light they shed upon Turkish character and upon Teutonic methods.

One afternoon I was sitting with Talaat, discussing routine matters, when his telephone rang.

"Pour vous," said the Minister, handing me the receiver.

It was one of my secretaries. He told me that Bedri had arrested Sir Edwin Pears, had thrown him into prison, and had seized all his papers. Sir Edwin was one of the best-known British residents of Constantinople. For forty years he had practised law in the Ottoman capital; he had also written much for the press during that period, and had published several books which had given him fame as an authority on Oriental history and politics. He was about eighty years old and of venerable and distinguished appearance. When the war started I had exacted a special promise from Talaat and Bedri that, in no event, should Sir Edwin Pears and Prof. Van Millingen of Robert College be disturbed. This telephone message which I now received---curiously enough, in Talaat's presence---seemed to indicate that this promise had been broken.

I now turned to Talaat and spoke in a manner that made no attempt to conceal my displeasure.

"Is this all your promises are worth?" I' asked. "Can't you find anything better to do than to molest such a respectable old man as Sir Edwin Pears? What has he ever done to you? "

"Come, come, don't get excited," rejoined Talaat. "He's only been in prison for a few hours, and I will see that he is released."

He tried to get Bedri on the wire, but failed. By this time I knew Bedri well enough to understand his methods of operation. When Bedri really wished to be reached on the telephone, he was the most accessible man in the world; when his presence at the other end of the wire might prove embarrassing, the most painstaking search could not reveal his whereabouts. As Bedri had given me his solemn promise that Sir Edwin, should not be disturbed, this was an occasion when the Prefect of Police preferred to keep himself inaccessible.

"I shall stay in this room until you get Bedri," I now told Talaat. The big Turk took the situation good-humouredly. We waited a considerable period, but Bedri succeeded in avoiding an encounter. Finally I called up one of my secretaries and told him to go out and hunt for the missing prefect.

"Tell Bedri," I said, "that I have Talaat under arrest in his own office and that I shall not let him leave it until he has been able to instruct Bedri to release Sir Edwin Pears."

Talaat was greatly enjoying the comedy of the situation; he knew Bedri's ways even better than I did and he was much interested in seeing whether I should succeed in finding him. But in a few moments the telephone rang. It was Bedri. I told Talaat to tell him that I was going to the prison in my own automobile to get Sir Edwin Pears.

"Please don't let him do that," replied Bedri. "Such an occurrence would make me personally ridiculous and destroy my influence."

"Very well," I replied, "I shall wait until 6.15. If Sir Edwin is not restored to his family by that time, I shall go to the Police Headquarters and get him."

As I returned to the Embassy I stopped at the Pears residence and attempted to soothe Lady Pears and her daughter.

"If your father is not here at 6.15," I told Miss Pears, "please let me know immediately!"

Promptly at that time my telephone rang. It was Miss Pears, who informed me that Sir Edwin had just reached home.

The next day Sir Edwin called at the Embassy to thank me for my efforts in his behalf. He told me that the German Ambassador had also worked for his release. This latter statement somewhat surprised me, as I knew no one else had had a chance to make a move, since everything transpired while I had been in Talaat's office. Half an hour afterward I met Wangenheim. himself; he dropped in at Mrs. Morgenthau's reception. I referred to the Pears case and asked him whether he had used any influence in obtaining his freedom. My question astonished him greatly.

"What?" he said. "I helped you to secure that man's release! Der alte Gauner I (The old rascal.) Why, I was the man who had him arrested!"

"What have you got against him?" I asked.

"In 1876," Wangenheim replied, "that man was pro-Russian and against Turkey! "

Such are the long memories of the Germans! In 1876, Sir Edwin wrote several articles for the London Daily News, describing the Bulgarian massacres. At that time the reports of these fiendish atrocities were generally disbelieved and Sir Edwin's letters placed all the incontrovertible facts before the English-speaking peoples, and had much to do with the emancipation of Bulgaria from Turkish rule. This act of humanity and journalistic statesmanship had brought Sir Edwin much fame and now, after forty years, Germany proposed to punish him by casting him into a Turkish prison! Again the Turks proved more considerate than their German allies, for they not only gave Sir Edwin his liberty and his papers, but permitted him to return to London.

Bedri, however, was a little mortified at my successful intervention in this instance and decided to even up the score. Next to Sir Edwin Pears, the most prominent English-speaking barrister in Constantinople was Dr. Mizzi, a Maltese, 70 years old. The ruling powers had a grudge against him, for he was the proprietor of the Levant Herald, a paper which had published articles criticizing the Union and Progress Committee. On the very night of the Pears episode, Bedri went to Dr. Mizzi's house at eleven o'clock, routed the old gentleman out of bed, arrested him, and placed him on a train for Angora, in Asia Minor. As a terrible epidemic of typhus was raging in Angora, this was not a desirable place of residence for a man of Dr. Mizzi's years. The next morning, when I heard of it for the first time, Dr. Mizzi was well on the way to his place of exile.

"This time I got ahead of you!" said Bedri, with a triumphant laugh. He was as good-natured about it and as pleased as a boy. At last he had "put one over" on the American Ambassador, who had been unguardedly asleep in his bed when this old man had been railroaded to a fever camp in Asia Minor.

But Bedri's success was not so complete, after all. At my request Talaat had Dr. Mizzi sent to Konia, instead of to Angora. There one of the American missionaries, Dr. Dodd, had a splendid hospital. He arranged that Dr. Mizzi could have a nice room in this building, and here he lived for several months, with congenial associates, good food, a healthy atmosphere, all the books he wanted, and one thing without which he would have been utterly miserable---a piano. So I still thought that the honours between Bedri and myself were a little better than even.

Early in January, 1916, word was received that the English were maltreating Turkish war prisoners in Egypt. Soon afterward I received letters from two Australians, Commander Stoker and Lieutenant Fitzgerald, telling me that they had been confined for eleven days in a miserable, damp dungeon at the War Office, with no companions except a monstrous swarm of vermin. These two naval officers had come to Constantinople on one of that famous fleet of American-built submarines which had made the daring trip from England, dived under the mines in the Dardanelles, and arrived in the Marmora, where for several weeks they terrorized and dominated this inland sea, practically putting an end to all shipping. The particular submarine on which my correspondents arrived, the E-15, had been caught in the Dardanelles, and its crew and officers had been sent to the Turkish military prison at Afium Kara Hissar in Asia Minor. When news of the alleged maltreatment of Turkish prisoners in Egypt was received, lots were drawn among these prisoners to see which two should be taken to Constantinople and imprisoned in reprisal. Stoker and Fitzgerald drew the unlucky numbers, and had been lying in this terrible underground cell for eleven days. I immediately took the matter up with Enver and suggested that a neutral doctor and officer examine the Turks in Egypt and report on the truth of the stories. We promptly received word that the report was false, and that, as a matter of fact, the Turkish prisoners in English hands were receiving excellent treatment.

About this time I called on Monsignor Dolci, the Apostolic Delegate to Turkey. He happened to refer to a Lieutenant Fitzgerald, who, he said, was then a prisoner of war at Afium Kara Hissar.

"I am much interested in him," said Monsignor Dolci, "because he is engaged to the daughter of the British Minister to the Vatican. I spoke to Enver about him and he promised that he would receive special treatment."

" What is his first name? " I asked.

"Jeffrey."

"He's receiving 'special treatment' indeed," I answered. "Do you know that he is in a dungeon in Constantinople this very moment? "

Naturally M. Dolci was much disturbed but I reassured him, saying that his prot?g? would be released in a few days.

"You see how shamefully you treated these young men," I now said to Enver, " you should do something to make amends."

"All right, what would you suggest?

Stoker and Fitzgerald were prisoners of war, and, according to the usual rule, would have been sent back to the prison camp after being released from their dungeon. I now proposed that Enver should give them a vacation of eight days in Constantinople. He entered into the spirit of the occasion and the men were released. They certainly presented a sorry sight; they had spent twenty-five days in the dungeon, with no chance to bathe or to shave, with no change of linen or any of the decencies of life. But Mr. Philip took charge., furnished them the necessaries, and in a brief period we had before us two young and handsome British naval officers. Their eight days' freedom turned out to be a triumphal procession, notwithstanding that they were always accompanied by an English-speaking Turkish officer. Monsignor Dolci and the American Embassy entertained them at dinner and they had a pleasant visit at the Girls' College. When the time came to return to their prison camp, the young men declared that they would be glad to spend another month in dungeons if they could have a corresponding period of freedom in the city when liberated.

In spite of all that has happened I shall always have one kindly recollection of Enver for his treatment of Fitzgerald. I told the Minister of War about the Lieutenant's engagement.

"Don't you think he's been punished enough?" I asked. " Why don't you let the boy go home and marry his sweetheart?'"

The proposition immediately appealed to Enver's sentimental side.

"I'll do it," he replied, "if he will give me his word of honour not to fight against Turkey any more."

Fitzgerald naturally gave this promise, and so his comparatively brief stay in the dungeon had the result of freeing him from imprisonment and restoring him to happiness. As poor Stoker had formed no romantic attachments that would have justified a similar plea in his case, he had to go back to the prison in Asia Minor. He did this, however, in a genuinely sporting spirit that was worthy of the best traditions of the British navy.

Chapter XXI - Bulgaria on the Auction Block

The failure of the Allied fleet at the Dardanelles did not definitely settle, the fate of Constantinople. Naturally the Turks and the Germans felt immensely relieved when the fleet sailed away. But they were by no means entirely easy in their minds. The most direct road to the ancient capital still remained available to their enemies.

In early September, 1915, one of the most influential Germans in the city gave me a detailed explanation of the prevailing military situation. He summed up the whole matter in the single phrase:

"We cannot hold the Dardanelles without the military support of Bulgaria."

This meant, of course, that unless Bulgaria aligned herself with Turkey and the Central Empires, the Gallipoli expedition would succeed, Constantinople would fall, the Turkish Empire would collapse, Russia would be reestablished as an economic and military power, and the war, in a comparatively brief period, would terminate in a victory for the Entente. Not improbably the real neutrality of Bulgaria would have had the same result. It is thus perhaps not too much to say that, in September and October of 1915, the Bulgarian Government held the duration of the war in its hands.

This fact is of such preeminent importance that I call hardly emphasize it too strongly. I suggest that my readers take down the map of a part of the world with which they are not very familiar---that of the Balkan States, as determined by the Treaty of Bucharest. All that remains of European Turkey is a small irregular area stretching about one hundred miles west of Constantinople. The nation whose land is contiguous to European Turkey is Bulgaria. The main railroad line to Western Europe starts at Constantinople and runs through Bulgaria, by way of Adrianople, Philippopolis, and Sofia. At that time Bulgaria could muster an army of 500,000 well-trained, completely organized troops. Should these once start marching toward Constantinople, there was practically nothing to bar their way. Turkey had a considerable army, it is true, but it was then finding plenty of employment repelling the Allied forces at the Dardanelles and the Russians in the Caucasus. With Bulgaria hostile, Turkey could obtain neither troops nor munitions from Germany. Turkey would have been completely isolated and, under the pounding of Bulgaria, would have disappeared as a military force, and as a European state, in one very brief campaign.

I wish to direct particular attention to this railroad, for it was, after all, the main strategic prize for which Germany was contending. After leaving Sofia it crosses northeastern Serbia, the most important stations being at Nish and Belgrade. From the latter point it crosses the River Save and later the River Danube, and thence pursues its course to Budapest and Vienna and thence to Berlin. Practically all the military operations that took place in the Balkans in 1915-16 had for their ultimate object the possession of this road. Once holding this line Turkey and Germany would no longer be separated; economically and militarily they would become a unit. The Dardanelles, as I have described, was the link that connected Russia with her allies; with this passage closed Russia's collapse rapidly followed. The valleys of the Morava and the Maritza, in which this railroad is laid, constituted for Turkey a kind of waterless Dardanelles. In her possession it gave her access to her allies; in the possession of her enemies, the Ottoman Empire would go to pieces. Only the accession of Bulgaria to the Teutonic cause could give the Turks and Germans this advantage. As soon as Bulgaria entered, that section of the railroad extending to the Serbian frontier would at once become available. If Bulgaria joined the Central Powers as an active participant, the conquest of Serbia would inevitably follow, and this would give the link extending from Nish to Belgrade to the Teutonic powers. Thus the Bulgarian alliance would make Constantinople a suburb of Berlin, place all the resources of the Krupps at the disposal of the Turkish army, make inevitable the failure of the Allied attack on Gallipoli, and lay the foundation of that Oriental Empire which had been for thirty years the mainspring of German policy.

It is thus apparent what my German friend meant when, in early September, he said that, "without Bulgaria we cannot hold the Dardanelles." Everybody sees this so clearly now that there is a prevalent belief that Germany had arranged this Bulgarian alliance before the outbreak of the war. On this point I have no definite knowledge. That the Bulgarian king and the Kaiser may have arranged this cooperation in advance is not unlikely. But we must not make the mistake of believing that this settled the matter, for the experience of the last few years shows us that treaties are not to be taken too seriously. Whether there was an understanding or not, I know that the Turkish officials and the Germans by no means regarded it as settled that Bulgaria would take their side. In their talks with me they constantly showed the utmost apprehension over the outcome; and at one time the fear was general that Bulgaria would take the side of the Entente.

I had my first personal contact with the Bulgarian negotiations in the latter part of May, when I was informed that M. Koloucheff, the Bulgarian Minister, had notified Robert College that the Bulgarian students could not remain until the end of the college year, but would have to return home by June 5th. The Constantinople College for Women had also received word that all the Bulgarian girls must return at the same time. Both these American institutions had many Bulgarian students, in most cases splendid representatives of their country; it is through these colleges, indeed, that the distant United States and Bulgaria had established such friendly relations. But they had never had such an experience before.

Everybody was discussing the meaning of this move., It seemed quite apparent. The chief topic of conversation at that time was Bulgaria. Would she enter the war? If so, on which side would she cast her fortunes? One day it was reported that she would join the Entente; the next day that she had decided to ally herself with the Central Powers. The prevailing belief was that she was actively bargaining with both sides and looking for the highest terms. Should Bulgaria go with the Entente, however, it would be undesirable to have any Bulgarian subjects marooned in Turkey. As the boys and girls in the American colleges usually came from important Bulgarian

122

families---one of them was the daughter of General Ivanoff, who led the Bulgarian armies in the Balkan wars---the Bulgarian Government might naturally have a particular interest in their safety.

The conclusion reached by most people was that Bulgaria had decided to take the side of the Entente. The news rapidly spread throughout Constantinople. The Turks were particularly impressed. Dr. Patrick, President of Constantinople College for Women, arranged a hurried commencement for her Bulgarian students, which I attended. It was a sad occasion, more like a funeral than the festivity that usually took place.

I found the Bulgarian girls almost immediately, most in a hysterical state; they all believed that war was coming and that they were being bundled home merely to prevent them from failing into the clutches of the Turks. My sympathies were so aroused that we brought them down to the American Embassy, where we all spent a delightful evening. After dinner the girls dried their eyes and entertained us by singing many of their beautiful Bulgarian songs, and what had started as a mournful day thus had a happy ending. Next morning the girls all left for Bulgaria.

A few weeks afterward the Bulgarian Minister told me that the Government had summoned the students home merely for political effect. There was no immediate likelihood of war, he said. But Bulgaria wished Germany and Turkey to understand that there was still a chance that she might join the Entente. Bulgaria, as all of us suspected, was apparently on the auction block. The one fixed fact in the Bulgarian position was the determination to have Macedonia. Everything, said Koloucheff, depended upon that. His conversations reflected the general Bulgarian view that Bulgaria had fairly won this territory in the first Balkan war, that the Powers had unjustly permitted her to be deprived of it, that it was Bulgarian by race, language, and tradition, and that there could be no permanent peace in the Balkans until it was returned to its rightful possessors. But Bulgaria insisted on more than a promise, to be redeemed after the war was over; she demanded immediate occupation. Once Macedonia were turned over to Bulgaria, she would join her forces to those of the Entente. There were two great prizes in the game then being played in the Balkans: one was Macedonia, which Bulgaria must have; and the other Constantinople, which Russia was determined to get. Bulgaria was entirely willing that Russia should have Constantinople if she herself could obtain Macedonia.

I was given to understand that the Bulgarian General Staff had plans all completed for the capture of Constantinople, and that they had shown these plans to the Entente. Their programme called for a Bulgarian army of about 300,000 men who would besiege Constantinople twenty-three days from the time the signal to start should be given. But promises of Macedonia would not suffice; the Bulgarian must have possession.

Bulgaria recognized the difficulties of the Allied position. She did not believe that Serbia and Greece would voluntarily surrender Macedonia, nor did she believe that the Allies would dare to take this country away from them by force. In that event, she thought that there was a danger that Serbia might make a separate peace with the Central Powers. On the other hand, Bulgaria would object if Serbia received Bosnia and Herzegovina as compensation for the loss of Macedonia---she felt that an enlarged Serbia would be a constant menace to her, and hence a future menace to peace in the Balkans. Thus the situation was extremely difficult and complicated.

123

One of the best-informed men in Turkey was Paul Weitz, the correspondent of the Frankfurter Zeitung. Weitz was more than a journalist; he had spent thirty years in Constantinople; he had the most intimate personal knowledge of Turkish affairs, and he was the confidant and adviser of the German Embassy. His duties there were actually semi-diplomatic. Weitz had really been one of the most successful agencies in the German penetration of Turkey; it was common talk that he knew every important man in the Turkish Empire, the best way to approach him, and his price. I had several talks with Weitz about Bulgaria during those critical August and early September days. He said many times that it was not at all certain that she would join her forces with Germany. Yet on September 7th Weitz came to me with important news. The situation had changed over night. Baron Neurath, the Conseiller of the German Embassy at Constantinople, had gone to Sofia, and, as a result of his visit, an agreement had been signed that would make Bulgaria Germany's ally.

Germany, said Weitz, had won over Bulgaria by doing something which the Entente had not been able and willing to do. It had secured her the possession at once of a piece of coveted territory. Serbia had refused to give Bulgaria immediate possession of Macedonia; Turkey, on the other hand, had now surrendered a piece of the Ottoman Empire. The amount of land in question, it is true, was apparently insignificant, yet it had great strategic advantages and represented a genuine sacrifice by Turkey. The Maritza River, a few miles north of Enos, bends to the east, to the north, and then to the west again, creating a block of territory, with an area of nearly 1,000 square miles, including the important cities of Demotica, Kara Agatch, and half of Adrianople. What makes this land particularly important is that it contains about fifty miles of the railroad which runs from Dedeagatch to Sofia. All this railroad, that is, except this fifty miles, is laid in Bulgarian territory; this short strip, extending through Turkey, cuts Bulgaria's communications with the Mediterranean. Naturally Bulgaria yearned for this piece of land; and Turkey now handed it over to her. This cession changed the whole Balkan situation and it made Bulgaria an ally of Turkey and the Central Powers. Besides the railroad, Bulgaria obtained that part of Adrianople which lay west of the Maritza River. In addition, of course, Bulgaria was to receive Macedonia, as soon as that province could be occupied by Bulgaria and her allies.

I vividly remember the exultation of Weitz when this agreement was signed.

"It's all settled," he told me. "Bulgaria has decided to join us. It was all arranged last night at Sofia."

The Turks also were greatly relieved. For the first time they saw the way out of their troubles. The Bulgarian arrangement, Enver told me, had taken a tremendous weight off their minds.

"We Turks are entitled to the credit," he said, "of bringing Bulgaria in on the side of the Central Powers. She would never have come to our assistance if we hadn't given her that slice of land. By surrendering it immediately and not waiting till the end of the war, we showed our good faith. It was very hard for us to do it, of course, especially to give up part of the city of Adrianople, but it was worth the price. We really surrendered this territory in exchange for Constantinople, for if Bulgaria had not come in on our side, we would have lost this city. Just think how enormously we have improved our position. We have had to keep more than 200,000 men at the Bulgarian frontier, to protect us against any possible attack from that quarter. We can now transfer all these troops to the Gallipoli peninsula, and thus make it absolutely impossible that the Allies' expedition can succeed. We are also greatly hampered at the Dardanelles by the lack of ammunition. But Bulgaria, Austria, and Germany are to make a joint attack on Serbia and will completely control that country in a few weeks. So we shall have a direct railroad line from Constantinople into Austria and Germany and can get all the war supplies which we need. With Bulgaria on our side no attack can be made on Constantinople from the north---we have created an impregnable bulwark against Russia. I do not deny that the situation had caused us great anxiety. We were afraid that Greece and Bulgaria would join hands, and that would also bring in Rumania. Then Turkey would have been lost; they would have had us between a pair of pincers. But now we have only one task before us, that is to drive the English and French at the Dardanelles into the sea. With all the soldiers and all the ammunition which we need, we shall do this in a very short time. We gave up a small area because we saw that that was the way to win the war."

The outcome justified Enver's prophecies in almost every detail. Three months after Bulgaria accepted the Adrianople bribe, the Entente admitted defeat and withdrew its forces from the Dardanelles; and, with this withdrawal, Russia, which was the greatest potential source of strength to the Allied cause and the country which, properly organized and supplied, might have brought the Allies a speedy triumph, disappeared as a vital factor in the war. When the British and French withdrew from Gallipoli that action turned adrift this huge hulk of a country to flounder to anarchy, dissolution, and ruin.

The Germans celebrated this great triumph in a way that was characteristically Teutonic. In their minds, January 17, 1916, stands out as one of the big dates in the war. There was great rejoicing in Constantinople, for the first Balkan express---or, as the Germans called it, the Balkanzug---was due to arrive that afternoon! The railroad station was decorated with flags and flowers, and the whole German and Austrian population of Constantinople, including the Embassy staffs, assembled to welcome the incoming train. As it finally rolled into the station, thousands of "hochs" went up from as many raucous throats.

Since that January 17, 1916, the Balkanzug has ran regularly from. Berlin to Constantinople. The Germans believe that it is as permanent a feature of the new Germanic Empire as the line from Berlin to Hamburg.

Chapter XXII - The Turk Reverts to the Ancestral Type

The withdrawal of the Allied fleet from the Dardanelles had consequences which the world does not yet completely understand. The practical effect of the event, as I have said, was to isolate the Turkish Empire from all the world excepting Germany and Austria. England, France, Russia, and Italy, which for a century had held a restraining hand over the Ottoman Empire, had finally lost all power to influence or control. The Turks now perceived that a series of dazzling events had changed them from cringing dependents of the European Powers into free agents. For the first time in two centuries they could now live their national life according to their own inclinations, and govern their peoples according to their own will. The first expression of this rejuvenated national life was an episode which, so far as I know, is the most terrible in the history of the world. New Turkey, freed from European tutelage, celebrated its national rebirth by murdering not far from a million of its own subjects.

I can hardly exaggerate the effect which the repulse of the Allied fleet produced upon the Turks. They believed that they had won the really great decisive battle of the war. For several centuries, they said, the British fleet had victoriously sailed the seas and had now met its first serious reverse at the hands of the Turks. In the first moments of their pride, the Young Turk leaders saw visions of the complete resurrection of their empire. What had for two centuries been a decaying nation had suddenly started on a new and glorious life. In their pride and arrogance the Turks began to look with disdain upon the people that had taught them what they knew of modern warfare, and nothing angered them so much as any suggestion that they owed any part of their success to their German allies.

"Why should we feel any obligation to the Germans? " Enver would say to me. "What have they done for us which compares with what we have done for them? They have lent us some money and sent us a few officers, it is true, but see what we have done! We have defeated the British fleet---something which neither the Germans nor any other nation could do. We have stationed armies on the Caucasian front, and so have kept busy large bodies of Russian troops that would have been used on the western front. Similarly we have compelled England to keep large armies in Egypt, in Mesopotamia, and in that way we have weakened the Allied armies in France. No, the Germans could never have achieved their military successes without us; the shoe of obligation is entirely on their foot."

This conviction possessed the leaders of the Union and Progress Party and now began to have a determining effect upon Turkish national life and Turkish policy. Essentially the Turk is a bully and a coward; he is brave as a lion when things are going his way, but cringing, abject, and nerveless when reverses are overwhelming him. And now that the fortunes of war were apparently favouring the empire, I began to see an entirely new Turk unfolding before my eyes. The hesitating and fearful Ottoman, feeling his way cautiously amid the mazes of European diplomacy, and seeking opportunities to find an advantage for himself in the divided counsels of the European powers, gave place to an upstanding, almost dashing figure, proud and assertive, determined to live his own life and absolutely contemptuous of his Christian foes. I was really witnessing a remarkable development in race psychology---an almost classical instance of reversion to type. The ragged, unkempt Turk of the twentieth century was vanishing and in his place was appearing the Turk of the fourteenth and the fifteenth, the Turk who had swept out of his Asiatic fastnesses, conquered all the powerful peoples in his way, and founded in Asia, Africa, and Europe one of the most extensive empires that history has known. If we are properly to appreciate this new Talaat and Enver and the events which now took place, we must understand the Turk who, under Osman and his successors, exercised this mighty but devastating influence in the world. We must realize that the basic fact underlying the Turkish mentality is its utter contempt for all other races. A fairly insane pride is the element that largely explains this strange human species. The common term applied by the Turk to the Christian is "dog," and in his estimation this is no mere rhetorical figure; he actually looks upon his European neighbours as far less worthy of consideration than his own domestic animals. "My son," an old Turk once said, "do you see that herd of swine? Some are white, some are black, some are large, some are small---they differ from each other in some respects, but they are all swine. So it is with Christians. Be not deceived, my son. These Christians may wear fine clothes, their women may be very beautiful to look upon; their skins are white and splendid; many of them are very intelligent and they build wonderful cities and create what seem to be great states. But remember that underneath all this dazzling exterior they are all the same---they are, all swine."

Practically all foreigners, while in the presence of a Turk, are conscious of this attitude. The Turk may be obsequiously polite, but there is invariably an almost unconscious. feeling that he is mentally shrinking from his Christian friend as something unclean. And this fundamental conviction for centuries directed the Ottoman policy toward its subject peoples. This wild horde swept from the plains of Central Asia and, like a whirlwind, overwhelmed the nations of Mesopotamia and Asia Minor; it conquered Egypt, Arabia, and practically all of northern Africa and then poured into Europe, crushed the Balkan nations, occupied a large part of Hungary, and even established the outposts of the Ottoman Empire in the southern part of Russia. So far as I can discover, the Ottoman Turks had only one great quality, that of military genius. They had several military leaders of commanding ability, and the early conquering Turks were brave, fanatical, and tenacious fighters, just as their descendants are today. I think that these old Turks present the most complete illustration in history of the brigand idea in politics. They were lacking in what we may call the fundamentals of a civilized community. They had no alphabet and no art of writing; no books, no poets, no art, and no architecture; they built no cities and they established no lasting state. They knew no law except the rule of might, and they had practically no agriculture and no industrial organization. They were simply wild and marauding horsemen, whose one conception of tribal success was to pounce upon people who were more civilized than themselves and plunder them. In the fourteenth and fifteenth centuries these tribes overran the cradles of modern civilization, which have given Europe its religion and, to a large extent, its civilization. At that time these territories were the seats of many peaceful and prosperous nations. The Mesopotamian valley supported a large industrious agricultural population; Bagdad was one of the largest and most flourishing cities in existence; Constantinople had a greater population than Rome, and the Balkan region and Asia Minor contained several powerful states. Over all this part of the world the Turk now swept as a huge, destructive force. Mesopotamia in a few years became a desert; the great cities of the Near East were reduced to misery, and the subject peoples became slaves. Such graces of civilization as the Turk has acquired in five centuries have practically all been taken from the subject peoples whom he so greatly despises. His religion comes from the Arabs; his language has acquired a certain literary value by borrowing certain Arabic and Persian elements; and his writing is Arabic. Constantinople's finest architectural monument, the Mosque of St. Sophia, was originally a Christian church, and all so-called Turkish architecture is derived from the Byzantine. The mechanism of business and industry has always rested in the hands of the subject peoples, Greeks, Jews, Armenians, and Arabs. The Turks have learned little of European art or science, they have established very few educational institutions, and illiteracy is the prevailing rule.

The result is that poverty has attained a degree of sordidness and misery in the Ottoman Empire which is almost unparalleled elsewhere. The Turkish peasant lives in a mud hut; he sleeps on a dirt floor; he has no chairs, no tables, no eating utensils, no clothes except the few scant garments which cover his back and which he usually wears for many years.

In the course of time these Turks might learn certain things from their European and Arab neighbours, but there was one idea which they could never even faintly grasp. They could not understand. that a conquered people were anything except slaves. When they took possession of a land, they found it occupied by a certain number of camels, horses, buffaloes., dogs, swine, and human beings. Of all these living things the object that physically most resembled themselves they regarded as the least important. It became a common saying with them that a horse or a camel was far more valuable than a man; these animals cost money, whereas "infidel Christians" were plentiful in the Ottoman countries and could easily be forced to labour. It is true that the early Sultans gave the subject peoples and the Europeans in the empire certain rights, but these in themselves really reflected the contempt in which all non-Moslems were held. I have already described the "Capitulations," under which foreigners in Turkey had their own courts, prisons, post offices, and other institutions. Yet the early sultans gave these privileges not from a spirit of tolerance, but merely because they looked upon the Christian nations as unclean and therefore unfit to have any contact with the Ottoman administrative and judicial system. The sultans similarly erected the several peoples, such as the Greeks and the Armenians, into separate "millets," or nations, not because they desired to promote their independence and welfare, but because they regarded them as vermin, and therefore disqualified for membership in the Ottoman state. The attitude of the Government toward their Christian subjects was illustrated by certain regulations which limited their freedom of action. The buildings in which Christians lived should not be conspicuous and their churches should have no belfry. Christians could not ride a horse in the city, for that was the exclusive right of the noble Moslem. The Turk had the right to test the sharpness of his sword upon the neck of any Christian.

Imagine a great government year in and year out maintaining this attitude toward many millions of its own subjects! And for centuries the Turks simply lived like parasites upon these overburdened and industrious people. They taxed them to economic extinction, stole their most beautiful daughters and forced them into their harems, took Christian male infants by the hundreds of thousands and brought them up as Moslem soldiers. I have no intention of describing the terrible vassalage and oppression that went on for five centuries; my purpose is merely to emphasize this innate attitude of the Moslem Turk to people not of his own race and religion---that they are not human beings with rights, but merely chattels, which may be permitted to live when they promote the interest of their masters, but which may be pitilessly destroyed when they have ceased to be useful. This attitude is intensified by a total disregard for human life and an intense delight in inflicting physical human suffering which are not unusually the qualities of primitive peoples.

Such were the mental characteristics of the Turk in his days of military greatness. In recent times his attitude toward foreigners and his subject peoples had superficially changed. His own military decline and the ease with which the infidel nations defeated his finest armies bad apparently given the haughty descendants of Osman a respect at least for their prowess. The rapid disappearance of his own empire in a hundred years, the creation out of the Ottoman Empire of new states like Greece, Serbia, Bulgaria, and Rumania, and the wonderful improvement which had followed the destruction of the Turkish yoke in these benighted lands, may have increased the Ottoman hatred for the unbeliever, but at least they had a certain influence in opening his eyes to his importance. Many Turks also now received their education in European universities; they studied in their professional schools, and they became physicians, surgeons, lawyers, engineers, and chemists of the modern kind. However much the more progressive Moslems might despise their Christian associates, they could not ignore the fact that the finest things, in this temporal world at least, were the products of European and American civilization.

And now that one development of modern history which seemed to be least understandable to the Turk began to force itself upon the consciousness of the more intelligent and progressive. Certain leaders arose who began to speak surreptitiously of such things as "Constitutionalism," "Liberty," "Self-government," and to whom the Declaration of Independence contained certain truths that might have a value even for Islam. These daring spirits began to dream of overturning the autocratic Sultan and of substituting a parliamentary system for his irresponsible rule. I have already described the rise and fall of this Young Turk movement under such leaders as Talaat, Enver, Djemal, and their associates in the Committee of Union and Progress. The point which I am emphasizing here is that this movement presupposed a complete transformation of Turkish mentality, especially in its attitude toward subject peoples. No longer, under the reformed Turkish state, were Greeks, Syrians, Armenians, and Jews to be regarded as " filthy giaours." All these peoples were henceforth to have equal rights and equal duties. A general love feast now followed the establishment of the new r?gime, and scenes of almost frenzied reconciliation, in which Turks and Armenians embraced each other publicly, apparently signalized the absolute union of the long antagonistic peoples. The Turkish leaders, including Talaat and Enver, visited Christian churches and sent forth prayers of thanksgiving for the new order, and went to Armenian cemeteries to shed tears of retribution over the bones of the martyred Armenians who lay there. Armenian priests reciprocally paid their tributes to the Turks in Mohammedan mosques. Enver Pasha visited several Armenian schools, telling the children that the old days of Moslem-Christian strife had passed forever and that the two peoples were now to live together as brothers and sisters. There were cynics who smiled at all these demonstrations and yet one development encouraged even them to believe that an earthly paradise had arrived. All through the period of domination only the master Moslem had been permitted to bear arms and serve in the Ottoman army. To be a soldier was an occupation altogether too manly and glorious for the despised Christian. But now the Young Turks encouraged all Christians to arm, and enrolled them in the army on an equality with Moslems. These Christians fought, both as officers and soldiers, in the Italian and the Balkan wars, winning high praise from the Turkish generals for their valour and skill. Armenian leaders had figured conspicuously in the Young Turk movement; these men apparently believed that a constitutional Turkey was possible. They were conscious of their own intellectual and industrial superiority to the Turks, and knew that they could prosper in the Ottoman Empire if left alone, whereas, under European control, they would have greater difficulty in meeting the competition of the more rigorous

European colonists who might come in. With the deposition of the Red Sultan, Abdul Hamid, and the establishment of a constitutional system, the Armenians now for the first time in several centuries felt themselves to be free men.

But, as I have already described, all these aspirations vanished like a dream. Long before the European War began, the Turkish democracy had disappeared. The power of the new Sultan had gone, and the hopes of regenerating Turkey on modern lines had gone also, leaving only a group of individuals, headed by Talaat and Enver, actually in possession of the state. Having lost their democratic aspirations these men now supplanted them with a new national conception. In place of a democratic constitutional state they resurrected the idea of Pan-Turkism; in place of equal treatment of all Ottomans, they decided to establish a country exclusively for Turks. I have called this a new conception; yet it was new only to the individuals who then controlled the destiny of the empire, for, in reality, it was simply an attempt to revive the most barbaric ideas of their ancestors. It represented, as I have said, merely an atavistic reversion to the original Turk. We now saw that the Turkish leaders, in talking about liberty, equality, fraternity, and constitutionalism, were merely children repeating phrases; that they had used the word "democracy" merely as a ladder by which to climb to power. After five hundred years' close contact with European civilization, the Turk remained precisely the same individual as the one who had emerged from the steppes of Asia in the Middle Ages. He was clinging just as tenaciously as his ancestors to that conception of a state as consisting of a few master individuals whose right it is to enslave and plunder and maltreat any peoples whom they can subject to their military control. Though Talaat and Enver and Djemal all came of the humblest families, the same fundamental ideas of master and slave possessed them that formed the statecraft of Osman and the early Sultans. We now discovered that a paper constitution and even tearful visits to Christian churches and cemeteries could not uproot the inborn preconception of this nomadic tribe that there are only two kinds of people in the world---the conquering and the conquered.

When the Turkish Government abrogated the Capitulations, and in this way freed themselves from the domination of the foreign powers, they were merely taking one step toward realizing this Pan-Turkish ideal. I have alluded to the difficulties which I had with them over the Christian schools. Their determination to uproot these, or at least to transform them into Turkish institutions, was merely another detail in the same racial progress. Similarly, they attempted to make all foreign business houses employ only Turkish labour, insisting that they should discharge their Greek, Armenian, and Jewish clerks, stenographers, workmen, and other employees. They ordered all foreign houses to keep their books in Turkish; they wanted to furnish employment for Turks, and enable them to acquire modern business methods. The Ottoman Government even refused to have any dealings with the representative of the largest Austrian munition maker unless he admitted a Turk as a partner. They developed a mania for suppressing all languages except Turkish. For decades French had been the accepted language of foreigners in Constantinople; most street signs were printed in both French and Turkish. One morning the astonished foreign residents discovered that all these French signs had been removed and that the names of streets, the directions on street cars, and other public notices, appeared only in those strange Turkish characters, which very few of them understood. Great confusion re-

130

sulted from this change, but the ruling powers refused to restore the detested foreign language.

These leaders not only reverted to the barbaric conceptions of their ancestors, but they went to extremes that had never entered the minds of the early sultans. Their fifteenth and sixteenth century predecessors treated the subject peoples as dirt under their feet, yet they believed that they had a certain usefulness and did not disdain to make them their slaves. But this Committee of Union and Progress, led by Talaat and Enver, now decided to do away with them altogether. The old conquering Turks had made the Christians their servants, but their parvenu descendants bettered their instruction, for they determined to exterminate them wholesale and Turkify the empire by massacring the non-Moslem elements. Originally this was not the statesmanlike conception of Talaat and Enver; the man who first devised it was one of the greatest monsters known to history, the "Red Sultan", Abdul Hamid. This man came to the throne in 1876, at a critical period in Turkish history. In the first two years of his reign, he lost Bulgaria as well as important provinces in the Caucasus, his last remaining vestiges of sovereignty in Montenegro, Serbia, and Rumania, and all his real powers in Bosnia and Herzegovina. Greece had long since become an independent nation, and the processes that were to wrench Egypt from the Ottoman Empire had already began. As the Sultan took stock of his inheritance, he could easily foresee the day when all the rest of his domain would pass into the hand of the infidel. What had caused this disintegration of this extensive Turkish Empire? The real cause, of course, lay deep in the character of the Turk, but Abdul Hamid saw only the more obvious fact that the intervention of the great European Powers had brought relief to these imprisoned nations. Of all the new kingdoms which had been carved out of the Sultan's dominions, Serbia---let us remember this fact to her everlasting honour---is the only one that has won her own independence. Russia, France, and Great Britain have set free all the rest. And what had happened several times before might happen again. There still remained one compact race in the Ottoman Empire that had national aspirations and national potentialities. In the northeastern part of Asia Minor, bordering on Russia, there were six provinces in which the Armenians formed the largest element in the population. From the time of Herodotus this portion of Asia has borne the name of Armenia. The Armenians of the present day are the direct descendants of the people who inhabited the country three thousand years ago. Their origin is so ancient that it is lost in fable and mystery. There are still undeciphered cuneiform inscriptions on the rocky hills of Van, the, largest Armenian city, that have led certain scholars---though not many, I must admit---to identify the Armenian race with the Hittites of the Bible. What is definitely known about the Armenians, however, is that for ages they have constituted the most civilized and most industrious race in the eastern section of the Ottoman Empire. From their mountains they have spread over the Sultan's dominions, and form a considerable element in the population of all the large cities. Everywhere they are known for their industry, their intelligence, and their decent and orderly lives. They are so superior to the Turks intellectually and morally that much of the business and industry had passed into their hands. With the Greeks, the Armenians constitute the economic strength of the empire. These people became Christians in the fourth century and established the Armenian Church as their state religion. This is said to be the oldest Christian Church in existence.

In face of persecutions which have had no parallel elsewhere these people have clung to their early Christian faith with the utmost tenacity. For fifteen hundred years they have lived there in Armenia, a little island of Christians surrounded by backward peoples of hostile religion and hostile race. Their long existence has been one unending martyrdom. The territory which they inhabit forms the connecting link between Europe and Asia, and all the Asiatic invasions---Saracens, Tartars, Mongols, Kurds, and Turks---have passed over their peaceful country. For centuries they have thus been the Belgium of the East. Through all this period the Armenians have regarded themselves not as Asiatics, but as Europeans. They speak an Indo-European language, their racial origin is believed by scholars to be Aryan, and the fact that their religion is the religion of Europe has always made them turn their eyes westward. And out of that western country, they have always hoped, would some day come the deliverance that would rescue them from their murderous masters. And now, as Abdul Hamid, in 1876, surveyed his shattered domain, he saw that its most dangerous spot was Armenia. He believed, rightly or wrongly, that these Armenians, like the Rumanians, the Bulgarians, the Greeks, and the Serbians, aspired to restore their independent medieval nation, and he knew that Europe and America sympathized with this ambition. The Treaty of Berlin, which had definitely ended the Turco-Russian War, contained an article which gave the European Powers a protecting hand over the Armenians. How could the Sultan free himself permanently from this danger? An enlightened administration, which would have transformed the Armenians into free men and made them safe in their lives and property and civil and religious rights, would probably have made them peaceful and loyal subjects. But the Sultan could not rise to such a conception of statesmanship as this. Instead, Abdul Hamid apparently thought that there was only one way of ridding Turkey of the Armenian problem--- and that was to rid her of the Armenians. The physical destruction of 2,000,000 men, women, and children by massacres, organized and directed by the state, seemed to be the one sure way of forestalling the further disruption of the Turkish Empire.

And now for nearly thirty years Turkey gave the world an illustration of government by massacre. We in Europe and America heard of these events when they reached especially monstrous proportions, as they did in 1895-96, when nearly 200,000 Armenians were most atrociously done to death. But through all these years the existence of the Armenians was one continuous nightmare. Their property was stolen, their men were murdered, their women were ravished, their young girls were kidnapped and forced to live in Turkish harems. Yet Abdul Hamid was not able to accomplish his full purpose. Had he had his will, he would have massacred the whole nation in one hideous orgy. He attempted to exterminate the Armenians in 1895 and 1896, but found certain insuperable obstructions to his scheme. Chief of these were England, France, and Russia. These atrocities called Gladstone, then eighty-six years old, from his retirement, and his speeches, in which he denounced the Sultan as "the great assassin," aroused the whole world to the enormities that were taking place. It became apparent that unless the Sultan desisted, England, France, and Russia would intervene, and the Sultan well knew, that, in case this intervention took place, such remnants of Turkey as had survived earlier partitions would disappear. Thus Abdul Hamid had to abandon his satanic enterprise of destroying a whole race by murder, yet Armenia continued to suffer the slow agony of pitiless persecution. Up to the outbreak of the European War not a day had passed in the Armenian vilayets without its outrages and its murders. The Young Turk r?gime, despite its promises of universal brotherhood, brought no respite to the Armenians. A few months after the love feastings already described, one of the worst massacres took place at Adana, in which 35,000 people were destroyed.

And now the Young Turks, who had adopted so many of Abdul Hamid's ideas, also made his Armenian policy their own. Their passion for Turkifying the nation seemed to demand logically the extermination of all Christians---Greeks, Syrians, and Armenians. Much as they admired the Mohammedan conquerors of the fifteenth and sixteenth centuries, they stupidly believed that these great warriors had made one fatal mistake, for they had had it in their power completely to obliterate the Christian populations and had neglected to do so. This policy in their opinion was a fatal error of statesmanship and explained all the woes from which Turkey has suffered in modern times. Had these old Moslem chieftains, when they conquered Bulgaria, put, all the Bulgarians to the sword, and peopled the Bulgarian country with Moslem Turks, there would never have been any modern Bulgarian problem and Turkey would never have lost this part of her empire. Similarly, had they destroyed all the Rumanians, Serbians, and Greeks, the provinces which are now occupied by these races would still have remained integral parts of the Sultan's domain. They felt that the mistake had been a terrible one, but that something might be saved from the ruin. They would destroy all Greeks, Syrians, Armenians, and other Christians, move Moslem families into their homes and into their farms, and so make sure that these territories would not similarly be taken away from Turkey. In order to accomplish this great reform, it would not be necessary to murder every living Christian. The most beautiful and healthy Armenian girls could be taken, converted forcibly to Mohammedanism, and made the wives or concubines of devout followers of the Prophet. Their children would then automatically become Moslems and so strengthen the empire, as the Janissaries had strengthened it formerly. These Armenian girls represent a high type of womanhood and the Young Turks, in their crude, intuitive way, recognized that the mingling of their blood with the Turkish population would exert a eugenic influence upon the whole. Armenian boys of tender years could be taken into Turkish families and be brought up in ignorance of the fact that they were anything but Moslems. These were about the only elements, however, that could make any valuable contributions to the new Turkey which was now being planned. Since all precautions must be taken against the development of a new generation of Armenians, it would be necessary to kill outright all men who were in their prime and thus capable of propagating the accursed species. Old men and women formed no great danger to the future of Turkey, for they had already fulfilled their natural function of leaving descendants; still they were nuisances and therefore should be disposed of.

Unlike Abdul Hamid, the Young Turks found themselves in a position where they could carry out this holy enterprise. Great Britain, France, and Russia had stood in the way of their predecessor. But now these obstacles had been removed. The Young Turks, as I have said, believed that they had defeated these nations and that they could therefore no longer interfere with their internal affairs. Only one power could successfully raise objections and that was Germany. In 1898, when all the rest of Europe was ringing with Gladstone's denunciations and demanding intervention, Kaiser Wilhelm the Second had gone to Constantinople, visited Abdul Hamid, pinned his finest decorations on that bloody tyrant's breast, and kissed him on both cheeks. The same Kaiser who had done this in 1898 was still sitting on the throne in 1915, and was now Turkey's ally. Thus for the first time in two centuries the Turks, in 1915, had their Christian populations utterly at their mercy. The time had finally come to make Turkey exclusively the country of the Turks.

Chapter XXIII - The "Revolution" at Van

The Turkish province of Van lies in the remote northeastern corner of Asia Minor; it touches the frontiers of Persia on the east and its northern boundary looks toward the Caucasus. It is one of the most beautiful and most fruitful parts of the Turkish Empire and one of the richest in historical associations. The city of Van, which is the capital of the vilayet, lies on the eastern shores of the lake of the same name; it is the one large town in Asia Minor in which the Armenian population is larger than the Moslem.

In the fall of 1914, its population of about 30,000 people represented one of the most peaceful and happy and prosperous communities in the Turkish Empire. Though Van, like practically every other section where Armenians lived, had had its periods of oppression and massacre, yet the Moslem yoke, comparatively speaking, rested upon its people rather lightly. Its Turkish governor, Tahsin Pasha, was one of the more enlightened type of Turkish officials. Relations between the Armenians, who lived in the better section of the city, and the Turks and the Kurds, who occupied the mud huts in the Moslem quarter, had been tolerably agreeable for many years.

The location of this vilayet, however, inevitably made it the scene of military operations, and made the activities of its Armenian population a matter of daily suspicion. Should Russia attempt an invasion of Turkey one of the most accessible routes lay through this province. The war had not gone far when causes of irritation arose. The requisitions of army supplies fell far more heavily upon the Christian than upon the Mohammedan elements in Van, just as they did in every other part of Turkey. The Armenians had to stand quietly by while the Turkish officers appropriated all their cattle, all their wheat, and all their goods of every kind, giving them only worthless pieces of paper in exchange. The attempt at general disarmament that took place also aroused their apprehension, which was increased by the brutal treatment visited upon Armenian soldiers in the Caucasus. On the other hand, the Turks made many charges against the Christian population, and, in fact, they attributed to them the larger share of the blame for the reverses which the Turkish armies had suffered in the Caucasus. The fact that a considerable element in the already changed forces was composed of Armenians aroused their unbridled wrath. Since about half the Armenians in the world inhabit the Russian provinces in the Caucasus and are liable, like all Russians, to military service, there were certainly no legitimate grounds for complaint, so far as these Armenian levies were bona fide subjects of the Czar. But the Turks asserted that large numbers of Armenian soldiers in Van and other of their Armenian provinces deserted, crossed the border, and joined the Russian army, where their knowledge of roads and the terrain was an important factor in the Russian victories. Though the exact facts are not yet ascertained, it seems not unlikely that such desertions, perhaps a few hundred, did take place. At the beginning of the war, Union and Progress agents appeared in Erzeroum and Van and appealed to the Armenian leaders to go into Russian Armenia and attempt to start revolutions against the Russian Government; and the fact that the Ottoman Armenians refused to do this contributed further to the prevailing irritation. The Turkish Government has made much of the "treasonable" behaviour of the Armenians of Van and have even urged it as an excuse for their subsequent treatment of the whole race. Their attitude illustrates once more the perversity of the Turkish mind. After massacring hundreds of thousands of Armenians in the course of thirty years, outraging their women and girls, and robbing and maltreating them in every conceivable way, the Turks still apparently believed that they had the right to expect from them the most enthusiastic "loyalty". That the Armenians all over Turkey sympathized with the Entente was no secret. "If you want to know how the war is going," wrote a humorous Turkish newspaper, "all you need to do is to look in the face of an Armenian. If he is smiling, then the Allies are winning; if he is downcast, then the Germans are successful." If an Ottoman Armenian soldier should desert and join the Russians, that would unquestionably constitute a technical crime against the state, and might be punished without violating the rules of all civilized countries. Only the Turkish mind, however---and possibly the Junker---could regard it as furnishing an excuse for the terrible barbarities that now took place.

Though the air, all during the autumn and winter of 1914-15, was filled with premonitions of trouble, the Armenians behaved with remarkable self-restraint. For years it had been the Turkish policy to provoke the Christian population into committing overt acts, and then seizing upon such misbehaviour as an excuse for massacres. The Armenian clergy and political leaders saw many evidences that the Turks were now up to their old tactics, and they therefore went among the people, cautioning them to keep quiet, to bear all insults and even outrages patiently, so as not to give the Moslems the opening which they were seeking. "Even though they burn a few of our villages," these leaders would say, "do not retaliate, for it is better that a few be destroyed than that the whole nation be massacred."

When the war started, the Central Government recalled Tahsin Pasha, the conciliatory governor of Van, and replaced him with Djevdet Bey, a brother-in-law of Enver Pasha. This act in itself was most disquieting. Turkish officialdom has always contained a minority of men who do not believe in massacre as a state policy and cannot be depended upon to carry out strictly the most bloody orders of the Central Government. Whenever massacres have been planned, therefore, it has been customary first to remove such "untrustworthy" public servants and replace them by men who are regarded as more reliable. The character of Tahsin's successor made his displacement still more alarming. Djevdet had spent the larger part of his life at Van; he was a man of unstable character, friendly to non-Moslems one moment, hostile the next, hypocritical, treacherous, and ferocious according to the worst traditions of his race. He hated the Armenians and cordially sympathized with the long-established Turkish plan of solving the Armenian problem. There is little question that he came to Van with definite instructions to exterminate all Armenians in this province, but, for the first few months, conditions did not facilitate such operations. Djevdet himself was absent fighting the Russians in the Caucasus and the near approach of the enemy made it a wise policy for the Turks to refrain from maltreating the Armenians of Van. But early in the spring the Russians temporarily retreated. It is generally recognized as good military tactics for a victorious army to follow up the retreating enemy. In the eyes of the Turkish generals, however, the withdrawal of the Russians was a happy turn of war mainly because it deprived the Armenians of their protectors and left them at the mercies of the Turkish army. Instead of following the retreating foe, therefore, the Turks' army turned aside and invaded their own territory of Van. Instead of fighting the trained Russian army of men, they turned their rifles, machine guns, and other weapons upon the Armenian women, children, and old men in the villages of Van. Following their usual custom, they distributed the most beautiful Armenian women among the Moslems, sacked and burned the Armenian villages, and massacred uninterruptedly for days. On April 15th, about 500 young Armenian men of Akantz were mustered to hear an order of the Sultan; at sunset they were marched outside the town and every man shot in cold blood. This procedure was repeated in about eighty Armenian villages in the district north of Lake Van, and in three days 24,000 Armenians were murdered in this atrocious fashion. A single episode illustrates the unspeakable depravity of Turkish methods. A conflict having broken out at Shadak, Djevdet Bey, who had meanwhile returned to Van, asked four of the leading Armenian citizens to go to this town and attempt to quiet the multitude. These men made the trip, stopping at all Armenian villages along the way, urging everybody to keep public order. After completing their work these four Armenians were murdered in a Kurdish village.

And so when Djevdet Bey, on his return to his official post, demanded that Van furnish him immediately 4,000 soldiers, the people were naturally in no mood to accede to his request. When we consider what had happened before and what happened subsequently, there remains little doubt concerning the purpose which underlay this demand. Djevdet, acting in obedience to orders from Constantinople, was preparing to wipe out the whole population, and his purpose in calling for 4,000 able-bodied men was merely to massacre them, so that the rest of the Armenians might have no defenders. The Armenians, parleying to gain time, offered to furnish five hundred soldiers and to pay exemption money for the rest; now, however, Djevdet began to talk aloud about "rebellion," and his determination to "crush" it at any cost. "If the rebels fire a single shot," he declared, "I shall kill every Christian man, woman, and" (pointing to his knee) "every child, up to here." For sometime the Turks had been constructing entrenchments around the Armenian quarter and filling them with soldiers and, in response to this provocation, the Armenians began to make preparations for a defense. On April 20th, a band of Turkish soldiers seized several Armenian women who were entering the city; a couple of Armenians ran to their assistance and were shot dead, The Turks now opened fire on the Armenian quarters with rifles and artillery; soon a large part of the town was in flames and a regular siege had started. The whole Armenian fighting force consisted of only 1,500 men; they had only 300 rifles and a most inadequate supply of ammunition, while Djevdet had an army of 5,000 men, completely equipped and supplied. Yet the Armenians fought with the utmost heroism and skill; they had little chance of holding off their enemies indefinitely, but they knew that a Russian army was fighting its way to Van and their utmost hope was that they would be able to defy the besiegers until these Russians arrived. As I am not writing the story of sieges and battles, I cannot describe in detail the numerous acts of individual heroism, the cooperation of the Armenian women, the ardour and energy of the Armenian children, the self-sacrificing zeal of the American missionaries, especially Doctor Ussher and his wife and Miss Grace H. Knapp, and the thousand other circumstances that made this terrible month one of the most glorious pages in modern Armenian history. The wonderful thing about it is that the Armenians triumphed. After nearly five weeks of sleepless fighting, the Russian army suddenly appeared and the Turks fled into the surrounding country, where they found appeasement for their anger by further massacres of unprotected Armenian villagers. Doctor Ussher, the American medical missionary whose hospital at Van was destroyed by bombardment, is authority for the statement that, after driving off the Turks, the Russians began to collect and to cremate the bodies of Armenians who had been murdered in the province, with the result that 55,000 bodies were burned.

I have told this story of the "Revolution" in Van not only because it marked the first stage in this organized attempt to wipe out a whole nation, but because these events are always brought forward by the Turks as a justification of their subsequent crimes. As I shall relate, Enver, Talaat, and the rest, when I appealed to them in behalf of the Armenians, invariably instanced the "revolutionists" of Van as a sample of Armenian treachery. The famous "Revolution," as this recital shows, was merely the determination of the Armenians to save their women's honour and their own lives, after the Turks, by massacring thousands of their neighbours, had shown them the fate that awaited them.

Chapter XXIV - The Murder of a Nation

The destruction of the Armenian race in 1915 involved certain difficulties that had not impeded the operations of the Turks in the massacres of 1895 and other years. In these earlier periods the Armenian men had possessed little power or means of resistance. In those days Armenians had not been permitted to have military training, to serve in the Turkish army, or to possess arms. As I have already said, these discriminations were withdrawn when the revolutionists obtained the upper hand in 1908. Not only were the Christians now permitted to bear arms, but the authorities, in the full flush of their enthusiasm for freedom and equality, encouraged them to do so. In the early part of 1915, therefore, every Turkish city contained thousands of Armenians who had been trained as soldiers and who were supplied with rifles, pistols, and other weapons of defense. The operations at Van once more disclosed that these men could use their weapons to good advantage. It was thus apparent that an Armenian massacre this time would generally assume more the character of warfare than those wholesale butcheries of defenseless men and women which the Turks had always found so congenial. If this plan of murdering a race were to succeed, two preliminary steps would therefore have to be taken: it would be necessary to render all Armenian soldiers powerless and to deprive of their arms the Armenians in every city and town. Before Armenia could be slaughtered, Armenia must be made defenseless.

In the early part of 1915, the Armenian soldiers in the Turkish army were reduced to a new status. Up to that time most of them had been combatants, but now they were all stripped of their arms and transformed into workmen. Instead of serving their country as artillerymen and cavalrymen, these former soldiers now discovered that they had been transformed into road labourers and pack animals. Army supplies of all kinds were loaded on their backs, and, stumbling under the burdens and driven by the whips and bayonets of the Turks, they were forced to drag their weary bodies into the mountains of the Caucasus. Sometimes they would have to plough their way, burdened in this fashion, almost waist high through snow. They had to spend practically all their time in the open, sleeping on the bare ground---whenever the ceaseless prodding of their taskmasters gave them an occasional opportunity to sleep. They were given only scraps of food; if they fell sick they were left where they had dropped, their Turkish oppressors perhaps stopping long enough to rob them of all their possessions---even of their clothes. If any stragglers succeeded in reaching their destinations, they were not infrequently massacred. In many instances Armenian soldiers were disposed of in even more summary fashion, for it now became almost the general practice to shoot them in cold blood. In almost all cases the procedure was the same. Here and there squads of 50 or 100 men would be taken, bound together in groups of four, and then marched out to a secluded spot a short distance from the village. Suddenly the sound of rifle shots would fill the air, and the Turkish soldiers who had acted as the escort would sullenly return to camp. Those sent to bury the bodies would find them almost invariably stark naked, for, as usual, the Turks had stolen all their clothes. In cases that came to my attention, the murderers had added a refinement to their victims' sufferings by compelling them to dig their graves before being shot.

Let me relate a single episode which is contained in one of the reports of our consuls and which now forms part of the records of the American State Department. Early in July, 2,000 Armenian "ameles" (such is the Turkish word for soldiers who have been reduced to workmen) were sent from Harpoot to build roads. The Armenians in that town understood what this meant and pleaded with the Governor for mercy. But this official insisted that the men were not to be harmed, and he even called upon the German missionary, Mr. Ehemann, to quiet the panic, giving that gentleman his word of honour that the ex-soldiers would be protected. Mr. Ehemann believed the Governor and assuaged the popular fear. Yet practically every man of these 2,000 was massacred, and his body thrown into a cave. A few escaped, and it was from these that news of the massacre reached the world. A few days afterward another 2,000 soldiers were sent to Diarbekir. The only purpose of sending these men out in the open country was that they might be massacred. In order that they might have no strength to resist or to escape by flight, these poor creatures were systematically starved. Government agents went ahead on the road, notifying the Kurds that the caravan was approaching and ordering them to do their congenial duty. Not only did the Kurdish tribesmen pour down from the mountains upon this starved and weakened regiment, but the Kurdish women came with butcher's knives in order that they might gain that merit in Allah's eyes that comes from killing a Christian. These massacres were not isolated happenings; I could detail many more episodes just as horrible as the one related above; throughout the Turkish Empire a systematic attempt was made to kill all able-bodied men, not only for the purpose of removing all males who might propagate a new generation of Armenians, but for the purpose of rendering the weaker part of the population an easy prey.

Dreadful as were these massacres of unarmed soldiers, they were mercy and justice themselves when compared with the treatment which was now visited upon those Armenians who were suspected of concealing arms. Naturally the Christians became alarmed when placards were posted in the villages and cities ordering everybody to bring their arms to headquarters. Although this order applied to all citizens, the Armenians well understood what the result would be, should they be left defenseless while their Moslem neighbours were permitted to retain their arms. In many cases, however, the persecuted people patiently obeyed the command; and then the Turkish officials almost joyfully seized their rifles as evidence that a "revolution" was being planned and threw their victims into prison on a charge of treason. Thousands failed to deliver arms simply because they had none to deliver, while an even greater number tenaciously refused to give them up, not because they were plotting an uprising, but because they proposed to defend their own lives and their women's honour against the outrages which they knew were being planned. The punishment inflicted upon these recalcitrants forms one of the most hideous chapters of modern history. Most of us believe that torture has long ceased to be an administrative and judicial measure, yet I do not believe that the darkest ages ever presented scenes more horrible than those which now took place all over Turkey. Nothing was sacred to the Turkish gendarmes; under the plea of searching for hidden arms, they ransacked churches, treated the altars and sacred utensils with the utmost indignity, and even held mock ceremonies in imitation of the Christian sacraments. They would beat the priests into insensibility, under the pretense that they were the centres of sedition. When they could discover no weapons in the churches, they would sometimes arm the bishops and priests with guns, pistols, and swords, then try them before courts-martial for possessing weapons against the law, and march them in this condition through the streets, merely to arouse the fanatical wrath of the mobs. The gendarmes treated women with the same cruelty and indecency as the men. There are cases on record in which women accused of concealing weapons were stripped naked and whipped with branches freshly cut from trees, and these beatings were even inflicted on women who were with child. Violations so commonly accompanied these searches that Armenian women and girls, on the approach of the gendarmes, would flee to the woods, the hills, or to mountain eaves.

As a preliminary to the searches everywhere, the strong men of the villages and towns were arrested and taken to prison. Their tormentors here would exercise the most diabolical ingenuity in their attempt to make their victims declare themselves to be "revolutionists" and to tell the hiding places of their arms. A common practice was to place the prisoner in a room, with two Turks stationed at each end and each side. The examination would then begin with the bastinado. This is a form of torture not uncommon in the Orient; it consists of beating the soles of the feet with a thin rod. At first the pain is not marked; but as the process goes slowly on, it develops into the most terrible agony, the feet swell and burst, and not infrequently, after being submitted to this treatment, they have to be amputated. The gendarmes would bastinado their Armenian victim until he fainted; they would then revive him by sprinkling water on his face and begin again. If this did not succeed in bringing their victim to terms, they had numerous other methods of persuasion. They would pull out his eyebrows and beard almost hair by hair; they would extract his finger nails and toe nails; they would apply red-hot irons to his breast, tear off his flesh with red-hot pincers, and then pour boiled butter into the wounds. In some cases the gendarmes would nail hands and feet to pieces of wood---evidently in imitation of the Crucifixion, and then, while the sufferer writhed in his agony, they would cry: " Now let your Christ come and help you!

These cruelties---and many others which I forbear to describe---were usually inflicted in the night time. Turks would be stationed around the prisons, beating drums and blowing whistles, so that the screams of the sufferers would not reach the villagers.

In thousands of cases the Armenians endured these agonies and refused to surrender their arms simply because they had none to surrender. However, they could not persuade their tormentors that this was the case. It therefore became customary, when news was received that the searchers were approaching, for Armenians to purchase arms from their Turkish neighbours so that they might be able to give them up and escape these frightful punishments.

One day I was discussing these proceedings with a responsible Turkish official, who was describing the tortures inflicted. He made no secret of the fact that the Government had instigated them, and, like an Turks of the official classes, he enthusiastically approved this treatment of the detested race. This official told me that all these details were matters of nightly discussion at the headquarters of the Union and Progress Committee. Each new method of inflicting pain was hailed as a splendid discovery, and the regular attendants were constantly ransacking their brains in the effort to devise some new torment. He told me that they even delved into the records of the Spanish Inquisition and other historic institutions of torture and adopted all the suggestions found there. He did not tell me who carried off the prize in this gruesome competition, but common reputation throughout Armenia gave a preeminent infamy to Djevdet Bey, the Vali of Van, whose activities in that section I have already described. All through this country Djevdet was generally known as the "horseshoer of Bashkale" for this connoisseur in torture had invented what was perhaps the masterpiece of all---that of nailing horseshoes to the feet of his Armenian victims.

Yet these happenings did not constitute what the newspapers of the time commonly referred to as the Armenian atrocities; they were merely the preparatory steps in the destruction of the race. The Young Turks displayed greater ingenuity than their predecessor, Abdul Hamid. The injunction of the deposed Sultan was merely "to kill, kill", whereas the Turkish democracy hit upon an entirely new plan. Instead of massacring outright the Armenian race, they now decided to deport it. In the south and southeastern section of the Ottoman Empire lie the Syrian desert and the Mesopotamian valley. Though part of this area was once the scene of a flourishing civilization, for the last five centuries it has suffered the blight that becomes the lot of any country that is subjected to Turkish rule; and it is now a dreary, desolate waste, without cities and towns or life of any kind, populated only by a few wild and fanatical Bedouin tribes. Only the most industrious labour, expended through many years, could transform this desert into the abiding place of any considerable population. The Central Government now announced its intention of gathering the two million or more Armenians living in the several sections of the empire and transporting them to this desolate and inhospitable region. Had they undertaken such a deportation in good faith it would have represented the height of cruelty and injustice. As a matter of fact, the Turks never had the slightest idea of reestablishing the Armenians in this new country. They knew that the great majority would never reach their destination and that those who did would either die of thirst and starvation, or be murdered by the wild Mohammedan desert tribes. The real purpose of the deportation was robbery and destruction; it really represented a new method of massacre. When the Turkish authorities gave the orders for these deportations, they were merely giving the death warrant to a whole race; they understood this well, and, in their conversations with me, they made no particular attempt to conceal the fact.

All through the spring and summer of 1915 the deportations took place. Of the larger cities, Constantinople, Smyrna, and Aleppo were spared; practically all other places where a single Armenian family lived now became the scenes of these unspeakable tragedies. Scarcely a single Armenian, whatever his education or wealth, or whatever the social class to which he belonged, was exempted from the order. In some villages placards were posted ordering the whole Armenian population to present itself in a public place at an appointed time-usually a day or two ahead, and in other places the town crier would go through the streets delivering the order vocally. In still others not the slightest warning was given. The gendarmes would appear before an Armenian house and order all the inmates to follow them. They would take women engaged in their domestic tasks without giving them the chance to change their clothes. The police fell upon them just as the eruption of Vesuvius fell upon Pompeii; women were taken from the washtubs, children were snatched out of bed, the bread was left half baked in the oven, the family meal was abandoned partly eaten, the children were taken from the schoolroom, leaving their books open at the daily task, and the men were forced to abandon their ploughs in the fields and their cattle on the mountain side. Even women who had just given birth to children would be forced to leave their beds and join the panic-stricken throng, their sleeping babies in their arms. Such things as they hurriedly snatched up---a shawl, a blanket, perhaps a few scraps of food---were all that they could take of their household belongings. To their frantic questions " Where are we going? " the gendarmes would vouchsafe only one reply: "To the interior."

In some cases the refugees were given a few hours, in exceptional instances a few days, to dispose of their property and household effects. But the proceeding, of course, amounted simply to robbery. They could sell only to Turks, and since both buyers and sellers knew that they had only a day or two to market the accumulations of a lifetime, the prices obtained represented a small fraction of their value. Sewing machines would bring one or two dollars---a cow would go for a dollar, a houseful of furniture would be sold for a pittance. In many cases Armenians were prohibited from selling or Turks from buying even at these ridiculous prices; under pretense that the Government intended to sell their effects to pay the creditors whom they would inevitably leave behind, their household furniture would be placed in stores or heaped up in public places, where it was usually pillaged by Turkish men and women. The government officials would also inform the Armenians that, since their deportation was only temporary, the intention being to bring them back after the war was over, they would not be permitted to sell their houses. Scarcely had the former possessors left the village, when Mohammedan mohadjirs---immigrants from other parts of Turkey---would be moved into the Armenian quarters. Similarly all their valuables---money, rings, watches, and jewellery---would be taken to the police stations for "safe keeping, pending their return, and then parcelled out among the Turks. Yet these robberies gave the refugees little anguish, for far more terrible and agonizing scenes were taking place under their eyes. The systematic extermination of the men continued; such males as the persecutions which I have already described had left were now violently dealt with. Before the caravans were started, it became the regular practice to separate the young men from the families, tie them together in groups of four, lead them to the outskirts, and shoot them. Public hangings without trial (the only offense being that the victims were Armenians) were taking place constantly. The gendarmes showed a particular desire to annihilate the educated and the influential. From American consuls and missionaries I was constantly receiving reports of such executions, and many of the events which they described will never fade from my memory. At Angora all Armenian men from fifteen to seventy were arrested, bound together in groups of four, and sent on the road in the direction of Caesarea. When they had travelled five or six hours and had reached a secluded valley, a mob of Turkish peasants fell upon them with clubs, hammers, axes, scythes, spades, and saws. Such instruments not only caused more agonizing deaths than guns and pistols, but, as the Turks themselves boasted, they were more economical, since they did not involve the waste of powder and shell. In this way they exterminated the whole male population of Angora, including all its men of wealth and breeding, and their bodies, horribly mutilated, were left in the valley, where they were devoured by wild beasts. After completing this destruction, the peasants and gendarmes gathered in the local tavern, comparing notes and boasting of the number of "'giaours" that each had slain. In Trebizond the men were placed in boats and sent out on the Black Sea; gendarmes would follow them in boats, shoot them down, and throw their bodies into the water.

When the signal was given for the caravans to move, therefore, they almost invariably consisted of women, children, and old men. Any one who could possibly have protected them from the fate that awaited them had been destroyed. Not infrequently the prefect of the city, as the mass started on its way, would wish them a derisive "pleasant journey." Before the caravan moved the women were sometimes offered the alternative of becoming Mohammedans. Even though they accepted the new faith, which few of them did, their earthly troubles did not end. The converts were compelled to surrender their children to a so-called "Moslem Orphanage," with the agreement that they should be trained as devout followers of the Prophet, They themselves must then show the sincerity of their conversion by abandoning their Christian husbands and marrying Moslems. If no good Mohammedan offered himself as a husband, then the new convert was deported, however strongly she might protest her devotion to Islam.

At first the Government showed some inclination to protect these departing throngs. The officers usually divided them into convoys, in some cases numbering several hundred, in others several thousand. The civil authorities occasionally furnished ox-carts which carried such household furniture as the exiles had succeeded in scrambling together. A guard of gendarmerie accompanied each convoy, ostensibly to guide and protect it. Women, scantily clad, carrying babies in their arms or on their backs, marched side by side with old men hobbling along with canes. Children would run along, evidently regarding the procedure, in the early stages, as some new lark. A more prosperous member would perhaps have a horse or a donkey, occasionally a farmer had rescued a cow or a sheep, which would trudge along at his side, and the usual assortment of family pets---dogs, cats, and birds---became parts of the variegated procession. From thousands of Armenian cities and villages these despairing caravans now set forth; they filled all the roads leading southward; everywhere, as they moved on, they raised a huge dust, and abandoned d?bris, chairs, blankets, bed-clothes, household utensils, and other impedimenta, marked the course of the pro-cessions. When the caravans first started, the individuals bore some resemblance to human beings; in a few hours, however, the dust of the road plastered their faces and clothes, the mud caked their lower members, and the slowly advancing mobs, fre-quently bent with fatigue and crazed by the brutality of their "protectors," resembled some new .and strange animal species. Yet for the better part of six months, from April to October, 1915, practically all the highways in Asia Minor were crowded with these unearthly bands of exiles. They could be seen winding in and out of every val-ley and climbing up the sides of nearly every mountain---moving on and on, they scarcely knew whither, except that every road led to death. Village after village and town after town was evacuated of its Armenian population, under the distressing circumstances already detailed. In these six months, as far as can be ascertained, about 1,200,000 people started on this journey to the Syrian desert.

"Pray for us," they would say as they left their homes---the homes in which their ancestors had lived for 2,500 years. "We shall not see you in this world again, but sometime we shall meet. Pray for us!"

The Armenians had hardly left their native villages when the persecutions began. The roads over which they travelled were little more than donkey paths; and what had started a few hours before as an orderly procession soon became a dishevelled and scrambling mob. Women were separated from their children and husbands from their wives. The old people soon lost contact with their families and became exhaust-ed and footsore. The Turkish drivers of the ox-carts, after extorting the last coin from their charges, would suddenly dump them and their belongings into the road, turn around, and return to the village for other victims. Thus in a short time practically everybody, young and old, was compelled to travel on foot. The gendarmes whom the Government had sent, supposedly to protect the exiles, in a very few hours became their tormentors. They followed their charges with fixed bayonets, prodding any one who showed any tendency to slacken the pace. Those who attempted to stop for rest, or who fell exhausted on the road, were compelled, with the utmost brutality, to re-join the moving throng. They even prodded pregnant women with bayonets; if one, as frequently happened, gave birth along the road, she was immediately forced to get up and rejoin the marchers. The whole course of the journey became a perpetual struggle with the Moslem inhabitants. Detachments of gendarmes would go ahead, notifying the Kurdish tribes that their victims were approaching, and Turkish peas-ants were also informed that their long-waited opportunity had arrived. The Gov-ernment even opened the prisons and set free the convicts, on the understanding that they should behave like good Moslems to the approaching Armenians. Thus eve-ry caravan had a continuous battle for existence with several classes of enemies---their accompanying gendarmes, the Turkish peasants and villagers, the Kurdish tribes and bands of Chetes or brigands. And we must always keep in mind that the men who might have defended these wayfarers had nearly all been killed or forced into the army as workmen, and that the exiles themselves had been systematically deprived of all weapons before the journey began.

When the victims had travelled a few hours from their starting place, the Kurds would sweep down from their mountain homes. Rushing up to the young girls, they would lift their veils and carry the pretty ones off to the hills. They would steal such children as pleased their fancy and mercilessly rob all the rest of the throng. If the exiles had started with any money or food, their assailants would appropriate it, thus leaving them a hopeless prey to starvation. They would steal their clothing, and sometimes even leave both men and women in a state of complete nudity. All the time that they were committing these depradations the Kurds would freely massacre, and the screams of women and old men would add to the general horror. Such as escaped these attacks in the open would find new terrors awaiting them in the Moslem villages. Here the Turkish roughs would fall upon the women, leaving them sometimes dead from their experiences or sometimes ravingly insane. After spending a night in a hideous encampment of this kind, the exiles, or such as had survived, would start again the next morning. The ferocity of the gendarmes apparently increased as the journey lengthened, for they seemed almost to resent the fact that part of their charges continued to live. Frequently any one who dropped on the road was bayoneted on the spot. The Armenians began to die by hundreds from hunger and thirst. Even when they came to rivers, the gendarmes, merely to torment them, would sometimes not let them drink. The hot sun of the desert burned their scantily clothed bodies, and their bare feet, treading the hot sand of the desert, became so sore that thousands fell and died or were killed where they lay. Thus, in a few days, what had been a procession of normal human beings became a stumbling horde of dust-covered skeletons, ravenously looking for scraps of food, eating any offal that came their way, crazed by the hideous sights that filled every hour of their existence, sick with all the diseases that accompany such hardships and privations, but still prodded on and on by the whips and clubs and bayonets of their executioners.

And thus, as the exiles moved, they left behind them another caravan---that of dead and unburied bodies, of old men and of women dying in the last stages of typhus, dysentery, and cholera, of little children lying on their backs and setting up their last piteous wails for food and water. There were women who held up their babies to strangers, begging them to take them and save them from their tormentors, and failing this, they would throw them into wells or leave them behind bushes., that at least they might die undisturbed. Behind was left a small army of girls who had been sold as slaves---frequently for a medjidie, or about eighty cents---and who, after serving the brutal purposes of their purchasers, were forced to lead lives of prostitution. A string of encampments, filled by the sick and the dying, mingled with the unburied or half-buried bodies of the dead, marked the course of the advancing throngs. Flocks of vultures followed them in the air, and ravenous dogs, fighting one another for the bodies of the dead, constantly pursued them. The most terrible scenes took place at the rivers, especially the Euphrates. Sometimes, when crossing this stream, the gendarmes would push the women into the water, shooting all who attempted to save themselves by swimming. Frequently the women themselves would save their honour by jumping into the river, their children in their arms.

"In the last week in June," I quote from a consular report, "several parties of Erzeroum Armenians were deported on successive days and most of them massacred on the way, either by shooting or drowning. One, Madame Zarouhi, an elderly lady of means, who was thrown into the Euphrates, saved herself by clinging to a boulder in the river. She succeeded in approaching the bank and returned to Erzeroum. to hide herself in a Turkish friend's house. She told Prince Argoutinsky, the representative of the 'All-Russian Urban Union' in Erzeroum, that she shuddered to recall how hundreds of children were bayoneted by the Turks and thrown into the Euphrates, and how men and women were stripped naked, tied together in hundreds, shot, and then hurled into the river. In a loop of the river near Erzinghan, she said, the thousands of dead bodies created such a barrage that the Euphrates changed its course for about a hundred yards."

It is absurd for the Turkish Government to assert that it ever seriously intended to "deport the Armenians to new homes"; the treatment which was given the convoys clearly shows that extermination was the real purpose of Enver and Talaat. How many exiled to the south under these revolting conditions ever reached their destinations? The experiences of a single caravan show how completely this plan of deportation developed into one of annihilation. The details in question were furnished me directly by the American Consul at Aleppo, and are now on file in the State Department at Washington. On the first of June a convoy of three thousand Armenians, mostly women, girls, and children, left Harpoot. Following the usual custom the Government provided them an escort of seventy gendarmes, under the command of a Turkish leader, a Bey. In accordance with the common experience these gendarmes proved to be not their protectors, but their tormentors and their executioners. Hardly had they got well started on the road when Bey took 400 liras from the caravan, on the plea that he was keeping it safely until their arrival at Malatia; no sooner had he robbed them of the only thing that might have provided them with food than he ran away, leaving them all to the tender mercies of the gendarmes.

All the way to Ras-ul-Ain, the first station on the Bagdad line, the existence of these wretched travellers was one prolonged horror. The gendarmes went ahead, informing the half-savage tribes of the mountains that several thousand Armenian women and girls were approaching. The Arabs and Kurds began to carry off the girls, the mountaineers fell upon them repeatedly, violating and killing the women, and the gendarmes themselves joined in the orgy. One by one the few men who accompanied the convoy were killed. The women had succeeded in secreting money from their persecutors, keeping it in their mouths and hair; with this they would buy horses, only to have them repeatedly stolen by the Kurdish tribesmen. Finally the gendarmes, having robbed and beaten and violated and killed their charges for thirteen days, abandoned them altogether. Two days afterward the Kurds went through the party and rounded up all the males who still remained alive. They found about 150, their ages varying from 15 to 90 years, and these, they promptly took away and butchered to the last man. But that same day another convoy from Sivas joined---this one from Harpoot, increasing the numbers of the whole caravan to 18,000 people.

Another Kurdish Bey now took command, and to him, as to all men placed in the same position, the opportunity was regarded merely as one for pillage, outrage, and murder. This chieftain summoned all his followers from the mountains and invited them to work their complete will upon this great mass of Armenians. Day after day and night after night the prettiest girls were carried away; sometimes they returned in a pitiable condition that told the full story of their sufferings. Any stragglers, those who were so old and infirm and sick that they could not keep up with the marchers, were promptly killed. Whenever they reached a Turkish village all the local vaga-

145

bonds were permitted to prey upon the Armenian girls. When the diminishing band reached the Euphrates they saw the bodies of 200 men floating upon the surface. By this time they had all been so repeatedly robbed that they had practically nothing left except a few ragged clothes, and even these the Kurds now took; and the larger part of the convoy marched for five days almost completely naked under the scorching desert sun. For another five days they did not have a morsel of bread or a drop of water. "Hundreds fell dead on the way," the report reads, "their tongues were turned to charcoal., and when, at the end of five days, they reached a fountain, the whole convoy naturally rushed toward it. But here the policemen barred the way and forebade them to take a single drop of water. Their purpose was to sell it at from one to three liras a cup and sometimes they actually withheld the water after getting the money. At another place, where there were wells, some women threw themselves into them, as there was no rope or pail to draw up the water. These women were drowned and, in spite of that, the rest of the people drank from that well, the dead bodies still remaining there and polluting the water. Sometimes, when the wells were shallow and the women could go down into them and come out again, the other people would rush to lick or suck their wet, dirty clothes, in the effort to quench their thirst. When they passed an Arab village in their naked condition the Arabs pitied them and gave them old pieces of cloth to cover themselves with. Some of the exiles who still had money bought some clothes; but some still remained who travelled thus naked all the way to the city of Aleppo. The poor women could hardly walk for shame; they all walked bent double.

On the seventieth day a few creatures reached Aleppo. Out of the combined convoy of 18,000 souls just 150 women and children reached their destination. A few of the rest, the most attractive, were still living as captives of the Kurds and Turks; all the rest were dead.

My only reason for relating such dreadful things as this is that, without the details, the English-speaking public cannot understand precisely what this nation is which we call Turkey. I have by no means told the most terrible details, for a complete narration of the sadistic orgies of which these Armenian men and women were the victims can never be printed in an American publication . Whatever crimes the most perverted instincts of the human mind can devise, and whatever refinements of persecution and injustice the most debased imagination can conceive, became the daily misfortunes of this devoted people. I am confident that the whole history of the human race contains no such horrible episode as this. The great massacres and persecutions of the past seem almost insignificant when compared with the sufferings of the Armenian race in 1915. The slaughter of the Albigenses in the early part of the thirteenth century has always been regarded as one of the most pitiful events in history. In these outbursts of fanaticism about 60,000 people were killed. In the massacre of St. Bartholomew about 30,000 human beings lost their lives. The Sicilian Vespers, which has always figured as one of the most fiendish outbursts of this kind, caused the destruction of 8,000. Volumes have been written about the Spanish Inquisition under Torquemada, yet in the eighteen years of his administration only a little more than 8,000 heretics were done to death. Perhaps the one event in history that most resembles the Armenian deportations was the expulsion of the Jews from Spain by Ferdinand and Isabella. According to Prescott 160,000 were uprooted from their homes and scattered broadcast over Africa and Europe. Yet all these previous persecutions seem almost trivial when we compare them with the sufferings of the Armenians, in which at least 600,000 people were destroyed and perhaps as many as 1,000,000. And these earlier massacres, when we compare them with the spirit that directed the Armenian atrocities, have one feature that we can almost describe as an excuse: they were the product of religious fanaticism and most of the men and women who instigated them sincerely believed that they were devoutly serving their Maker. Undoubtedly religious fanaticism was an 'Impelling motive with the Turkish and Kurdish rabble who slew Armenians as a service to Allah, but the men who really conceived the crime had no such motive. Practically all of them were atheists, with no more respect for Mohammedanism than for Christianity, and with them the one motive was cold-blooded, calculating state policy.

The Armenians are not the only subject people in Turkey which have suffered from this policy of making Turkey exclusively the country of the Turks. The story which I have told about the Armenians I could also tell with certain modifications about the Greeks and the Syrians. Indeed the Greeks were the first victims of this nationalizing idea. I have already described how, in the few months preceding the European War, the Ottoman Government began deporting its Greek subjects along the coast of Asia Minor. These outrages aroused little interest in Europe or the United States, yet in the space of three or four months more than 100,000 Greeks were taken from their age-long homes in the Mediterranean littoral and removed to the Greek Islands and the interior. For the larger part these were bona-fide deportations; that is, the Greek inhabitants were actually removed to new places and were not subjected to wholesale massacre. it was probably for the reason that the civilized world did not protest against these deportations that the Turks afterward decided to apply the same methods on a larger scale not only to the Greeks but to the Armenians, Syrians, Nestorians, and others of its subject peoples. In fact, Bedri Bey, the Prefect of Police at Constantinople, himself told one of my secretaries that the Turks had expelled the Greeks so successfully that they had decided to apply the same method to all the other races in the empire.

The martyrdom of the Greeks, therefore, comprised two periods: that antedating the war, and that which began in the early part of 1915. The first affected chiefly the Greeks on the seacoast of Asia Minor. The second affected those living in Thrace and in the territories surrounding the Sea of Marmora, the Dardanelles, the Bosphorus, and the coast of the Black Sea. These latter, to the extent of several hundred thousand, were sent to the interior of Asia Minor. The Turks adopted almost identically the same procedure against the Greeks as that which they had adopted against the Armenians. They began by incorporating the Greeks into the Ottoman army and then transforming them into labour battalions, using them to build roads in the Caucasus and other scenes of action. These Greek soldiers, just like the Armenians, died by thousands from cold, hunger, and other privations. The same house-to-house searches for hidden weapons took place in the Greek villages, and Greek men and women were beaten and tortured just as were their fellow Armenians. The Greeks had to submit to the same forced requisitions, which amounted in their case, as in the case of the Armenians, merely to plundering on a wholesale scale. The Turks attempted to force the Greek subjects to become Mohammedans; Greek girls, just like Armenian girls, were stolen and taken to Turkish harems and Greek boys were kidnapped and placed in Moslem households. The Greeks, just like the Armenians, were accused of disloyalty to the Ottoman Government; the Turks accused them of furnishing supplies to the English submarines in the Marmora and also of acting as spies. The Turks also declared that the Greeks were not loyal to the Ottoman Government, and that they also looked forward to the day when the Greeks inside of Turkey would become part of Greece. These latter charges were unquestionably true; that the Greeks, after suffering for five centuries the most unspeakable outrages at the hands of the Turks, should look longingly to the day when their territory should be part of the fatherland, was to be expected. The Turks, as in the case of the Armenians, seized upon this as an excuse for a violent onslaught on the whole race. Everywhere the Greeks were gathered in groups and, under the so-called protection of Turkish gendarmes, they were transported, the larger part on foot, into the interior. Just how many were scattered in this fashion is not definitely known, the estimates varying anywhere from 200,000 up to 1,000,000. These caravans suffered great privations, but they were not submitted to general massacre as were the Armenians, and this is probably the reason why the outside world has not heard so much about them. The Turks showed them this greater consideration not from any motive of pity. The Greeks, unlike the Armenians, had a government which was vitally interested in their welfare. At this time there was a general apprehension among the Teutonic Allies that Greece would enter the war on the side of the Entente, and a wholesale massacre of Greeks in Asia Minor would unquestionably have produced such a state of mind in Greece that its pro-German king would have been unable longer to keep his country out of the war. It was only a matter of state policy, therefore, that saved these Greek subjects of Turkey from all the horrors that befell the Armenians. But their sufferings are still terrible, and constitute another chapter in the long story of crimes for which civilization will hold the Turk responsible.

Chapter XXV - Talaat Tells Why He "Deports" the Armenians

It was some time before the story of the Armenian atrocities reached the American Embassy in all its horrible details. In January and February fragmentary reports began to filter in, but the tendency was at first to regard them as mere manifestations of the disorders that had prevailed in the Armenian provinces for many years. When the reports came from Urumia, both Enver and Talaat dismissed them as wild exaggerations, and when, for the first time, we heard of the disturbances at Van, these Turkish officials declared that they were nothing more than a mob uprising which they would soon have under control. I now see what was not apparent in those early months, that the Turkish Government was determined to keep the news, as long as possible, from the outside world. It was clearly the intention that Europe and America should hear of the annihilation of the Armenian race only after that annihilation had been accomplished. As the country which the Turks particularly wished to keep in ignorance was the United States, they resorted to the most shameless prevarications when discussing the situation with myself and with my staff.

In early April the authorities arrested about two hundred Armenians in Constantinople and sent them into the interior. Many of those who were then deported were educational and social leaders and men who were prominent in industry and in finance. I knew many of these men and therefore felt a personal interest in their misfortunes. But when I spoke to Talaat about their expulsion, he replied that the Government was acting in self-defense. The Armenians at Van, he said, had already shown their abilities as revolutionists; he knew that these leaders in Constantinople were corresponding with the Russians and he had every reason to fear that they would start an insurrection against the Central Government. The safest plan, therefore, was to send them to Angora and other interior towns. Talaat denied that this was part of any general concerted scheme to rid the city of its Armenian population, and insisted that the Armenian masses in Constantinople would not be disturbed.

But soon the accounts from the interior became more specific and more disquieting. The withdrawal of the Allied fleet from the Dardanelles produced a distinct change in the atmosphere. Until then there were numerous indications that all was not going well in the Armenian provinces; when it at last became definitely established, however, that the traditional friends of Armenia, Great Britain, France, and Russia, could do nothing to help that suffering people, the mask began to disappear. In April I was suddenly deprived of the privilege of using the cipher for communicating with American consuls. The most rigorous censorship also was applied to letters. Such measures could mean only that things were happening in Asia Minor which the authorities were determined to conceal. But they did not succeed. Though all sorts of impediments were placed to travelling, certain Americans, chiefly missionaries, succeeded in getting through.

For hours they would sit in my office and, with tears streaming down their faces, they would tell me of the horrors through which they had passed. Many of these, both men and women, were almost broken in health from the scenes which they had witnessed. In many cases they brought me letters from American consuls, confirming the most dreadful of their narrations and adding many unprintable details. The general purport of all these first-hand reports was that the utter depravity and fiendishness of the Turkish nature, already sufficiently celebrated through the centuries, had now surpassed themselves. There was only one hope of saving nearly 2,000,000 people from massacre, starvation, and even worse, I was told, that was the moral power of the United States. These spokesmen of a condemned nation declared that, unless the American Ambassador could persuade the Turk to stay his destroying arm, the whole Armenian nation would disappear. It was not only American and Canadian missionaries who made this personal appeal. Several of their German associates begged me to intercede. These men and women confirmed all the worst things which I had heard, and they were unsparing in denouncing their own fatherland. They did not conceal the humiliation which they felt, as Germans, in the fact that their own nation was allied with a people that could perpetrate such infamies, but they understood German policy well enough to know that Germany would not intercede. There was no use in expecting aid from the Kaiser, they said-America must stop the massacres, or they would go on.

Technically, of course, I had no right to interfere. According to the cold-blooded legalities of the situation, the treatment of Turkish subjects by the Turkish Government was purely a domestic affair; unless it directly affected American lives and

149

American interests, it was outside the concern of the American Government. When I first approached Talaat on the subject, he called my attention to this fact in no uncertain terms. This interview was one of the most exciting which I had had up to that time. Two missionaries had just called upon me, giving the full details of the frightful happenings at Konia. After listening to their stories, I could not restrain myself, and went immediately to the Sublime Porte. I saw at once that Talaat was in one of his most ferocious states of mind. For months he had been attempting to secure the release of one of his closest friends, Ayoub Sabri, and Zinnoun, who were held as prisoners by the English at Malta. His failure in this matter was a constant grievance and irritation; he was always talking about it, always making new suggestions for getting his friends back to Turkey, and always appealing to me for help. So furious did the Turkish Boss become when thinking about his absent friends that we usually referred to these manifestations as Talaat in his "Ayoub Sabri moods," This particular morning the Minister of the Interior was in one of his worst "Ayoub Sabri moods." Once more he had been working for the release of the exiles and once more he had failed. As usual, he attempted to preserve outer calm and courtesy to me, but his short, snappy phrases, his bull-dog rigidity, and his wrists, planted on the table, showed that it was an unfavourable moment to stir him to any sense of pity or remorse. I first spoke to him about a Canadian missionary, Dr. McNaughton, who was receiving harsh treatment in Asia Minor.

"The man is an English agent," he replied, "and we have the evidence for it."

"Let me see it, " I asked.

"We'll do nothing for any Englishman or any Canadian," he replied, "until they release Ayoub and Zinnoun."

"But you promised to treat English in the employ of Americans as Americans," I replied.

"That may be," rejoined the Minister, "but a promise is not made to be kept forever. I withdraw that promise now. There is a time limit on a promise."

"But if a promise is not binding, what is?" I asked.

"A guarantee," Talaat answered quickly.

This fine Turkish distinction had a certain metaphysical interest, but I had more practical matters to discuss at that time. So I began to talk about the Armenians at Konia. I had hardly started when Talaat's attitude became even more belligerent. His eyes lighted up, he brought his jaws together, leaned over toward me, and snapped out:

"Are they Americans?"

The implications of this question were hardly diplomatic; it was merely a way of telling me that the matter was none of my business. In a moment Talaat said this in so many words.

"The Armenians are not to be trusted, " he said, "besides, what we do with them does not concern the United States."

I replied that I regarded myself as the friend of the Armenians and was shocked at the way that they were being treated. But he shook his head and refused to discuss the matter. I saw that nothing could be gained by forcing the issue at that time. I spoke in behalf of another British subject who was not being treated properly.

"He's English, isn't he?" answered Talaat. "Then I shall do as I like with him!"

"Eat him, if you wish!" I replied.

"No," said Talaat, "he would go against my digestion."

He was altogether in a reckless mood. "Gott strafe England!" he shouted-using one of the few German phrases that he knew. "As to your Armenians, we don't give a rap for the future! We live only in the present! As to the English, I wish you would telegraph Washington that we shall not do a thing for them until they let out Ayoub Sabri and Zinnoun!"

Then leaning over, he struck a pose, pressed his hand to his heart, and said, in English---I think this must have been almost all the English he knew:

"Ayoub Sabri-he-my-brudder!"

Despite this I made another plea for Dr. McNaughton.

"He's not American," said Talaat, "he's a Canadian."

"It's almost the same thing, " I said.

"Well," replied Talaat, "if I let him go, will you promise that the United States will annex Canada? "

"I promise," said I, and we both laughed at this little joke.

"Every time you come here," Talaat finally said, "you always steal something from me. All right, you can have your McNaughton!"

Certainly this interview was not an encouraging beginning, so far as the Armeniens were concerned. But Talaat was not always in an "Ayoub Sabri mood."

He went from one emotion to another as lightly as a child; I would find him fierce and unyielding one day, and uproariously good-natured and accommodating the next. Prudence indicated, therefore, that I should await one of his more congenial moments before approaching him on the subject that aroused all the barbarity in his nature. Such an opportunity was soon presented. One day, soon after the interview chronicled above, I called on Talaat again. The first thing he did was to open his desk and pull out a handful of yellow cablegrams.

"Why don't you give this money to us? " he said, with a grin.

"What money? " I asked.

"Here is a cablegram for you from America, sending you a lot of money for the Armenians. You ought not to use it that way; give it to us Turks, we need it as badly as they do."

"I have not received any such cablegram," I replied.

"Oh, no, but you will," he answered. "I always get all your cablegrams first, you know. After I have finished reading them I send them around to you.

This statement was the literal truth. Every morning all uncoded cablegrams received in Constantinople' were forwarded to Talaat, who read them, before consenting to their being forwarded to their destinations. Even the cablegrams of the ambassadors were apparently not exempt, though, of course, the ciphered messages were not interfered with. Ordinarily I might have protested against this infringement of my rights, but Talaat's engaging frankness about pilfering my correspondence and in even waving my own cablegrams in my face gave me an excellent opening to introduce the forbidden subject.

But on this occasion, as on many others, Talaat was evasive and non-committal and showed much hostility to the interest which the American people were manifesting in the Armenians. He explained his policy on the ground that the Armenians were in constant correspondence with the Russians. The definite conviction which these conversations left upon my mind was that Talaat was the most implacable enemy of this persecuted race. "He gave me the impression," such is the entry which I find in my diary on August 3d, "that Talaat is the one who desires to crush the poor Armenians." He told me that the Union and Progress Committee had carefully considered the matter in all its details and that the policy which was being pursued was that which they had officially adopted. He said that I must not get the idea that the deportations had been decided upon hastily; in reality, they were the result of prolonged and careful deliberation. To my repeated appeals that he should show mercy to these people, he sometimes responded seriously, sometimes angrily, and sometimes flippantly.

"Some day," he once said, "I will come and discuss the whole Armenian subject with you," and then he added, in a low tone in Turkish: "But that day will never come!"

"Why are you so interested in the Armenians, anyway?" he said, on another occasion. "You are a Jew; these people are Christians. The Mohammedans and the Jews always get on harmoniously. We are treating the Jews here all right. What have you to complain of? Why can't you let us do with these Christians as we please?"

I had frequently remarked that the Turks look upon practically every question as a personal matter, yet this point of view rather stunned me. However, it was a complete revelation of Turkish mentality; the fact that, above all considerations of race and religion, there are such things as humanity and civilization, never for a moment enters their mind. They can understand a Christian fighting for a Christian and a Jew fighting for a Jew, but such abstractions as justice and decency form no part of their conception of things.

"You don't seem to realize," I replied, "that I am not here as a Jew but as American Ambassador. My country contains something more than 97,000,000 Christians and something less than 3,000,000 Jews. So, at least in my ambassadorial capacity, I am 97 per cent. Christian. But after all, that is not the point. I do not appeal to you in the name of any race or any religion, but merely as a human being. You have told me many times that you want to make Turkey a part of the modern progressive world. The way you are treating the Armenians will not help you to realize that ambition; it puts you in the class of backward, reactionary peoples."

"We treat the Americans all right, too," said Talaat. "I don't see why you should complain."

"But Americans are outraged by your persecutions of the Armenians," I replied. "You must base your principles on humanitarianism, not racial discrimination, or the United States will not regard you as a friend and an equal. And you should understand the great changes that are taking place among Christians all over the world. They are forgetting their differences and all sects are coming together as one. You look down on American missionaries, but don't forget that it is the best element in America that supports their religious work, as well as their educational institutions. Americans are not mere materialists, always chasing money---they are broadly humanitarian, and interested in the spread of justice and civilization throughout the world. After this war is over you will face a new situation. You say that, if victorious, you can defy the world, but you are wrong. You will have to meet public opinion everywhere, especially in the United States. Our people will never forget these massacres. They will always resent the wholesale destruction of Christians in Turkey. They will look upon it as nothing but wilful murder and will seriously condemn all the men who are responsible for it. You will not be able to protect yourself under your political status and say that you acted as Minister of the Interior and not as Talaat. You are defying all ideas of justice as we understand the term in our country."

Strangely enough, these remarks did not offend Talaat, but they did not shake his determination. I might as well have been talking to a stone wall. From my abstractions he immediately came down to something definite.

"These people," he said, "refused to disarm when we told them to. They opposed us at Van and at Zeitoun, and they helped the Russians. There is only one way in which we can defend ourselves against them in the future, and that is just to deport them."

"Suppose a few Armenians did betray you," I said. "Is that a reason for destroying a whole race? Is that an excuse for making innocent women and children suffer?"

"Those things are inevitable," he replied.

This remark to me was not quite so illuminating as one which Talaat made subsequently to a reporter of the Berliner Tageblatt, who asked him the same question. "We have been reproached," he said, according to this interviewer, "for making no distinction between the innocent Armenians and the guilty; but that was utterly impossible, in view of the fact that those who were innocent to-day might be guilty to-morrow"!

One reason why Talaat could not discuss this matter with me freely, was because the member of the embassy staff who did the interpreting was himself an Armenian. In the early part of August, therefore, he sent a personal messenger to me, asking if I could not see him alone---he said that he himself would provide the interpreter. This was the first time that Talaat had admitted that his treatment of the Armenians was a matter with which I had any concern. The interview took place two days afterward. It so happened that since the last time I had visited Talaat I had shaved my beard. As soon as I came in the burly Minister began talking in his customary bantering fashion.

"You have become a young man again," he said; "you are so young now that I cannot go to you for advice any more."

"I have shaved my beard," I replied, "because it had become very gray---made gray by your treatment of the Armenians."

After this exchange of compliments we settled down to the business in hand. "I have asked you to come to-day," began Talaat, "so that I can explain our position on the whole Armenian subject. We base our objections to the Armenians on three distinct grounds. In the first place, they have enriched themselves at the expense of the Turks. In the second place, they are determined to domineer over us and to establish a separate state. In the third place, they have openly encouraged our enemies. They have assisted the Russians in the Caucasus and our failure there is largely explained by their actions. We have therefore come to the irrevocable decision that we shall make them powerless before this war is ended."

On every one of these points I had plenty of arguments in rebuttal. Talaat's first objection was merely an admission that the Armenians were more industrious and more able than the dull-witted and lazy Turks. Massacre as a means of destroying business competition was certainly an original conception! His general charge that the Armenians were "conspiring" against Turkey and that they openly sympathized with Turkey's enemies merely meant, when reduced to its original elements, that the Armenians were constantly appealing to the European Powers to protect them

153

against robbery, murder, and outrage. The Armenian problem, like most race problems, was the result of centuries of ill-treatment and injustice. There could be only one solution for it, the creation of an orderly system of government, in which all citizens were to be treated upon an equality, and in which all offenses were to be punished as the acts of individuals and not as of peoples. I argued for a long time along these and similar lines.

"It is no use for you to argue," Talaat answered, "we have already disposed of three quarters of the Armenians; there are none at all left in Bitlis, Van, and Erzeroum. The hatred between the Turks and the Armenians is now so intense that we have got to finish with them. If we don't, they will plan their revenge."

"If you are not influenced by humane considerations," I replied, "think of the material loss. These people are your business men. They control many of your industries. They are very large tax-payers. What would become of you commercially without them?"

"We care nothing about the commercial loss," replied Talaat. "We have figured all that out and we know that it will not exceed five million pounds. We don't worry about that. I have asked you to come here so as to let you know that our Armenian policy is absolutely fixed and that nothing can change it. We will not have the Armenians anywhere in Anatolia. They can live in the desert but nowhere else."

I still attempted to persuade Talaat that the treatment of the Armenians was destroying Turkey in the eyes of the world, and that his country would never be able to recover from this infamy.

"You are making a terrible mistake," I said, and I repeated the statement three times.

"Yes, we may make mistakes," he replied, "but" ---and he firmly closed his lips and shook his head---"we never regret."

I had many talks with Talaat on the Armenians, but I never succeeded in moving him to the slightest degree. He always came back to the points which he had made in this interview. He was very willing to grant any request I made in behalf of the Americans or even of the French and English, but I could obtain no general concessions for the Armenians. He seemed to me always to have the deepest personal feeling in this matter, and his antagonism to the Armenians seemed to increase as their sufferings increased. One day, discussing a particular Armenian, I told Talaat that he was mistaken in regarding this man as an enemy of the Turks; that in reality he was their friend.

"No Armenian," replied Talaat, "can be our friend after what we have done to them."

One day Talaat made what was perhaps the most astonishing request I had ever heard. The New York Life Insurance Company and the Equitable Life of New York had for years done considerable business among the Armenians. The extent to which this people insured their lives was merely another indication of their thrifty habits.

"I wish," Talaat now said, "that you would get the American life insurance companies to send us a complete list of their Armenian policy holders. They are practically all dead now and have left no heirs to collect the money. It of course all escheats to the State. The Government is the beneficiary now. Will you do so?"

This was almost too much, and I lost my temper.

"You will get no such list from me," I said, and I got up and left him.

154

One other episode involving the Armenians stirred Talaat to one of his most ferocious moods. In the latter part of September, Mrs. Morgenthau left for America. The sufferings of the Armenians had greatly preyed upon her mind and she really left for home because she could not any longer endure to live in such a country. But she determined to make one last intercession for this poor people on her own account. Her way home took her through Bulgaria, and she had received an intimation that Queen Eleanor of that country would be glad to receive her. Perhaps it was Mrs. Morgenthau's well-known interest in social work that led to this invitation. Queen Eleanor was a high-minded woman, who had led a sad and lonely existence, and who was spending most of her time attempting to improve the condition of the poor in Bulgaria. She knew all about social work in American cities, and, a few years before, she had made all her plans to visit the United States in order to study our settlements at first hand. At the time of Mrs. Morgenthau's visit the Queen had two American nurses from the Henry Street Settlement of New York instructing a group of Bulgarian girls in the methods of the American Red Cross.

My wife was mainly interested in visiting the Queen in order that, as one woman to another, she might make a plea for the Armenians. At that time the question of Bulgaria's entrance into the war had reached a critical stage, and Turkey was prepared to make concessions to gain her as an ally. It was therefore a propitious moment to make such an appeal.

The Queen received Mrs. Morgenthau informally, and my wife spent about an hour telling her all about the Armenians. Most of what she said was entirely new to the Queen. Little had yet appeared in the European press on this subject, and Queen Eleanor was precisely the kind of woman from whom the truth would be concealed as long as possible. Mrs. Morgenthau gave her all the facts about the treatment of Armenian women and children and asked her to intercede in their behalf. She even went so far as to suggest that it would be a terrible thing if Bulgaria, which in the past had herself suffered such atrocities at the hands of the Turks, should now become their allies in war. Queen Eleanor was greatly moved. She thanked my wife for telling her these truths and said that she would investigate immediately and see if something could not be done.

Just as Mrs. Morgenthau was getting ready to leave she saw the Duke of Mecklenburg standing near the door. The Duke was in Sofia at that time attempting to arrange for Bulgaria's participation in the war. The Queen introduced him to Mrs. Morgenthau; His Highness was polite, but his air was rather cold and injured. His whole manner, particularly the stern glances which he cast on Mrs. Morgenthau, showed that he had heard a considerable part of the conversation. As he was exerting all his efforts to bring Bulgaria in on Germany's side, it is not surprising that he did not relish the plea which Mrs. Morgenthau was making to the Queen that Bulgaria should not ally herself with Turkey.

Queen Eleanor immediately interested herself in the Armenian cause, and, as a result, the Bulgarian Minister to Turkey was instructed to protest against the atrocities. This protest accomplished nothing, but it did arouse Talaat's momentary wrath against the American Ambassador. A few days afterward, when routine business called me to the Sublime Porte; I found him in an exceedingly ugly humour. He answered most of my questions savagely and in monosyllables, and I was afterward told that Mrs. Morgenthau's intercession with the Queen had put him into this mood.

In a few days, however, he was as good-natured as ever, for Bulgaria had taken sides with Turkey.

Talaat's attitude toward the Armenians was summed up in the proud boast which he made to his friends: "I have accomplished more toward solving the Armenian problem in three months than Abdul Hamid accomplished in thirty years!"

Chapter XXVI - Enver Pasha Discusses the Armenians

All this time I was bringing pressure upon Enver also. The Minister of War, as I have already indicated, was a different type of man from Talaat. He concealed his real feelings much more successfully; he was usually suave, cold-blooded, and scrupulously polite. And at first he was by no means so callous as Talaat in discussing the Armenians. He dismissed the early stories as wild exaggerations, declared that the troubles at Van were merely ordinary warfare, and attempted to quiet my fears that the wholesale annihilation of the Armenians had been decided on. Yet all the time that Enver was attempting to deceive me, he was making open admissions to other people---a fact of which I was aware. In particular he made no attempt to conceal the real situation from Dr. Lepsius, a representative of German missionary interests. Dr. Lepsius was a high-minded Christian gentleman. He had been all through the Armenian massacres of 1895, and he had raised considerable sums of money to build orphanages for Armenian children who had lost their parents at that time. He came again in 1915 to investigate the Armenian situation in behalf of German missionary interests. He asked for the privilege of inspecting the reports of American consuls and I granted it. These documents, supplemented by other information which Dr. Lepsius obtained, largely from German missionaries in the interior, left no doubt in his mind as to the policy of the Turks. His feelings were aroused chiefly against his own government. He expressed to me the humiliation which he felt, as a German, that the Turks should set about to exterminate their Christian subjects, while Germany, which called itself a Christian country, was making no endeavours to prevent it. From him Enver scarcely concealed the official purpose. Dr. Lepsius was simply staggered by his frankness, for Enver told him in so many words that they at last had an opportunity to rid themselves of the Armenians and that they proposed to use it.

By this time Enver had become more frank with me---the circumstantial reports which I possessed made it useless for him to attempt to conceal the true situation further---and we had many long and animated discussions on the subject. One of these I recall with particular vividness. I notified Enver that I intended to take up the matter in detail and he laid aside enough time to go over the whole situation.

"The Armenians had a fair warning," Enver began, "of what would happen to them in case they joined our enemies. Three months ago I sent for the Armenian Patriarch and I told him that if the Armenians attempted to start a revolution or to assist the Russians, I would be unable to prevent mischief from happening to them. My warning produced no effect and the Armenians started a revolution and helped the Russians. You know what happened at Van. They obtained control of the city, used bombs against government buildings, and killed a large number of Moslems. We knew that they were planning uprisings in other places. You must understand that we are now fighting for our lives at the Dardanelles and that we are sacrificing thousands of men. While we are engaged in such a struggle as this, we cannot permit people in our own country to attack us in the back. We have got to prevent this no matter what means we have to resort to. It is absolutely true that I am not opposed to the Armenians as a people. I have the greatest admiration for their intelligence and industry, and I should like nothing better than to see them become a real part of our nation. But if they ally themselves with our enemies, as they did in the Van district, they will have to be destroyed. I have taken pains to see that no injustice is done; only recently I gave orders to have three Armenians who had been deported returned to their homes, when I found that they were innocent. Russia, France, Great Britain, and America are doing the Armenians no kindness by sympathizing with and encouraging them. I know what such encouragement means to a people who are inclined to revolution. When our Union and Progress Party attacked Abdul Hamid, we received all our moral encouragement from the outside world. This encouragement was of great help to us and had much to do with our success. It might similarly now help the Armenians and their revolutionary programme. I am sure that if these outside countries did not encourage them, they would give up all their efforts to oppose the present government and become law-abiding citizens. We now have this country in our absolute control and we can easily revenge ourselves on any revolutionists."

"After all," I said, "suppose what you say is true, why not punish the guilty? Why sacrifice a whole race for the alleged crimes of individuals?"

"Your point is all right during peace times," replied Enver. "We can then use Platonic means to quiet Armenians and Greeks, but in time of war we cannot investigate and negotiate. We must act promptly and with determination. I also think that the Armenians are making a mistake in depending upon the Russians. The Russians really would rather see them killed than alive. They are as great a danger to the Russians as they are to us. If they should form an independent government in Turkey, the Armenians in Russia would attempt to form an independent government there. The Armenians have also been guilty of massacres; in the entire district around Van only 30,000 Turks escaped, all the rest were murdered by the Armenians and Kurds. I attempted to protect the non-combatants at the Caucasus; I gave orders that they should not be injured, but I found that the situation was beyond my control. There are about 70,000 Armenians in Constantinople and they will not be molested, except those who are Dashnaguists and those who are plotting against the Turks. However, I think you can ease your mind on the whole subject as there will be no more massacres of Armenians."

I did not take seriously Enver's concluding statement. At the time that he was speaking, massacres and deportations were taking place all over the Armenian provinces and they went on almost without interruption for several months.

As soon as the reports reached the United States the question of relief became a pressing one. In the latter part of July, I heard that there were 5,000 Armenians from Zeitoun and Sultani? who were receiving no food whatever. I spoke about them to Enver, who positively declared that they would receive proper food. He did not receive favourably any suggestion that American representatives should go to that part of the country and assist and care for the exiles.

"For any American to do this," he said, "would encourage all Armenians and make further trouble. There are twenty-eight million people in Turkey and one million Armenians, and we do not propose to have one million disturb the peace of the rest of the population. The great trouble with the Armenians is that they are separatists. They are determined to have a kingdom of their own, and they have allowed themselves to be fooled by the Russians. Because they have relied upon the friendship of the Russians, they have helped them in this war. We are determined that they shall behave just as Turks do. You must remember that when we started this revolution in Turkey there were only two hundred of us. With these few followers we were able to deceive the Sultan and the public, who thought that we were immensely more numerous and powerful than we were. We really prevailed upon him and the public through our sheer audacity, and in this way we established the Constitution. It is our own experience with revolutions which makes us fear the Armenians. If two hundred Turks could overturn the Government, then a few hundred bright, educated Armenians could do the same thing. We have therefore deliberately adopted the plan of scattering them so that they can do us no harm. As I told you once before, I warned the Armenian Patriarch that if the Armenians attacked us while we were engaged in a foreign war, that we Turks would hit back and that we would hit back indiscriminately."

Enver always resented any suggestion that American missionaries or other friends of the Armenians should go to help or comfort them. "They show altogether too much sympathy for them," he said over and over again.

I had suggested that particular Americans should go to Tarsus and Marsovan.

"If they should go there, I am afraid that the local people in those cities would become angry and they would be inclined to start some disturbance which might create an incident. It is better for the Armenians themselves, therefore, that the American missionaries should keep away from them."

"But you are ruining the country economically." I said at another time, making the same point that I had made to Talaat. And he answered it in almost the same words, thus showing that the subject had been completely canvassed by the ruling powers.

"Economic considerations are of no importance at this time. The only important thing is to win. That's the only thing we have on our mind. If we win, everything will be all right; if we lose, everything will be all wrong anyhow. Our situation is desperate, I admit it, and we are fighting as desperate men fight. We are not going to let the Armenians attack us in the rear."

The question of relief to the starving Armenians became every week a more pressing one, but Enver still insisted that Americans should keep away from the Armenian provinces.

"How can we furnish bread to the Armenians," Enver declared, "when we can't get enough for our own people? I know that they are suffering and that it is quite likely that they cannot get bread at all this coming winter. But we have the utmost difficulty in getting flour and clothing right here in Constantinople."

I said that I had the money and that American missionaries were anxious to go and use it for the benefit of the refugees.

"We don't want the Americans to feed the Armenians," he flatly replied. "That is one of the worst things that could happen to them. I have already said that it is their belief that they have friends in other countries which leads them to oppose the Government and so brings down upon them all their miseries. If you Americans begin to distribute food and clothing among them, they will. then think that they have powerful friends in the United States. This will encourage them to rebellion again and then we shall have to punish them still more. If you will give such money as you have received to the Turks, we shall see that it is used for the benefit of the Armenians."

Enver made this proposal with a straight face, and he made it not only on this occasion but on several others. At the very moment that Enver suggested this mechanism of relief, the Turkish gendarmes and the Turkish officials were not only robbing the Armenians of all their household possessions, of all their food and all their money, but they were even stripping women of their last shreds of clothing and prodding their naked bodies with bayonets as they staggered across the burning desert. And the Minister of War now proposed that we give our American money to these same guardians of the law for distribution among their charges! However, I had to be tactful.

"If you or other heads of the Government would become personally responsible for the distribution," I said, "of course we would be glad to entrust the money to you. But naturally you would not expect us to give this money to the men who have been killing the Armenians and outraging their women."

But Enver returned to his main point. "They must never know," he said, "that they have a friend in the United States. That would absolutely ruin them! It is far better that they starve, and in saying this I am really thinking of the welfare of the Armenians themselves. If they can only be convinced that they have no friends in other countries, then they will settle down, recognize that Turkey is their only refuge, and become quiet citizens. Your country is doing them no kindness by constantly showing your sympathy. You are merely drawing upon them greater hardships."

In other words, the more money which the Americans sent to feed the Armenians, the more Armenians Turkey intended to massacre! Enver's logic was fairly maddening; yet he did relent at the end and permit me to help the sufferers through certain missionaries. In all our discussions he made this hypocritical plea that he was really a friend of this distracted nation and that even the severity of the measures which he had adopted was mercy in disguise. Since Enver always asserted that he wished to treat the Armenians with justice---in this his attitude to me was quite different from that of Talaat, who openly acknowledged his determination to deport them---I went to the pains of preparing an elaborate plan for bettering their condition. I suggested that, if he wished to be just, he should protect the innocent refugees and lessen this suffering as much as possible, and that for that purpose he should appoint a special committee of Armenians to assist him and send a capable Armenian, such as Oskan Effendi, formerly Minister of Posts and Telegraphs, to study conditions and submit suggestions for remedying the existing evils. Enver did not approve either of my proposals; as to the first, he said that his colleagues would misunderstand it, and, as to Oskan, he said that he admired him for his good work while he had been in the Cabinet and had backed him in his severity toward the inefficient officials, yet he could not trust him because he was a member of the Armenian Dashnaguist Society.

In another talk with Enver I began by suggesting that the Central Government was probably not to blame for the massacres. I thought that this would not be displeasing to him.

"Of course I know that the Cabinet would never order such terrible things as have taken place," I said. "You and Talaat and the rest of the Committee can hardly be held responsible. Undoubtedly your subordinates have gone much further than you have ever intended. I realize that it is not always easy to control your underlings."

Enver straightened up at once. I saw that my remarks, far from smoothing the way to a quiet and friendly discussion, had greatly offended him. I had intimated that things could happen in Turkey for which he and his associates were not responsible.

"You are greatly mistaken," he said. "We have this country absolutely under our control. I have no desire to shift the blame on to our underlings and I am entirely willing to accept the responsibility myself for everything that has taken place. The Cabinet itself has ordered the deportations. I am convinced that we are completely justified in doing this owing to the hostile attitude of the Armenians toward the Ottoman Government, but we are the real rulers of Turkey, and no underling would dare proceed in a matter of this kind without our orders."

Enver tried to mitigate the barbarity of his general attitude by showing mercy in particular instances. I made no progress in my efforts to stop the programme of wholesale massacre, but I did save a few Armenians from death. One day I received word from the American Consul at Smyrna that seven Armenians had been sentenced to be hanged. These men had been accused of committing some rather vague political offense in 1909; yet neither Rahmi Bey, the Governor General of Smyrna, nor the Military Commander believed that they were guilty. When the order for execution reached Smyrna these authorities wired Constantinople that under the Ottoman law the accused had the right to appeal for clemency to the Sultan. The answer which was returned to this communication well illustrated the extent to which the rights of the Armenians were regarded at that time:

"Technically, you are right; hang them first and send the petition for pardon afterward."

I visited Enver in the interest of these men on Bairam, which is the greatest Mohammedan religious festival; it is the day that succeeds Ramadan, their month of fasting. Bairam has one feature in common with Christmas, for on that day it is customary for Mohammedans to exchange small presents, usually sweets. So after the usual remarks of felicitation, I said to Enver:

"To-day is Bairam. and you haven't sent me any present yet."

Enver laughed.

"What do you want? Shall I send you a box of candies?

"Oh, no," I answered, "I am not so cheap as that. I want the pardon of the seven Armenians whom the court-martial has condemned at Smyrna."

The proposition apparently struck Enver as very amusing.

"That's a funny way of asking for a pardon," he said. " However, since you put it that way, I can't refuse."

He immediately sent for his aide and telegraphed to Smyrna, setting the men free.

Thus fortuitously is justice administered and decision involving human lives made in Turkey. Nothing could make clearer the slight estimation in which the Turks hold life, and the slight extent to which principle controls their conduct. Enver spared these men not because he had the slightest interest in their cases, but simply as a personal favour to me and largely because of the whimsical manner in which I had asked it. In all my talks on the Armenians the Minister of War treated the whole matter more or less casually; he could discuss the fate of a race in a parenthesis, and refer to the massacre of children as nonchalantly as we would speak of the weather.

One day Enver asked me to ride with him in the Belgrade forest. As I was losing no opportunities to influence him, I accepted this invitation. We autoed to Buyukdere, where four attendants with horses met us. In our ride through the beautiful forest, Enver became rather more communicative in his conversation than ever before. He spoke affectionately of his father and mother; when they were married, he said, his father had been sixteen and his mother only eleven, and he himself had been born when his mother was fifteen. In talking of his wife, the Imperial Princess, he disclosed a much softer side to his nature than I had hitherto seen. He spoke of the dignity with which she graced his home, regretted that Mohammedan ideas of propriety prohibited her from entering social life, but expressed a wish that she and Mrs. Morgenthau could meet. He was then furnishing a beautiful new palace on the Bosphorus; when this was finished, he said, the Princess would invite my wife to breakfast. Just then we were passing the house and grounds of Senator Abraham Pasha, a very rich Armenian. This man had been an intimate friend of the Sultan Abdul Aziz, and, since in Turkey a man inherits his father's friends as well as his property, the Crown Prince of Turkey, a son of Abdul Aziz, made weekly visits to this distinguished Senator. As we passed through the park, Enver noticed with disgust that woodmen were cutting down trees and stopped them. When I heard afterward that the Minister of War had bought this park, I understood one of the reasons for his anger. Since Abraham Pasha was an Armenian, this gave me an opportunity to open the subject again.

I spoke to him of the terrible treatment from which the Armenian women were suffering.

"You said that you wanted to protect women and children," I remarked, "but I know that your orders are not being carried out."

"Those stories can't be true," he said. "I cannot conceive that a Turkish soldier would ill-treat a woman who is with child."

Perhaps, if Enver could have read the circumstantial reports which were then lying in the archives of the American Embassy, he might have changed his mind.

Shifting the conversation once more, he asked me about my saddle, which was the well-known "General McClellan" type. Enver tried it and liked it so much that he afterward borrowed it, had one made exactly like it for himself---even including the number in one corner and adopted it for one of his regiments. He told me of the railroads which he was then building in Palestine, said how well the Cabinet was working, and pointed out that there were great opportunities in Turkey now for real-estate speculation. He even suggested that he and I join hands in buying land that was sure to rise in value! But I insisted in talking about the Armenians. However, I made no more progress than before.

"We shall not permit them to cluster in places where they can plot mischief and help our enemies. So we are going to give them new quarters."

This ride was so successful, from Enver's point of view, that we took another a few days afterward, and this time Talaat and Dr. Gates, the President of Robert College, accompanied us. Enver and I rode ahead, while our companions brought up the rear. These Turkish officials are exceedingly jealous of their prerogatives, and, since the Minister of War is the ranking member of the Cabinet, Enver insisted on keeping a decorous interval between ourselves and the other pair of horsemen. I was somewhat amused by this, for I knew that Talaat was the more powerful politician; yet he accepted the discrimination and only once did he permit his horse to pass Enver and myself. At this violation of the proprieties, Enver showed his displeasure, whereas Talaat paused, reined up his horse, and passed submissively to the rear.

"I was merely showing Dr. Gates the gait of my horse," he said, with an apologetic air.

But I was interested in more important matters than such fine distinctions in official etiquette; I was determined to talk about the Armenians. But again I failed to make any progress. Enver found more interesting subjects of discussion.

He began to talk of his horses, and now another incident illustrated the mercurial quality of the Turkish mind---the readiness with which a Turk passes from acts of monstrous criminality to acts of individual kindness. Enver said that the horse races would take place soon and regretted that he had no jockey.

"I'll give you an English jockey," I said. "Will you make a bargain? He is a prisoner of war; if he wins will you give him his freedom?"

"I'll do it," said Enver.

This man, whose name was Fields., actually entered the races as Enver's jockey, and came in third. He rode for his freedom, as Mr. Philip said! Since he did not come in first, the Minister was not obliged, by the terms of his agreement, to let him return to England, but Enver stretched a point and gave him his liberty.

On this same ride Enver gave me an exhibition of his skill as a marksman.

At one point in the road I suddenly heard a pistol shot ring out in the air. It was Enver's aide practising on a near-by object. Immediately Enver dismounted, whipped out his revolver, and, thrusting his arm out rigidly and horizontally, he took aim.

"Do you see that twig on that tree?" he asked me. It was about thirty feet away.

When I nodded, Enver fired-and the twig dropped to the ground.

The rapidity with which Enver could whip his weapon out of his pocket, aim, and shoot, gave me one convincing explanation for the influence which he exercised with the piratical crew that was then ruling Turkey. There were plenty of stories floating around that Enver did not hesitate to use this method of suasion at certain critical moments of his career; how true these anecdotes were I do not know, but I can certainly testify to the high character of his marksmanship.

Talaat also began to amuse himself in the same way, and finally the two statesmen started shooting in competition and behaving as gaily and as carefree as boys let out of school.

"Have you one of your cards with you?" asked Enver. He requested that I pin it to a tree, which stood about fifty feet away.

Enver then fired first. His hand was steady; his eye went straight to the mark, and the bullet hit the card directly in the centre. This success rather nettled Talaat. He took aim, but his rough hand and wrist shook slightly---he was not an athlete like his younger, wiry, and straight-backed associate. Several times Talaat hit around the edges of the card, but he could not duplicate Enver's skill.

"If it had been a man I was firing at," said the bulky Turk, jumping on his horse again, "I would have hit him several times."

So ended my attempts to interest the two most powerful Turks of their day in the fate of one of the most valuable elements in their empire!

I have already said that Sa?d Halim, the Grand Vizier, was not an influential personage. Nominally, his office was the most important in the empire; actually, the Grand Vizier was a mere place-warmer, and Talaat and Enver controlled the present incumbent, precisely as they controlled the Sultan himself. Technically the ambassadors should have conducted their negotiations with Sa?d Halim, for he was Minister for Foreign Affairs; I early discovered, however, that nothing could be accomplished this way, and, though I still made my Monday calls as a matter of courtesy, I preferred to deal directly with the men who had the real power to decide all matters. In order that I might not be accused of neglecting any means of influencing the Ottoman Government, I brought the Armenian question several times to the Grand Vizier's attention. As he was not a Turk, but an Egyptian, and a man of education and breeding, it seemed not unlikely that he might have a somewhat different attitude toward the subject peoples. But I was wrong, The Grand Vizier was just as hostile to the Armenians as Talaat and Enver. I soon found that merely mentioning the subject irritated him greatly. Evidently he did not care to have his elegant case interfered with by such disagreeable and unimportant subjects. The Grand Vizier showed his attitude when the Greek Charg? d'Affaires spoke to him about the persecutions of the Greeks. Sa?d Halim. said that such manifestations did the Greeks more harm than good.

"We shall do with them just the opposite from what we are asked to do," said the Grand Vizier.

To my appeals the nominal chief minister was hardly more statesmanlike. I had the disagreeable task of sending him, in behalf of the British, French, and Russian governments, a notification that these Powers would hold personally responsible for the Armenian atrocities the men who were then directing Ottoman affairs. This meant, of course, that in the event of Allied success, they would treat the Grand Vizier, Talaat, Enver, Djemal and their companions as ordinary murderers. As I came into the room to discuss. this somewhat embarrassing message with this member of the royal house of Egypt, he sat there, as usual, nervously fingering his beads, and not in a particularly genial frame of mind. He at once spoke of this telegram; his face flushed with anger, and he began a long diatribe against the whole Armenian race. He declared that the Armenian "rebels" had killed 120,000 Turks at Van. This and other of his statements were so absurd that I found myself spiritedly defending the persecuted race, and this aroused the Grand Vizier's wrath still further, and, switching from the Armenians, he began to abuse my own country, making the usual charge that our sympathy with the Armenians was largely responsible for all their troubles.

Soon after this interview Sa?d Halim ceased to be Minister for Foreign Affairs; his successor was Halil Bey, who for several years had been Speaker of the Turkish Parliament. Halil was a very different type of man. He was much more tactful, much more intelligent, and much more influential in Turkish affairs. He was also a smooth and oily conversationalist, good natured and fat, and by no means so lost to all decent sentiments as most Turkish politicians of the time. It was generally reported that Halil did not approve the Armenian proceedings, yet his official position compelled him to accept them and even, as I now discovered, to defend them. Soon after obtaining his Cabinet post, Halil called upon me and made a somewhat rambling explanation of the Armenian atrocities. I had already had experiences with several official attitudes toward the persecutions; Talaat had been bloodthirsty and ferocious, Enver subtly calculating, while the Grand Vizier had been testy. Halil now regarded the elimination of this race with the utmost good humour. Not a single aspect of the proceeding, not even the unkindest things I could say concerning it, disturbed his equanimity in the least. He began by admitting that nothing could palliate these massacres, but, he added that, in order to understand them, there were certain facts that I should keep in mind.

"I agree that the Government has made serious mistakes in the treatment of the Armenians," said Halil, "but the harm has already been done. What can we do about it now? Still, if there are any errors we can correct, we should correct them. I deplore as much as you the excesses and violations which- have been committed. I wish to present to you the view of the Sublime Porte; I admit that this is no justification, but I think there are extenuating circumstances that you should take into consideration before judgment is passed upon the Ottoman Government."

And then, like all the others, he went back to the happenings at Van, the desire of the Armenians for independence, and the help which they had given the Russians. I had heard it all many times before.

"I told Vartkes" (an Armenian deputy who, like many other Armenian leaders, was afterward murdered), "that, if his people really aspired to an independent existence, they should wait for a propitious moment. Perhaps the Russians might defeat the Turkish troops and occupy all the Armenian provinces. Then I could understand that the Armenians might want to set up for themselves. Why not wait, I told Vartkes, until such a fortunate time had arrived? I warned him that we would not let the Armenians jump on our backs, and that, if they did engage in hostile acts against our troops, we would dispose of all Armenians who were in the rear of our army, and that our method would be to send them to a safe distance in the south. Enver, as you know, gave a similar warning to the Armenian Patriarch. But in spite of these friendly warnings, they started a revolution."

I asked about methods of relief, and told him that already twenty thousand pounds ($100,000) had reached me from America.

"It is the business of the Ottoman Government,"' he blandly answered, "to see that these people are settled, housed, and fed until they can support themselves. The Government will naturally do its duty! Besides, the twenty thousand pounds that you have is in reality nothing at all."

"That is true," I answered, "it is only a beginning, but I am sure that I can get all the money we need."

"It is the opinion of Enver Pasha," he replied, "that no foreigners should help the Armenians. I do not say that his reasons are right or wrong. I merely give them to you as they are. Enver says that the Armenians are idealists, and that the moment foreigners approach and help them, they will be encouraged in their national aspirations. He is utterly determined to cut forever all relations between the Armenians and foreigners."

"Is this Enver's way of stopping any further action on their part? " I asked.

Halil smiled most good-naturedly at this somewhat pointed question and answered: "The Armenians have no further means of action whatever!"

Since not far from 500,000 Armenians had been killed by this time, Halil's genial retort certainly had one virtue which most of his other statements in this interview had lacked---it was the truth.

"How many Armenians in the southern provinces are in need of help?" I asked.

"I do not know; I would not give you even an approximate figure."

"Are there several hundred thousand?"

"I should think so," Halil admitted, "but I cannot say how many hundred thousand."

"A great many suffered," he added, "simply because Enver could not spare troops to defend them. Some regular troops did accompany them and these behaved very well; forty even lost their lives defending the Armenians. But we had to withdraw most of the gendarmes for service in the army and put in a new lot to accompany the Armenians. It is true that these gendarmes committed many deplorable excesses."

"A great many Turks do not approve these measures," I said.

"I do not deny it," replied the ever-accommodating Halil, as he bowed himself out.

Enver, Halil, and the rest were ever insistent on the point which they constantly raised, that no foreigners should furnish relief to the Armenians. A few days after this visit the Under-Secretary of State called at the American Embassy. He came to deliver to me a message from Djemal to Enver. Djemal, who then had jurisdiction over the Christians in Syria, was much annoyed at the interest which the American consuls were displaying in the Armenians. He now asked me to order these officials "to stop busying themselves in Armenian affairs." Djemal could not distinguish between the innocent and the guilty, this messenger said, and so he had to punish them all! Some time afterward Halil complained to me that the American consuls were sending facts about the Armenians to America and that the Government insisted that they should be stopped.

As a matter of fact, I was myself sending most of this information, ---and I did not stop.

Chapter XXVII - "I Shall Do Nothing for the Armenians" Says the German Ambassador

Suppose that there is no phase of the Armenian question which has aroused more interest than this: Had the Germans any part in it? To what extent was the Kaiser responsible for the wholesale slaughter of this nation? Did the Germans favour it, did they merely acquiesce, or did they oppose the persecutions? Germany, in the last four years, has become responsible for many of the blackest pages in history; is she responsible for this, unquestionably the blackest of all?

I presume most people will detect in the remarks of these Turkish chieftains certain resemblances to the German philosophy of war. Let me repeat particular phrases used by Enver and other Turks while discussing the Armenian massacres: "The Armenians have brought this fate upon themselves." "They had a fair warning of what would happen to them." "We were fighting for our national existence ... .. We were justified, in resorting to any means that would accomplish these ends." "We have no time to separate the innocent from the guilty." "The only thing we have on our mind is to win the war."

These phrases somehow have a familiar ring, do they not? Indeed, I might rewrite all these interviews with Enver, use the word Belgium in place of Armenia, put the words in a German general's mouth instead of Enver's, and we should have almost a complete exposition of the German attitude toward subject peoples. But the teachings of the Prussians go deeper than this. There was one feature about the Armenian proceedings that was new---that was not Turkish at all. For centuries the Turks have ill-treated their Armenians and all their other subject peoples with inconceivable barbarity. Yet their methods have always been crude, clumsy, and unscientific. They excelled in beating out an Armenian's brains with a club, and this unpleasant illustration is a perfect indication of the rough and primitive methods which they applied to the Armenian problem. They have understood the uses of murder, but not of murder as a fine art. But the Armenian proceedings of 1915 and 1916 evidenced an entirely new mentality. This new conception was that of deportation. The Turks, in five hundred years, had invented innumerable ways of physically torturing their Christian subjects, yet never before had it occurred to their minds to move them bodily from their homes, where they had lived for many thousands of years, and send them hundreds of miles away into the desert. Where did the Turks get this idea? I have already described how, in 1914, just before the European War, the Government moved not far from 100,000 Greeks from their age-long homes along the Asiatic littoral to certain islands in the Aegean. I have also said that Admiral Usedom, one of the big German naval experts in Turkey, told me that the Germans had suggested this deportation to the Turks. But the all-important point is that this idea of deporting peoples en masse is, in modern times, exclusively Germanic. Any one who reads the literature of Pan-Germany constantly meets it. These enthusiasts for a German world have deliberately planned, as part of their programme, the ousting of the French from certain parts of France, of Belgians from Belgium, of Poles from Poland, of Slavs from Russia, and other indigenous peoples from the territories which they have inhabited for thousands of years, and the establishment in the vacated lands of solid, honest Germans. But it is hardly necessary to show that the Germans have advocated this as a state policy; they have actually been doing it in the last four years. They have moved we do not know how many thousands of Belgians and French from their native land. Austria-Hungary has killed a large part of the Serbian population and moved thousands of Serbian children into her own territories intending to bring them up as loyal subjects of the empire. To what degree this movement of populations has taken place we shall not know until the end of the war, but it has certainly gone on extensively.

Certain German writers have even advocated the application of this policy to the Armenians. According to the Paris Temps, Paul Rohrbach "in a conference held at Berlin, some time ago, recommended that Armenia should be evacuated of the Armenians. They should be dispersed in the direction of Mesopotamia and their places should be taken by Turks, in such a fashion that Armenia should be freed of all Russian influence and that Mesopotamia might be provided with farmers which it now lacked." The purpose of all this was evident enough. Germany was building the Bagdad railroad across the Mesopotamian desert. This was an essential detail in the achievement of the great new German Empire, extending from Hamburg to the Persian Gulf. But this railroad could never succeed unless there should develop a thrifty and industrious population to feed it. The lazy Turk would never become such a colonist. But the Armenian was made of just the kind of stuff which this enterprise needed. It was entirely in accordance with the German conception of statesmanship to seize these people in the lands where they had lived for ages and transport them violently to this dreary, hot desert. The mere fact that they had always lived in a temperate climate would furnish no impediment in Pan-German eyes. I found that Germany had been sowing those ideas broadcast for several years; I even found that German savants had been lecturing on this subject in the East. "I remember attending a lecture by a well-known German professor," an Armenian tells me. "His main point was that throughout their history the Turks had made a great mistake in being too merciful toward the non-Turkish population. The only way to insure the prosperity of the empire, according to this speaker, was to act without any sentimentality toward all the subject nationalities and races in Turkey who did not fall in with the plans of the Turks."

The Pan-Germanists are on record in the matter of Armenia. I shall content myself with quoting the words of the author of "Mittel-Europa, "Friedrich Naumann, perhaps the ablest propagator of Pan-German ideas. In his work on Asia, Naumann, who started life as a Christian clergyman, deals in considerable detail with the Armenian massacres of 1895-96. 1 need only quote a few passages to show the attitude of German state policy on such infamies: "If we should take into consideration merely the violent massacre of from 80,000 to 100,000 Armenians," writes Naumann, "we can come to but one opinion---we must absolutely condemn with all anger and vehemence both the assassins and their instigators. They have perpetrated the most abominable massacres upon masses of people, more numerous and worse than those inflicted by Charlemagne on the Saxons. The tortures which Lepsius has described surpass anything we have ever known. "What then prohibits us from falling upon the Turk and saying to him: 'Get thee gone, wretch!'? Only one thing prohibits us, for the Turk answers: 'I, too, I fight for my existence!'---and indeed, we believe him. We believe, despite the indignation which the bloody Mohammedan barbarism arouses in us, that the Turks are defending themselves legitimately, and before anything else we see in the Armenian question and Armenian massacres a matter of internal Turkish policy, merely an episode of the agony through which a great empire is passing, which does not propose to let itself die without making a last attempt to save itself by bloodshed. All the great powers, excepting Germany, have adopted a policy which aims to upset the actual state of affairs in Turkey. In accordance with this, they demand for the subject peoples of Turkey the rights of man, or of humanity, or of civilization, or of political liberty---in a word, something that will make them the equals of the Turks. But just as little as the ancient Roman despotic state could tolerate the Nazarene's religion, just as little can the Turkish Empire, which is really the political successor of the eastern Roman Empire, tolerate any representation of western free Christianity among its subjects. The danger for Turkey in the Armenian question is one of extinction. For this reason she resorts to an act of a barbarous Asiatic state; she has destroyed the Armenians to such an extent that they will not be able to manifest themselves as a political force for a considerable period. A horrible act, certainly, an act of political despair, shameful in its details, but still a piece of political history, in the Asiatic manner... In spite of the displeasure which the German Christian feels at these accomplished facts, he has nothing to do except quietly to heal the wounds so far as he can, and then to let matters take their course. For a long time our policy in the Orient has been determined: we belong to the group that protects Turkey, that is the fact by which we must regulate our conduct... We do not prohibit any zealous Christian from caring for the victims of these horrible crimes, from bringing up the children and nursing the adults. May God bless these good acts like all other acts of faith. Only we must take care that deeds of charity do not take the form of political acts which are likely to thwart our German policy. The internationalist, he who belongs to the English school of thought, may march with, the Armenians. The nationalist, he who does not intend to sacrifice the future of Germany to England, must, on questions of external policy, follow the path marked out by Bismarck, even if it is merciless in its sentiments... National policy: that is the profound moral reason why we must, as statesmen, show ourselves indifferent to the sufferings of the Christian peoples of Turkey, however painful that may be to our human feelings... That is our duty, which we must recognize and confess before God and before man. If for this reason we now maintain the existence of the Turkish state, we do it in our own self-interest, because what we have in mind is our great future... On one side lie our duties as a nation, on the other our duties as men. There are times, when, in a conflict of duties, we can choose a middle ground. That is all right from a human standpoint, but rarely right in a moral sense. In this instance, as in all analogous situations, we must clearly know on which side lies the greatest and most important moral duty. Once we have made such a choice we must not hesitate. William II has chosen. He has become the friend of the Sultan, because he is thinking of a greater, independent Germany."

Such was the German state philosophy as applied to the Armenians, and I had the opportunity of observing German practice as well. As soon as the early reports reached Constantinople, it occurred to me that the most feasible way of stopping the outrages would be for the diplomatic representatives of all countries to make a joint appeal to the Ottoman Government. I approached Wangenheim on this subject in the latter part of March. His antipathy to the Armenians became immediately apparent. He began denouncing them in unmeasured terms; like Talaat and Enver, he affected to regard the Van episode as an unprovoked rebellion, and, in his eyes, as in theirs, the Armenians were simply traitorous vermin.

"I will help the Zionists," he said, thinking that this remark would be personally pleasing to me, "but I shall do nothing whatever for the Armenians."

Wangenheim pretended to regard the Armenian question as a matter that chiefly affected the United States. My constant intercession in their behalf apparently created the impression, in his Germanic mind, that any mercy shown this people would be a concession to the American Government. And at that moment he was not disposed to do anything that would please the American people.

"The United States is apparently the only country that takes much interest in the Armenians," he said. "Your missionaries are their friends and your people have constituted themselves their guardians. The whole question of helping them is therefore an American matter. How, then, can you expect me to do anything as long as the United States is selling ammunition to the enemies of Germany? Mr. Bryan has just published his note, saying that it would be unneutral not to sell munitions to England and France. As long as your government maintains that attitude we can do nothing for the Armenians."

Probably no one except a German logician would ever have detected any relation between our sale of war materials to the Allies and Turkey's attacks upon hundreds of thousands of Armenian women and children. But that was about as much progress as I made with Wangenheim at that time. I spoke to him frequently, but he invariably offset my pleas for mercy to the Armenians by references to the use of American shells at the Dardanelles. A coolness sprang up between us soon afterward, the result of my refusal to give him "credit" for having stopped the deportation of French and British civilians to the Gallipoli peninsula. After our somewhat tart conversation over the telephone, when he had asked me to telegraph Washington that he had not het-zed the Turks in this matter, our visits to each other ceased for several weeks.

There were certain influential Germans in Constantinople who did not accept Wangenheim's point of view. I have already referred to Paul Weitz, for thirty years the correspondent of the Frankfurter Zeitung, who probably knew more about affairs in the Near East than any other German. Although Wangenheim constantly looked to Weitz for information, he did not always take his advice. Weitz did not accept the orthodox imperial attitude toward Armenia, for he believed that Germany's refusal effectively to intervene was doing his fatherland everlasting injury. Weitz was con-stantly presenting this view to Wangenheim, but he made little progress. Weitz told me about this himself, in January, 1916, a few weeks before I left Turkey. I quote his own words on this subject:

"I remember that you told me at the beginning," said Weitz, "what a mistake Ger-many was making in the Armenian matters. I agreed with you perfectly. But when I urged this view upon Wangenheim, he threw me twice out of the room!"

Another German who was opposed to the atrocities was Neurath, the Conseiller of the German Embassy. His indignation reached such a point that his language to Ta-laat and Enver became almost undiplomatic. He told me, however, that he had failed to influence them.

"They are immovable and are determined to pursue their present course," Neurath said.

Of course no Germans could make much impression on the Turkish Government as long as the German Ambassador refused to interfere. And, as time went on, it be-came more and more evident that Wangenheim had no desire to stop the deporta-tions. He apparently wished, however, to reestablish friendly relations with me, and soon sent third parties to ask why I never came to see him. I do not know how long this estrangement would have lasted had not a great personal affliction befallen him. In June, Lieutenant Colonel Leipzig, the German Military Attach?, died under the most tragic and mysterious circumstances in the railroad station at Lule Bourgas. He was killed by a revolver shot; one story said that the weapon had been accidentally dis-charged, another that the Colonel had committed suicide, still another that the Turks had assassinated him, mistaking him for Liman von Sanders. Leipzig was one of Wangenheim's intimate friends; as young men they had been officers in the same regiment, and at Constantinople they were almost inseparable. I immediately called on the Ambassador to express my condolences. I found him very dejected and care-worn. He told me that he had heart trouble, that he was almost exhausted, and that he had applied for a few weeks' leave of absence. I knew that it was not only his com-rade's death that was preying upon Wangenheim's mind. German missionaries were flooding Germany with reports about the Armenians and calling upon the Govern-ment to stop the massacres. Yet, overburdened and nervous as Wangenheim was this day, he gave many signs that he was still the same unyielding German militarist. A few days afterward, when he returned my visit, he asked:

"Where's Kitchener's army?

"We are willing to surrender Belgium now," he went on. "Germany intends to build an enormous fleet of submarines with great cruising radius. In the next war, we shall therefore be able completely to blockade England. So we do not need Belgium for its submarine bases. We shall give her back to the Belgians, taking the Congo in exchange."

I then made another plea in behalf of the persecuted Christians. Again we discussed this subject at length.

"The Armenians,'" said Wangenheim, "have shown themselves in this war to be enemies of the Turks. It is quite apparent that the two peoples can never live together in the same country. The Americans should move some of them to the United States, and we Germans will send some to Poland and in their place send Jewish Poles to the Armenian provinces---that is, if they will promise to drop their Zionist schemes."

Again, although I spoke with unusual earnestness, the Ambassador refused to help the Armenians.

Still, on July 4th, Wangenheim did present a formal note of protest. He did not talk to Talaat or Enver, the only men who had any authority, but to the Grand Vizier, who was merely a shadow. The incident had precisely the same character as his pro forma protest against sending the French and British civilians down to Gallipoli, to serve as targets for the Allied fleet. Its only purpose was to put Germans officially on record. Probably the hypocrisy of this protest was more apparent to me than to others, for, at the very moment when Wangenheim presented this so-called protest, he was giving me the reasons why Germany could not take really effective steps to end the massacres. Soon after this interview, Wangenheim received his leave and went to Germany.

Callous as Wangenheim showed himself to be, he was not quite so implacable toward the Armenians as the German naval attach? in Constantinople, Humann. This person was generally regarded as a man of great influence; his position in Constantinople corresponded to that of Boy-Ed in the United States. A German diplomat once told me that Humann was more of a Turk than Enver or Talaat. Despite this reputation I attempted to enlist his influence. I appealed to him particularly because he was a friend of Enver, and was generally looked upon as an important connecting link between the German Embassy and the Turkish military authorities. Humann was a personal emissary of the Kaiser, in constant communication with Berlin and undoubtedly he reflected the attitude of the ruling powers in Germany. He discussed the Armenian problem with the utmost frankness and brutality.

"I have lived in Turkey the larger part of my life," he told me, "and I know the Armenians. I also know that both Armenians and Turks cannot live together in this country. One of these races has got to go. And I don't blame the Turks for what they are doing to the Armenians. I think that they are entirely justified. The weaker nation must succumb. The Armenians desire to dismember Turkey; they are against the Turks and the Germans in this war, and they therefore have no right to exist here. I also think that Wangenheim went altogether too far in making a protest; at least I would not have done so."

I expressed my horror at such sentiments, but Humann went on abusing the Armenian people and absolving the Turks from all blame.

"It is a matter of safety," he replied; "the Turks have got to protect themselves, and, from this point of view, they are entirely justified in what they are doing. Why, we found 7,000 guns at Kadikeuy which belonged to the Armenians. At first Enver wanted to treat the Armenians with the utmost moderation, and four months ago he insisted that they be given another opportunity to demonstrate their loyalty. But after what they did at Van, he had to yield to the army, which had been insisting all along that it should protect its rear. The Committee decided upon the deportations and Enver reluctantly agreed. All Armenians are working for the destruction of Turkey's power and the only thing to do is to deport them. Enver is really a very kind-hearted man; he is incapable personally of hurting a fly! But when it comes to defending an idea in which he believes, he will do it fearlessly and recklessly. Moreover, the Young Turks have to get rid of the Armenians merely as a matter of self-protection. The Committee is strong only in Constantinople and a few other large cities. Everywhere else the people are strongly 'Old Turk'. And these old Turks are all fanatics. These Old Turks are not in favour of the present government, and so the Committee has to do everything in their power to protect themselves. But don't think that any harm will come to other Christians. Any Turk can easily pick out three Armenians among a thousand Turks!"

Humann was not the only important German who expressed this latter sentiment. Intimations began to reach me from many sources that my "meddling" in behalf of the Armenians was making me more and more unpopular in German officialdom. One day in October, Neurath, the German Conseiller, called and showed me a telegram which he had just received from the German Foreign Office. This contained the information that Earl Crewe and Earl Cromer had spoken on the Armenians in the House of Lords, had laid the responsibility for the massacres upon the Germans, and had declared that they had received their information from an American witness. The telegram also referred to an article in the Westminster Gazette, which said that the German consuls at certain places had instigated and even led the attacks, and particularly mentioned Resler of Aleppo. Neurath said that his government had directed him to obtain a denial of these charges from the American Ambassador at Constantinople. I refused to make such a denial, saying that I did not feel called upon to decide officially whether Turkey or Germany was to blame for these crimes.

Yet everywhere in diplomatic circles there seemed to be a conviction that the American Ambassador was responsible for the wide publicity which the Armenian massacres were receiving in Europe and the United States. I have no hesitation in saying that they were right about this. In December, my son, Henry Morgenthau, Jr., paid a visit to the Gallipoli peninsula, where he was entertained by General Liman von Sanders and other German officers. He had hardly stepped into German headquarters when an officer came up to him and said:

"Those are very interesting articles on the Armenian question which your father is writing in the American newspapers."

"My father has been writing no articles," my son replied.

"Oh," said this officer, "just because his name isn't signed to them doesn't mean that he is not writing them!"

Von Sanders also spoke on this subject.

"Your father is making a great mistake," he said, "giving out the facts about what the Turks are doing to the Armenians. That really is not his business."

As hints of this kind made no impression on me, the Germans evidently decided to resort to threats. In the early autumn, a Dr. Nossig arrived in Constantinople from Berlin. Dr. Nossig was a German Jew, and came to Turkey evidently to work against the Zionists. After he had talked with me for a few minutes, describing his Jewish activities, I soon discovered that he was a German political agent. He came to see me twice; the first time his talk was somewhat indefinite, the purpose of the call apparently being to make my acquaintance and insinuate himself into my good graces. The second time, after discoursing vaguely on several topics, he came directly to the point. He drew his chair close up to me and began to talk in the most friendly and confidential manner.

"Mr. Ambassador," he said, "we are both Jews and I want to speak to you as one Jew to another. I hope you will not be offended if I presume upon this to give you a little advice. You are very active in the interest of the Armenians and I do not think you realize how very unpopular you are becoming, for this reason, with the authorities here. In fact, I think that I ought to tell you that the Turkish Government is contemplating asking for your recall. Your protests for the Armenians will be useless. The Germans will not interfere for them and you are just spoiling your opportunity for usefulness and running the risk that your career will end ignominiously."

"Are you giving me this advice," I asked, "because you have a real interest in my personal welfare?"

"Certainly," he answered; "all of us Jews are proud of what you have done and we would hate to see your career end disastrously."

"Then you go back to the German Embassy," I said, "and tell Wangenheim what I say---to go ahead and have me recalled. If I am to suffer martyrdom, I can think of no better cause in which to be sacrificed. In fact, I would welcome it, for I can think of no greater honour than to be recalled because I, a Jew, have been exerting all my powers to save the lives of hundreds of thousands of Christians."

Dr. Nossig hurriedly left my office and I have never seen him since. When next I met Enver I told him that there were rumours that the Ottoman Government was about to ask for my recall. He was very emphatic in denouncing the whole story as a falsehood. "We would not be guilty of making such a ridiculous mistake," he said. So there was not the slightest doubt that this attempt to intimidate me had been hatched at the German Embassy.

Wangenheim. returned to Constantinople in early October. I was shocked at the changes that had taken place in the man. As I wrote in my diary, "he looked the perfect picture of Wotan." His face was almost constantly twitching; he wore a black cover over his right eye, and he seemed unusually nervous and depressed. He told me that he had obtained little rest; that he had been obliged to spend most of his time in Berlin attending to business. A few days after his return I met him on my way to Haskeuy; he said that he was going to the American Embassy and together we walked back to it. I had been recently told by Talaat that he intended to deport all the Armenians who were left in Turkey and this statement had induced me to make a final plea to the one man in Constantinople who had the power to end the horrors. I took Wangenheim. up to the second floor of the Embassy, where we could be entirely alone and uninterrupted, and there, for more than an hour, sitting together over the tea table, we had our last conversation on this subject.

"Berlin telegraphs me," he said, "that your Secretary of State tells them that you say that more Armenians than ever have been massacred since Bulgaria has come in on our side."

"No, I did not cable that," I replied. "I admit that I have sent a large amount of information to Washington. I have sent copies of every report and every statement to the State Department. They are safely lodged there, and whatever happens to me, the evidence is complete, and the American people are not dependent on my oral report for their information. But this particular statement you make is not quite accurate. I merely informed Mr. Lansing that any influence Bulgaria might exert to stop the massacres has been lost, now that she has become Turkey's ally."

We again discussed the deportations.

"Germany is not responsible for this," Wangenheim said.

"You can assert that to the end of time," I replied, "but nobody will believe it. The world will always hold Germany responsible; the guilt of these crimes will be your inheritance forever. I know that you have filed a paper protest. But what does that amount to? You know better than I do that such a protest will have no effect. I do not claim that Germany is responsible for these massacres in the sense that she instigated them. But she is responsible in the sense that she had the power to stop them and did not use it. And it is not only America and your present enemies that will hold you responsible. The German people will some day call your government to account. You are a Christian people and the time will come when Germans will realize that you have let a Mohammedan people destroy another Christian nation. How foolish is your protest that I am sending information to my State Department. Do you suppose that you can keep secret such hellish atrocities as these? Don't get such a silly, ostrich-like thought as that---don't think that by ignoring them yourselves, you can get the rest of the world to do so. Crimes like these cry to heaven. Do you think I could know about things like this and not report them to my government? And don't forget that German missionaries, as well as American, are sending me information about the Armenians."

"All that you say may be true," replied the German Ambassador, "but the big problem that confronts us is to win this war. Turkey has settled with her foreign enemies; she has done that at the Dardanelles and at Gallipoli. She is now trying to settle her internal affairs. They still greatly fear that the Capitulations will again be forced upon them. Before they are again put under this restraint, they intend to have their internal problems in such shape that there will be little chance of any interference from foreign nations. Talaat has told me that he is determined to complete this task before peace is declared. In the future they don't intend that the Russians shall be in a position to say that they have a right to intervene about Armenian matters because there are a large number of Armenians in Russia who are affected by the troubles of their coreligionists in Turkey. Giers used to be doing this an the time and the Turks do not intend that any ambassador from Russia or from any other country shall have such an opportunity in the future. The Armenians anyway are a very poor lot. You come in contact in Constantinople with Armenians of the educated classes, and you get your impressions about them from these men, but all the Armenians are not of that type. Yet I admit that they have been treated terribly. I sent a man to make investigations and he reported that the worst outrages have not been committed by Turkish officials but by brigands."

Wangenheim again suggested that the Armenians be taken to the United States, and once more I gave him the reasons why this would be impracticable.

"Never mind all these considerations," I said. "Let us disregard everything---military necessity, state policy, and all else---and let us look upon this simply as a human problem. Remember that most of the people who are being treated in this way are old men, old women, and helpless children. Why can't you, as a human being, see that these people are permitted to live? "

"At the present stage of internal affairs in Turkey," Wangenheim replied, "I shall not intervene."

I saw that it was useless to discuss the matter further. He was a man who was devoid of sympathy and human pity, and I turned from him in disgust. Wangenheim rose to leave. As he did so he gave a gasp, and his legs suddenly shot from under him. I jumped and caught the man just as he was falling. For a minute he seemed utterly dazed; he looked at me in a bewildered way, then suddenly collected himself and regained his poise. I took the Ambassador by the arm, piloted him down stairs, and put him into his auto. By this time he had apparently recovered from his dizzy spell and he reached home safely. Two days afterward, while sitting at his dinner table, he had a stroke of apoplexy; he was carried upstairs to his bed, but he never regained consciousness. On October 24th, I was officially informed that Wangenheim. was dead. And thus my last recollection of Wangenheim is that of the Ambassador as he sat in my office in the American Embassy, absolutely refusing to exert any influence to prevent the massacre of a nation. He was the one, and his government was the one government, that could have stopped these crimes, but, as Wangenheim told me many times, "our one aim is to win this war."

The Grand Vizier led the procession; I walked the whole way with Enver. All the officers of the Goeben and the Breslau, and all the German generals, dressed in full uniform, followed. It seemed as though the whole of Constantinople lined the streets, and the atmosphere had some of the quality of a holiday. We walked to the grounds of Dolma Bagtche, the Sultan's Palace, passing through the gate which the ambassadors enter when presenting their credentials. At the dock a steam launch lay awaiting our arrival, and in this stood Neurath, the German Conseiller, ready to receive the body of his dead chieftain. The coffin, entirely covered with flowers, was placed in the boat. As the launch sailed out into the stream Neurath, a six-foot Prussian, dressed in his military uniform, his helmet a waving mass of white plumes, stood erect and silent. Wangenheim was buried in the park of the summer embassy at Therapia, by the side of his comrade Colonel Leipzig. No final resting-place would have been more appropriate, for this had been the scene of his diplomatic successes, and it was from this place that, a little more than two years before, he had directed by wireless the Goeben and the Breslau, and safely brought them into Constantinople, thus making it inevitable that Turkey should join forces with Germany, and paving the way for all the triumphs and all the horrors that have necessarily followed that event.

Chapter XXVIII - Enver Again Moves for Peace Farewell to the Sultan and to Turkey

My failure to stop the destruction of the Armenians had made Turkey for me a place of horror, and I found intolerable my further daily association with men who, however gracious and accommodating and good-natured they might have been to the American Ambassador, were still reeking with the blood of nearly a million human beings. Could I have done anything more, either for Americans, enemy aliens, or the persecuted peoples of the empire, I would willingly have stayed. The position of Americans and Europeans, however, had now become secure and, so far as the subject peoples were concerned, I had reached the end of my resources. Moreover, an event was approaching in the United States which, I believed, would inevitably have the greatest influence upon the future of the world and of democracy---the presidential campaign. I felt that there was nothing so important in international politics as the reelection of President Wilson. I could imagine no greater calamity, for the United States and the world, than that the American nation should fail to indorse heartily this great statesman. If I could substantially assist in Mr. Wilson's reelection, I concluded that I could better serve my country at home at this juncture.

I had another practical reason for returning home, and that was to give the President and the State Department, by word of mouth, such first-hand information as I possessed on the European situation. It was especially important to give them the latest side lights on the subject of peace. In the latter part of 1915 and the early part of 1916 this was the uppermost topic in Constantinople. Enver Pasha was constantly asking me to intercede with the President to end the war. Several times he intimated that Turkey was war-weary and that its salvation depended on getting an early peace. I have already described the conditions that prevailed a few months after the outbreak of the war, but, by the end of 1915, they were infinitely worse. When Turkey decided on the deportation and massacre of her subject peoples, especially the Armenians and Greeks, she had signed her own economic death warrant. These were the people, as I have already said, who controlled her industries and her finances and developed her agriculture, and the material consequences of this great national crime now began to be everywhere apparent. The farms were lying uncultivated and daily thousands of peasants were dying of starvation. As the Armenians and Greeks were the largest taxpayers, their annihilation greatly reduced the state revenues, and the fact that practically all Turkish ports were blockaded had shut off customs collections. The mere statement that Turkey was barely taking in money enough to pay the interest on her debt, to say nothing of ordinary expenses and war expenses, gives a fair idea of her advanced degree of exhaustion. In these facts Turkey had abundant reasons for desiring a speedy peace.

Besides this, Enver and the ruling party feared a revolution, unless the war quickly came to an end. As I wrote the State Department about this time, "These men are willing to do almost anything to retain their power."

Still I did not take Enver's importunities for peace any too seriously. "Are you speaking for yourself and your party in this matter," I asked him, "or do you really speak for Germany also? I cannot submit a proposition from you unless the Germans are back of you. Have you consulted them about this?"

"No," Enver replied, "but I know how they feel."

"That is not sufficient," I answered. "You had better communicate with them directly through the German Embassy. I would not be willing to submit a proposition that was not indorsed by all the Teutonic Allies."

Enver thought that it would be almost useless to discuss the matter with the German Ambassador.

He said, however, that he was just leaving for Orsova, a town on the Hungarian and Rumanian frontier, where he was to have a conference with Falkenhayn, at that time the German Chief-of-Staff. Falkenhayn, said Enver, was the important man; he would take up the question of peace with him.

"Why do you think that it is a good time to discuss peace now? " I asked.

"Because in two weeks we shall have completely annihilated Serbia. We think that should put the Allies in a frame of mind to discuss peace. My visit to Falkenhayn is to complete arrangements for the invasion of Egypt. In a very few days we expect Greece to join us. We are already preparing tons of provisions and fodder to send to Greece. And when we get Greece, of course, Rumania will come in. When the Greeks and Rumanians join us, we shall have a million fresh troops. We shall get all the guns and ammunition we need from Germany as soon as the direct railroad is opened. All these things make it an excellent time for us to take up the matter of peace."

I asked the Minister of War to talk the matter over with Falkenhayn at his proposed interview, and report to me when he returned. In some way this conversation came to the ears of the new German Ambassador, Graf Wolf-Metternich, who immediately called to discuss the subject. He apparently wished to impress upon me two things: that Germany would never surrender Alsace-Lorraine, and that she would insist on the return of all her colonies. I replied that it was apparently useless to discuss peace until England first had won some great military victory.

"That may be so," replied the Graf, "but you can hardly expect that Germany shall let England win such a victory merely to put her in a frame of mind to consider peace. But I think that you are wrong. It is a mistake to say that Great Britain has not already won great victories. I think that she has several very substantial ones to her credit. Just consider what she has done. She has established her unquestioned supremacy of the seas and driven off all German commerce. She has not only not lost a foot of her own territory, but she has gained enormous new domains. She has annexed Cyprus and Egypt and has conquered all the German colonies. She is in possession of a considerable part of Mesopotamia. How absurd to say that England has gained nothing by the war!"

On December 1st, Enver came to the American Embassy and reported the results of his interview with Falkenhayn. The German Chief-of-Staff had said that Germany would very much like to discuss peace but that Germany could not state her terms in advance, as such an action would be generally interpreted as a sign of weakness. But one thing could be depended on; the Allies could obtain far more favourable terms at that moment than at any future time. Enver told me that the Germans would be willing to surrender all the territory they had taken from the French and practically all of Belgium. But the one thing on which they had definitely settled was the permanent dismemberment of Serbia. Not an acre of Macedonia would be returned to Serbia and even parts of old Serbia would be retained; that is, Serbia would become a much smaller country than she had been before the Balkan wars, and, in fact, she would practically disappear as an independent state. The meaning of all this was apparent, even then. Germany had won the object for which she had really gone to war; a complete route from Berlin to Constantinople and the East; part, and a good part, of the Pan-German "Mittel Europa" had thus become an accomplished military fact. Apparently Germany was willing to give up the overrun provinces of northern France and Belgium, provided that the Entente would consent to her retention of these conquests. The proposal which Falkenhayn made then did not materially differ from that which Germany had put forward in the latter part of 1914. This Enver-Falkenhayn interview, as reported to me, shows that it was no suddenly conceived German plan, but that it has been Germany's scheme from the first.

In all this I saw no particular promise of an early peace. Yet I thought that I should lay these facts before the President. I therefore applied to Washington for a leave of absence, which was granted.

I had my farewell interview with Enver and Talaat on the thirteenth of January. Both men were in their most delightful mood. Evidently both were turning over in their minds, as was I, all the momentous events that had taken place in Turkey, and in the world, since my first meeting with them two years before. Then Talaat and Enver were merely desperate adventurers who had reached high position by assassination and intrigue; their position was insecure, for at any moment another revolution might plunge them into the obscurity from which they had sprung. But now they were the unquestioned despots of the Ottoman Empire, the allies of the then strongest military power in the world, the conquerors---absurdly enough they so regarded themselves---of the British navy. At this moment of their great triumph---the Allied expedition to the Dardanelles had evacuated its positions only two weeks before--- both Talaat and Enver regarded their country again as a world power.

"I hear you are going home to spend a lot of money and reelect your President," said Talaat---this being a jocular reference to the fact that I was the Chairman of the Finance Committee of the Democratic National Committee. "That's very foolish; why don't you stay here and give it to Turkey? We need it more than your people do."

"'But we hope you are coming back soon," he added, in the polite (and insincere) manner of the oriental. You and we have really grown up together; you came here about the same time that we took office and we don't know how we could ever get so well acquainted with another man. We have grown fond of you, too. We have had our differences, and pretty lively ones at times, but we have always found you fair, and we respect American policy in Turkey as you have represented it. We don't like to see you go, even for a few months."

I expressed my pleasure at these words.

"It's very nice to hear you talk that way," I answered. "Since you flatter me so much, I know that you will be willing to promise me certain things. Since I have you both here together this is my chance to put you on record. Will you treat the people in my charge considerately, just the same as though I were here?"

"As to the American missionaries and colleges and schools," said Talaat---and Enver assented----"we give you an absolute promise. They will not be molested in the slightest degree, but can go on doing their work just the same as before. Your mind can rest easy on that score."

"How about the British and French? " I asked.

"Oh, well," said Talaat, smiling, "we may have to have a little fun with them now and then, but don't worry. We'll take good care of them."

And now for the last time I spoke on the subject that had rested so heavily on my mind for many months. I feared that another appeal would be useless, but I decided to make it.

"How about the Armenians?"

Talaat's geniality disappeared in an instant. His face hardened and the fire of the beast lighted up his eyes once more.

What's the use of speaking about them?" he said, waving his hand. "We are through with them. That's all over."

Such was my farewell with Talaat. "That's all over" were his last words to me.

The next day I had my farewell audience with the Sultan. He was the same gracious, kindly old gentleman whom I had first met two years before. He received me informally, in civilian European clothes, and asked me to sit down with him. We talked for twenty minutes, and discussed among other things the pleasant relations that prevailed between America and Turkey. He thanked me for the interest which I had taken in his country and hoped that I would soon return. Then he took up the question of war and peace.

"Every monarch naturally desires peace," he said. "None of us approves the shedding of blood. But there are times when war seems unavoidable. We may wish to settle our disputes amicably, but we cannot always do it. This seems to be one of them. I told the British Ambassador that we did not wish to go to war with his country. I tell you the same thing now. But Turkey had to defend her rights. Russia attacked us; and naturally we had to defend ourselves. Thus the war was not the result of any planning on our part; it was an act of Allah---it was fate."

I expressed the hope that it might soon be over.

"Yes, we wish peace also," replied His Majesty. "But it must be a peace that will guarantee the rights of our empire. I am sure that a civilized and flourishing country like America wants peace, and she should exert all her efforts to bring about a peace that shall be permanent."

One of the Sultan's statements at this interview left a lasting impression. This was his assertion that "Russia attacked us." That the simple-minded old gentleman believed this was apparent; it was also clear that he knew nothing of the real facts--- that Turkish warships, under German officers, had plunged Turkey into the war by bombarding Russian seaports. Instead of telling him the truth, the Young Turk leaders had foisted upon the Sultan this fiction of Russia as the aggressor. The interview showed precisely to what extent the ostensible ruler of Turkey was acquainted with the crucial facts in the government of his own empire.

In our interview Talaat and Enver had not said their final farewells, telling me that they would meet me at the station. A few minutes before the train started Bedri came up, rather pale-faced and excited, and brought me their apologies.

"They cannot come," he said, "the Crown Prince has just committed suicide."

I knew the Crown Prince well and I had expected to have him as a fellow passenger to Berlin; he had been about to make a trip to Germany, and his special car was attached to this train. I had seen much of Youssouf Izzeddin; he had several times invited me to call upon him, and we had spent many hours talking over the United States and American institutions, in which subject he had always displayed the keenest interest. Many times had he told me that he would like to introduce certain American governmental ideas in Turkey. This morning, when we were leaving for Berlin, the Crown Prince was found lying on the floor in his villa, bathed in a pool of blood, with his arteries cut. Youssouf was the son of Abdul-Aziz, Sultan from 1861 to 1876, who, gruesomely enough, had ended his days by opening his arteries forty years before. The circumstances surrounding the death of father and son were thus precisely the same. The fact that Youssouf was strongly pro-Ally, that he had opposed Turkey's participation in the war on Germany's side, and that he was extremely antagonistic to the Committee of Union and Progress gave rise to many suspicions. I know nothing about the stories that now went from mouth to mouth, and merely record that the official report on the death was that it was a case of "suicide."

"On l'a suicid?!" (they have suicided him!), remarked a witty Frenchman, when this verdict was reported.

This tragic announcement naturally cast a gloom over our party, as our train pulled out of Constantinople, but the journey proved to be full of interest. I was now on the famous Balkanzug, and this was only the second trip which it had made to Berlin. My room was No. 13; several people came to look at it, telling me that, on the outward trip, the train had been shot at, and a window of my compartment broken.

Soon after we started I discovered that Admiral Usedom was one of my fellow passengers. Usedom had had a distinguished career in the navy; among other things he had been captain of the Hohenzollern, the Kaiser's yacht, and thus was upon friendly terms with His Majesty. The last time I had seen Usedom was on my visit to the Dardanelles, where he had been Inspector General of the Ottoman defenses. As soon as we met again, the admiral began to talk about the abortive Allied attack. He again made no secret of the fears which he had then entertained that this attack would succeed.

"Several times," he said, "we thought that they were on the verge of getting through. All of us down there were very much distressed and depressed over the prospect. We owed much to the heroism of the Turks and their willingness to sacrifice an unlimited number of human lives. It is all over now---that part of our task is finished."

The Admiral thought that the British landing party had been badly prepared, though he spoke admiringly of the skill with which the Allies had managed their retreat. I also obtained further light on the German attitude toward the Armenian massacres. Usedom made no attempt to justify them; neither did he blame the Turks. He discussed the whole thing calmly, dispassionately, merely as a military problem, and one would never have guessed from his remarks that the lives of a million human beings had been involved. He simply said that the Armenians were in the way, that they were an obstacle to German success, and that it had therefore been necessary to remove them, just like so much useless lumber. He spoke about them as detachedly as one would speak about removing a row of houses in order to bombard a city.

Poor Serbia! As our train sped through her devastated districts I had a picture of what the war had meant to this brave little country. In the last two years this nation had stood alone, practically unassisted by her allies, attempting to stem the rush of Pan-German conquest, just as, for several centuries, she had stood as a bulwark against the onslaughts of the Turks. And she had paid the penalty. Many farms we passed were abandoned, overgrown with weeds and neglected, and the buildings were frequently roofless and sometimes razed to the ground. Whenever we crossed a stream we saw the remains of a dynamited bridge; in all cases the Germans had built new ones to replace those which had been destroyed. We saw many women and children, looking ragged and half starved, but significantly we saw very few men, for all had either been killed or they were in the ranks of Serbia's still existing and valiant little army. All this time trains full of German soldiers were passing us or standing on the switches at the stations where we slowed up, a sufficient explanation for all the misery and devastation we saw on our way.

Chapter XXIX - Von Jagow, Zimmermann, and German-Americans

Our train drew into the Berlin station on the evening of February 2, 1916. The date is worth mentioning, for that marked an important crisis in German-American relations. Almost the first man I met was my old friend and colleague, Ambassador James W. Gerard. Mr. Gerard told me that he was packing up and expected to leave Berlin at any moment, for he believed that a break between Germany and the United States was a matter only of days, perhaps of hours. At that time Germany and the United States were discussing the settlement of the Lusitania outrage. The negotiations had reached a point where the Imperial Government had expressed a willingness to express her regrets, pay an indemnity, and promise not to do it again. But the President and Mr. Lansing insisted that Germany should declare that the sinking of the Lusitania had been an illegal act. This meant that Germany at no time in the future could resume submarine warfare without stultifying herself and doing something which her own government had denounced as contrary to international law. But our government would accept nothing less and the two nations were, therefore, at loggerheads.

"I can do nothing more," said Mr. Gerard. "I want to have you talk with Zimmermann and Von Jagow, and perhaps you can give them a new point of view."

I soon discovered, from my many callers, that the atmosphere in Berlin was tense and exceedingly anti-American. Our country was regarded everywhere as practically an ally of the Entente, and I found that the most absurd ideas prevailed concerning the closeness of our relations with England. Thus it was generally believed that Sir Cecil Spring-Rice, the British Ambassador in Washington, met regularly with President Wilson's Cabinet and was consulted on all our national policies.

At three o'clock Mr. Gerard took me to Von Jagow's house and we spent more than an hour there with the Foreign Minister. Von Jagow was a small, slight man of nervous disposition. He lighted cigarette after cigarette during our interview. He was apparently greatly worried over the American situation. Let us not suppose that the German Government regarded lightly a break with the United States. At that time their newspapers were ridiculing and insulting us, and making fun of the idea that Uncle Sam would go to war. The contrast between these journalistic vapourings and the anxiety, even the fear, which this high German official displayed, much impressed me. The prospect of having our men and our resources thrown on the side of the Entente he did not regard indifferently, whatever the Berlin press might say.

"It seems to us a shame that Mr. Lansing should insist that we declare the Lusitania sinking illegal," Von Jagow began. "He is acting like a technical lawyer."

"If you want the real truth," I replied, "I do not think that the United States is particular or technical about the precise terms that you use. But you must give definite assurances that you are sorry for the act, say that you regard it as an improper one, and that it will not occur again. Unless you do this, the United States will not be satisfied."

"We cannot do that," he answered. "Public opinion in Germany would not permit it. If we should make a declaration such as you outline, the present Cabinet would fall."

"But I thought that you had public opinion here well under control?" I answered. "It may take a little time but certainly you can change public sentiment so that it would approve such a settlement."

"As far as the newspapers are concerned," said Von Jagow, "that is true. We can absolutely control them. However, that will take some time. The newspapers cannot reverse themselves immediately; they will have to do it gradually, taking two or three weeks. We can manage them. But there are members of Parliament whom we can't control and they would make so much trouble that we would all have to resign."

"Yet it seems to me," I rejoined, "that you could get these members together, explain to them the necessity of keeping the United States out of the war, and that they would be convinced. The trouble is that you Germans don't understand conditions in my country. You don't think that the United States will fight. You don't understand President Wilson; you think that he is an idealist and a peace man, and that, under no circumstances, will he take up arms. You are making the greatest and most costly mistake that any nation could make. The President has two sides to his nature. Do not forget that he has Scotch-Irish blood in him. Up to the present you have seen only the Scotch side of him. That makes him very cautious, makes him weigh every move, makes him patient and long-suffering. But he has also all the fire and combativeness of the Irish. Let him once set his jaws and it takes a crowbar to open them again. If he once decides to fight, he will fight with all his soul and to the bitter end. You can go just so far with your provocations but no farther. You are also greatly deceived because certain important members of Congress, perhaps even a member of the Cabinet, have been for peace. But there is one man who is going to settle this matter--- that is the President. He will settle it as he thinks right and just, irrespective of what other people may say or do."

Von Jagow said that I had given him a new impression of the President. But he still had one more reason to believe that the United States would not go to war.

"How about the German-Americans?" he asked.

"I can tell you all about them," I answered, "because I am one of them myself. I was born in Germany and spent the first nine years of my life here. I have always loved many things German, such as its music and its literature. But my parents left this country because they were dissatisfied and unhappy here. The United States gave us a friendly reception and a home, and made us prosperous and happy. There are many millions just like us; there is no business opportunity and no social position that is not open to us. I do not believe that there is a more contented people in the world than the German-Americans." I could not reveal to him my own state of mind, as I was still ambassador, but I could and did say:

"Take my own children. Their sympathies all through this war have been with England and her allies. My son is here with me; he tells me that, if the United States goes to war, he will enlist immediately. Do you suppose, in case we should go to war with Germany, that they would side with you? The idea is simply preposterous. And the overwhelming mass of German-Americans feel precisely the same way."

"But I am told," said Von Jagow, "that there will be an insurrection of German-Americans if your country makes war on us."

"Dismiss any such idea from your mind," I replied.

The first one who attempts it will be punished so promptly and so drastically that such a movement will not go far. And I think that the loyal German-Americans themselves will be the first to administer such punishment."

"We wish to avoid a rupture with the United States," said Von Jagow. "But we must have time to change public sentiment here. There are two parties here, holding diametrically opposed views on submarine warfare. One believes in pushing it to the limit, irrespective of consequences to the United States or any other power. The present Cabinet takes the contrary view; we wish to meet the contentions of your President, but the militaristic faction is pushing us hard. They will force us out of office if we declare the Lusitania sinking illegal or improper. I think that President Wilson should understand this. We are working with him, but we must go cautiously. I should suppose that Mr. Wilson, since he wishes to avoid a break, would prefer to have us in power. Why should he take a stand that will drive us out of office and put in here men who will make war inevitable between Germany and the United States?"

"Do you wish Washington to understand," I asked, "that your tenure of office depends on your not making this declaration?"

"We certainly do," replied Von Jagow. "I wish that you would telegraph Washington to that effect. Tell the President that, if we are displaced now, we shall be succeeded by men who advocate unlimited submarine warfare."

He expressed himself as amazed at my description of President Wilson and his willingness to fight. "We regard him," said Von Jagow, "as absolutely a man of peace. Nor do we believe that the American people will fight. They are far from the scene of action, and, what, after all, have they to fight for? Your material interests are not affected."

"But there is one thing that we will fight for," I replied, "and that is moral principle. It is quite apparent that you do not understand the American spirit You do not realize that we are holding off, not because we have no desire to fight, but because we wish to be absolutely fair. We first wish to have all the evidence in. I admit that we are reluctant to mix in foreign disputes, but we shall insist upon our right to use the ocean as we see fit and we don't propose to have Germany constantly interfering with that right and murdering our citizens. The American is still perhaps a great powerful youth, but once he gets his mind made up that he is going to defend his rights, he will do so irrespective of consequences. You seem to think that Americans will not fight for a principle; you apparently have forgotten that all our wars have been over matters of principle. Take the greatest of them all ---the Civil War, from 1861 to '65. We in the North fought to emancipate the slaves; that was purely a matter of principle; our material interests were not involved. And we fought that to the end, although we had to fight our own brothers."

"We don't want to be on bad terms with the United States," Von Jagow replied. "There are three nations on whom the peace of the world depends---England, the United States, and Germany. We three should get together, establish peace, and maintain it. I thank you for your explanation; I understand the situation much better now. But I still don't see why your Government is so hard on Germany and so easy with England." I made the usual explanation that we regarded our problem with each nation as a distinct matter and could not make our treatment of Germany in any way conditional on our treatment of England.

"Oh, yes," replied Von Jagow, rather plaintively.

"It reminds me of two boys playing in a yard. One is to be punished first and the other is waiting for his turn. Wilson is going to spank the German boy first, and, after he gets through, then he proposes to take up England."

"However," he concluded, "I wish you would cable the President that you have gone over the matter with me and now understand the German point of view. Won't you please ask him to do nothing until you have reached the other side and explained the whole thing personally?

I made this promise, and Mr. Gerard and I cabled immediately.

At four-thirty o'clock I had an engagement to take tea with Dr. Alexander and his wife at their home. I had been there about fifteen minutes when Zimmermann was announced! He was a different kind of man from Von Jagow. He impressed me as much stronger, mentally and physically. He was tall, even stately in his bearing, masterful in his manner, direct and searching in his questions, but extremely pleasing and insinuating.

Zimmermann, discussing the German-American situation, began with a statement which I presume he thought would be gratifying to me. He told me how splendidly the Jews had behaved in Germany during the war and how deeply under obligations the Germans felt to them.

"After the war," he said, "they are going to be much better treated in Germany than they have been."

Zimmermann told me that Von Jagow had told him about our talk and asked me to repeat part of it. He was particularly interested, he said, in my statements about the German-Americans, and he wished to learn from me himself the facts upon which I based my conclusions. Like most Germans, he regarded the Germanic elements in our population as almost a part of Germany.

"Are you sure that the mass of German-Americans would be loyal to the United States in case of war?" he asked. "Aren't their feelings for the Fatherland really dominant? "

"You evidently regard those German-Americans as a distinct part of the population," I replied, "living apart from the rest of the people and having very little to do with American life as a whole. You could not make a greater mistake. You can purchase a few here and there who will make a big noise and shout for Germany, but I am talking about the millions of Americans of German ancestry. These people regard themselves as Americans and nothing else. The second generation particularly resent being looked upon as Germans. It is practically impossible to make them talk German; they refuse to speak anything but English. They do not read German newspapers and will not go to German schools. They even resent going to Lutheran churches where the language is German. We have more than a million German-Americans in New York City, but it has been a great struggle to keep alive one German theatre; the reason is that these people prefer the theatres where English is the language. We have a few German clubs, but their membership is very small. The German-Americans prefer to belong to the clubs of general membership and there is not a single one in New York, even the finest, where they are not received upon their merits. In the political and social life of New York there are few German-Americans who, as such, have acquired any prominent position, though there are plenty of men of distinguished position who are German in origin. If the United States and Germany go to war, you will not only be surprised at the loyalty of our German people, but the whole world will be. Another point; if the United States goes in, we shall fight to the end, and it will be a very long and a very determined struggle."

After three years I have no reason to be ashamed of either of these prophecies. I sometimes wonder what Zimmermann now think of my statements.

After the explanation Zimmermann began to talk about Turkey. He seemed interested to find out whether the Turks were likely to make a separate peace. I bluntly told him that the Turks felt themselves to be under no obligations to the Germans. This gave me another opportunity.

"I have learned a good deal about German methods in Turkey," I said. "I think it would be a great mistake to attempt similar tactics in the United States. I speak of this because there has been a good deal of sabotage there already. This in itself is solidifying the German-Americans against you and is more than anything else driving the United States into the arms of England."

"But the German Government is not responsible," said Zimmermann. "We know nothing about it."

Of course I could not accept that statement on its face value---recent developments have shown how mendacious it was---but we passed to other topics. The matter of the submarine came up again.

"We have voluntarily interned our navy," said Zimmermann. "We can do nothing at sea except with our submarines. It seems to me that the United States is making a serious mistake in so strongly opposing the submarine. You have a long coast line and you may need the U-boat yourself some day. Suppose one of the European Powers, or particularly Japan, should attack you. You could use the submarine to good purpose then. Besides, if you insist on this proposed declaration in the Lusitania matter, you will simply force our government into the hands of the Tirpitz party."

Zimmermann now returned again to the situation in Turkey. His questions showed that he was much displeased with the new German Ambassador, Graf Wolf-Metternich. Metternich, it seemed, had failed in his attempt to win the good will of the ruling powers in Turkey and had been a trial to the German Foreign Office. Metternich had shown a different attitude toward the Armenians from Wangenheim, and he had made sincere attempts with Talaat and Enver to stop the massacres. Zimmermann now told me that Metternich had made a great mistake in doing this and had destroyed his influence at Constantinople. Zimmermann made no effort to conceal his displeasure over Metternich's manifestation of a humanitarian spirit. I now saw that Wangenheim had really represented the attitude of official Berlin, and I thus had confirmation, from the highest German authority, of my conviction that Germany had acquiesced in those deportations.

In a few days we had taken the steamer at Copenhagen, and, on February 22, 1916, I found myself once more sailing into New York harbour---and home.

www.ingramcontent.com/pod-product-compliance
Ingram Content Group UK Ltd.
Pitfield, Milton Keynes, MK11 3LW, UK
UKHW040642140425
5457UKWH00014B/62